RIPPED APART

RIPPED APART

UNSETTLING NARRATIVES OF TRANSNATIONAL MIGRATION

VANESSA DE VERITCH WOODSIDE

TEXAS TECH UNIVERSITY PRESS

This book is typeset in Unna. The paper used in this book meets the minimum requirements of ANSI/NISO Z39.48-1992 (R1997). ∞

Designed by Hannah Gaskamp
Cover design by Hannah Gaskamp

Library of Congress Control Number: 2020945335
ISBN: 978-1-68283-071-0 (cloth)
ISBN: 978-1-68283-072-7 (ebook)
Printed in the United States of America
20 21 22 23 24 25 26 27 28 / 9 8 7 6 5 4 3 2 1

Texas Tech University Press
Box 41037
Lubbock, Texas 79409-1037 USA
800.832.4042
ttup@ttu.edu

www.ttupress.org

Contents

Illustrations

RIPPED APART

Introduction

A mainstream media blitz ensued after the 2018 implementation of unabashedly severe policies directed toward immigrant families, many of whom had joined one of the first of various "migrant caravans" that continue to depart from Central America to present themselves at the US-Mexico border to request political asylum, as per US and international law. What began as a seemingly steady flow of network news proffering contrasting depictions of these migrants as, on the one hand, armies preparing for an imminent "invasion of our Country" (@realDonaldTrump 2018), and desperate refugees escaping inevitable poverty and death on the other, quickly evolved into a 24-hour cycle of reporting on the Trump administration's intention to deter continued migration of families by making good on the threat of family separation as an element of the zero-tolerance policy for individuals who crossed the border without papers.

Mincing no words, then Attorney General Jeff Sessions and Department of Homeland Security Secretary Kirstjen Nielsen justified the forcible separation of nearly 3,000 children as young as one year old from their parents, although it is evident that the logistics of such an operation were neither fully fleshed out nor apparent to those on the front lines of the impending "crisis" at the border. Jarring images of children crowded in chain-link cages began to permeate newspapers, television, and social media. When the Trump administration established a massive tent camp in Tornillo, Texas, to house unaccompanied minors in June 2018, images and descriptions of the haunting specter of internment and concentration camps of days gone by contributed to the mobilization of the general public, who were flabbergasted at the scope and intentionality of policies to create trauma among juveniles, a traditionally vulnerable population.

Amid the public outcry and a federal ruling, the administration reversed course and later in June indicated that children under the age of five would be reunited with their families by July 10 and that those over five would be reunited shortly thereafter on July 27. Nevertheless, there were still reportedly over 100 children separated from caretakers at the border even after the court order (Jordan 2019), as well as 500 minors in custody (Sacchetti 2018), generating additional controversy about gross underreporting of figures. As the Tornillo camp rapidly expanded—to a capacity of up to 3,000 youths prior to its ultimate closure in December 2018—community members across the nation no longer remained silent, horrified at the expansion of Tornillo and a similar camp in Homestead, Florida, particularly in light of the revelation of a simultaneous policy that resulted in the deportation of individuals who came forward to sponsor children in detention. Add to this the widespread concern about the death of two young Guatemalan migrants in US custody within three weeks in December 2018 and February 2019 reports indicating the implausibility of the Office of Refugee Resettlement's ability to reunite the thousands of remaining children with their families due to flaws in tracking (Congressional Research Service 2019; Soboroff and

Romero 2019) and it is logical that the public would take notice and express consternation and dissatisfaction at the state's intentional use of psychological violence on adults and children alike as a deterrent to immigration.

Yet, perhaps it was Kim Kyung-Hoon's November 2018 photograph of a mother and two diaper-clad children frantically fleeing tear gas launched by US border authorities that most broadly sparked outrage. Such imagery makes it difficult to deny the tangible evidence of violence perpetrated against migrants by the US government or the inherent risks of their journeys. Julia LeDuc's June 2019 image of Óscar Alberto Martínez Ramírez and his 23-month-old daughter who drowned while crossing the Río Bravo—that eerily recalls Nilüfer Demir's 2015 heart-wrenching image of drowned three-year-old Syrian refugee Alan Kurdi washed up on the beach—shook the international community. Similarly, although to a lesser degree, earlier images of unaccompanied minors in emergency shelters during the Obama administration's response to the alarming "humanitarian crisis" caused by the influx of thousands of unaccompanied and undocumented child migrants from Mexico and Central America in 2014 simultaneously sensationalized the seemingly recent phenomenon and captured the human element of migration by thrusting images of the most vulnerable victims into the limelight. Although recent media attention focuses on the sudden surge of child migrants, in historical terms, the displacement and movement of women and children across la línea is in no way new, nor are the traumas associated with immigration.

The renewed interest and emotion invested in discussions regarding the "problem" of immigration bring to the forefront the limited access the general public has had to the stories and experiences of the actors at the center of the political debates until relatively recently. Prior to the depiction of the 2018–2019 and earlier 2014 "crises" at the border, there was seemingly little attention paid to the personal stories of immigrants in the media until "undocumented and unafraid" students took to social media to share their stories as Congress was slated to consider the DREAM Act, a 2009 proposal to provide legal status to undocumented youth who were brought to the US as children, graduated from US high schools, and attend college or enter the military. "DREAMers" took advantage of social media to articulate and disseminate their stories and experiences, and some media outlets soon followed suit, revealing the human element of migration by covering the public protests that drew attention to the injustice of students' imminent deportations. However, mainstream attention to such matters remained relatively limited, even with an increasing number of activists speaking out, particularly after the proposal and April 2010 passage of Arizona's anti-immigrant Senate Bill 1070. Notably, most of the positive coverage demonstrating the personal impact of immigration policies and practices on individuals tended to focus on select "success stories" of migrants that reflected hegemonic narratives of progress and assimilation.

At the time, such stories stood out as being extraordinary and exceptional in the midst of acerbic political rhetoric and a veritable media frenzy depicting the influx of immigrants from Mexico and Latin America as a fearsome deluge of derelicts and drains on the United States government and society, yet they failed to provide authentic representations of more widespread migrant families' realities, which have largely been shaped by global factors beyond their control. Once again, these broader global factors—as well as a host of specific examples of US intervention in Latin America—that have driven waves of Latinx migration are omitted from most conversations about immigration in our current contentious climate of cultural confrontation that extends beyond political discourse exhorting the need to "Make America Great Again" to the broader propensity toward escalated interactions online and otherwise.

Some commentators attribute the increased tension to the rise of voices emboldened to articulate racist perspectives regarding immigrants to then presidential candidate Trump's denigrating references to Mexican nationals as "rapists" who "are bringing drugs . . . [and] crime" (2015) and explicit contrasts in his assessment of the worth of Latinx versus, say, Scandinavian migrants. Whether the current broader public articulation of such ideas is the result of the consumption of the inflammatory rhetoric or the manifestation of latent sentiments that couldn't be as openly shared in a more PC-conscious landscape, fear and hate-based discourse has, not surprisingly, undergirded specific immigration policies and practices. Nevertheless, this practice is not unique to the Trump administration, and various historians have addressed the unique ways that racialized conceptualizations of illegality have impacted Latinx families of migration since the late eighteenth century.

The public outcry and, in many cases, outrage that ensued in the wake of the circulation of images and stories of forced separation and immigrants' lack of due process within this last year is a timely reminder of the power of storytelling, one which US-based Latina authors have harnessed for decades. Whether the compelling stories be testimonies or fictionalized accounts of the trials and injustices endured by migrants, narrative portraits of individuals driven by desperation to cross the US-Mexico border are an effective means by which the US public may come to better understand the circumstances surrounding migration in order to view these human beings and their families as exactly that: human. In operating as a counter-discourse to criminalizing and stigmatizing representation of immigrants, Latina[1] texts have underscored the socioeconomic and psychological consequences of global market forces upon families as well as the violation of their basic human rights under US immigration policies, thereby functioning as oppositional representations to dominant views of immigration shaped by both global markets and the state.

More significantly, the Latina works that constitute the focus of this book are among the first to document more specifically the affront to immigrants' humanity vis-à-vis the constellation of interconnected layers or nodes of violence and trauma that have historically impacted women and children of migration before, during, and after the migratory journey. Engaging in the highly polemical social and political debate regarding undocumented immigration from the unique lens of literary analysis, *Ripped Apart* introduces readers to this growing body of Latina migrant narratives that capture the intersecting nodes of physical, psychological, sociocultural, and legal / structural violence. Readers will thus find a relatively extensive inclusion of summaries of relevant little-known works from the 1980s onward that portray the personal impact of the sociocultural phenomenon of the transnational[2] movement, as well as an explanation of the broader historical and legal contexts of the US-Mexico borderlands and transnational motherhood to more explicitly orient them to the manner in which Latina authors have utilized a variety of specific techniques in detailing the layers of trauma that are directly related to evolving US foreign policy (and political, economic, and military interventions) and immigration policies and practices as a means to constitute a more accurate or complete conceptualization of contemporary immigration and history and its impact on the individual.

Much as Chicana writers began to embrace the Chicana

woman and her intersectional "multiple voicings" as "theoretical subject" in the 1980s (N. Alarcón 1991, 38), contemporary Latina writers have shifted the focus to the migrant, namely the female migrant and the juvenile migrant, as the theoretical subjects of the new millennium through detailed depictions of their experiences and an emphasis on their qualities as human beings by turning public focus regarding immigration inward—within the confines of the home and the family. In doing so, this emerging corpus of texts promotes a shift from public consciousness, or awareness, of immigration to public conscience or conscientiousness, and exemplifies an interlocking of literature and social justice with migrant narratives as "resistance literature" (Harlow 1987). To delve into this notion of literature as resistance more deeply, *Ripped Apart* also incorporates a focus on empathy theory and cognitive approaches to literature and social justice, exploring how and why various genres of Latina narratives of migration (fiction and nonfiction alike) may be more effective than research studies or a historical overview in exposing readers to the atrocities related to the racialization of immigration and the policing of "the Other." As such, these Latina texts function as powerful tools that exemplify Dominick LaCapra's conceptualization of "empathic unsettlement" (2001, 41) and may ultimately prompt readers to engage in meaningful pro-social behaviors and actions, especially in the cases of texts geared toward juvenile audiences.

For the purposes of thematic organization, the chapters that follow begin with an overview of the constellation of overlapping nodes of the legal / structural, sociocultural, physical, and psychological violence that Latinx families of migration endure, drawing on theories of violence and trauma developed by Cathy Caruth, Dominick LaCapra, and Nicole M. Guidotti-Hernández, and offering an overview of trends within the field of trauma studies and the debate regarding the representability of trauma. Delineating broader historical and legal contexts that map on to legal / structural and sociocultural violence, the first chapter describes the creation of illegality, the racialization of immigration, and the policing of the nonwhite "Other." More specifically, I address the history of forcible separation of families as a result of immigration law, policies, and practices of policing, as connected to the manipulation of discourse and threat narratives about Latinxs and the economy, criminality, and "Americanness." This chapter also explores historical patterns of gendered immigration and the migration of unaccompanied minors, as well as the associated physical, psychological, and social vulnerabilities that the migration of women and youth entail.

Each subsequent chapter will elaborate upon the specific strategies that Latina authors implement to direct attention to the four intersecting nodes of violence and how these techniques foster reader empathy. Thus, the first chapter also introduces some basic concepts of Suzanne Keen's narrative empathy theory and elements of Mark Bracher's schema criticism to establish a foundation for deeper discussions throughout *Ripped Apart* of specific narrative techniques that contribute to the development of bounded strategic empathy, ambassadorial strategic empathy, and broadcast strategic empathy, as well as how these techniques may be particularly effective because of their potential for counteracting negative mental schemas and biased information processing through readers' systematic exposure to more adequate exemplars and prototypes that direct attention to characters' situatedness and malleability, the internal heterogeneity of marginalized groups, and the underlying solidarity or universality of human experience across social groups (Bracher 2013). In addition to exploring aspects of character identification (e.g., naming, relative flatness or round-ness, attributed speech, actions, and representation of con-sciousness) in the close analysis of the texts, I address narrative situation (e.g., point of view, perspective, the implicit location of the narrator with respect to other characters, and free indirect discourse). Moreover, I examine other factors that may affect empathetic responses in readers like metanarrative commen-tary, nested narrative levels, polyphony, repetitions, pace, order of plot events, and genre expectations.

Given the unique attributes of genres, *Ripped Apart* will undertake separate analyses of various examples of Latina literary production (novels, young adult novels, short stories, ethnographies, memoirs, theatrical works, and children's litera-ture) that document the ways in which families of Latinx migra-tion have historically been subject to a web of interconnected nodes of violence. Regardless of genre, Keen's and Bracher's respective ideas about narrative strategies to develop empathy and to retool faulty schemas related to autonomy, essentialism, atomism, and homogeneity are aptly suited to inform an anal-ysis of how Latina texts are effective instruments to combat erroneous conceptualizations regarding migrant families and their experiences and potentially lead to extratextual (i.e., "real-life") efforts to change policies and systems. Simultaneously, LaCapra's notion of "empathetic unsettlement" is particularly useful in understanding the power of texts to unsettle their readers to the degree that they experience a mediated reac-tion or response yet maintain textual or narrative distance and thereby avoid overidentification with characters and potential appropriation of the trauma.

Chapter 2 discusses four young adult novels that expose readers to specific historical moments—namely the Mexican Revolution and the repatriation of Mexicans and Mexican

Americans in the 1930s—and the profound impacts of displacement and family separations on the young characters. Published in the 1980s, Irene Beltrán Hernández's *Across the Great River* is a precursor to post-millennial works addressing issues of violence, immigration, and the family like Pam Muñoz Ryan's *Esperanza Rising* and Guadalupe García McCall's *Shame the Stars* and *All the Stars Denied*. These examples of Latina (and, more specifically, Chicana[3]) *Bildungsroman* present works of cultural resistance that interrogate both dominant notions of US-Mexico relations in the borderlands and patriarchal ideas and traditions within Mexican and Chicanx culture. This chapter thus analyzes how the texts document the various types of violence inflicted on Mexicans in the US in the context of the Mexican Revolution and the Great Depression as well as the triple oppression based on race, class, and gender that the female protagonists experience. Chapter 3 then directs attention to texts pertaining to Central American migration, namely Graciela Limón's *In Search of Bernabé* and *The River Flows North*, both of which condemn the violent ramifications of US political and economic intervention in Central America and its collateral damage on families. In conjunction with the short story "The Cariboo Café" by Helena María Viramontes, these works articulate the layers of personal trauma associated with overarching contexts of economic and sociopolitical instability in the region during the 1970s and '80s and exemplify Chicana texts that reflect the pan-ethnic solidarity of the Sanctuary Movement.

Chapter 4 focuses on similar themes of compounded layers of violence in fictional representations, in a more contemporary context, of the experiences of unaccompanied minors who seek opportunity, safety, and emotional fulfillment by crossing the border illegally. I explore divergences in youths' motivations for border crossing—whether rooted in a search for answers, unified families, or an escape from imminent death—in Reyna Grande's *Across a Hundred Mountains*, Ann Jaramillo's *La Línea*,[4] and Alexandra Diaz's *The Only Road*, and discuss how juvenile migrants present a paradox vis-à-vis their agency and the US legal system's simultaneous presumption of their vulnerability and/or criminality. In addition to analyzing the incorporation of the impacts of NAFTA and policies that led to the proliferation of violent gangs in Mexico and Central America, I establish a link between the depiction of characters' experiences with a variety of traumas and violence with psychological studies of migrant adolescents who struggle with adapting to evolving roles and familial configurations as a result of the inversion of typical mother-child relationships, family reunification after prolonged separation, and continued exposure to trauma in these examples of the *Bildungsroman*.

Chapter 5 continues the exploration of the relationship between intimate experiences and broader social, political, and cultural contexts of violence with a focus on motherhood, maternity, and migration in Latina novels. Through exposing the individual price of globalization and migration—namely the violence, exploitation, suffering, and injustice endured by migrants and their families—writers like Ana Castillo, Julia Álvarez, and Melinda Palacio cultivate transnational alliances in the fight for human rights while also invoking questions of amorphous identity, based on race, class, gender, and nationality. Due to the striking thematic parallels, I incorporate an analysis of Josefina López's play *Detained in the Desert* in this chapter, also explaining the unique features of theatrical works and genre-specific critique. As a whole, the texts examined in this chapter represent varied individual physical, emotional, and legal realities of border-crossing experiences and family separations and overtly interrogate and critique the hypocrisy of US immigration policy and practices and the dominant culture's indifference to the marginal position of migrants, much more so than the works discussed in the earlier chapters. *The Guardians* and *Return to Sender* focus on legal / structural, sociocultural, physical, and psychological violence in the wake of Operation Gatekeeper and Operation Return to Sender respectively. Alternatively, *Ocotillo Dreams* and *Detained in the Desert* reveal and contest the violence inherent in the policies and practices related to Arizona SB 1070 and racial profiling.

Chapter 6 shifts the focus to nonfiction, including Alicia Alarcón's collection of testimonials *La Migra me hizo los mandados*, Sonia Nazario's ethnographic text *Enrique's Journey: The Story of a Boy's Dangerous Odyssey to Reunite with His Mother*, and Diane Guerrero's memoir, *In the Country We Love: My Family Divided*, written with Michelle Burford. Each of these examples of life-writing reveals the profound personal impact of the varying types of violence that transnational and familial separation inflicts on women and children, during the migrant journey itself, when children are left behind in their country of origin by migrating parents, and when children remain in the US after parents' detention and deportation. Chapter 7 expands the scope to include analysis of recent children's (picture) books by Latinx[5] authors that similarly reveal the far-reaching consequences of the various layers of violence with which Latinx families of migration contend. Like texts geared toward adults, books written by Latinxs for small children and early readers bring the focus back to *la familia* and invoke consideration of what it means to be Latinx in the US, notions of cultural diversity within and beyond borders, and the importance of *transfrontera* alliances to combat and overcome layers of violence, thereby teaching empathy, cultural coalitions, and social change to the next generation.

The final chapter more broadly unites the contents of the previous chapters within the frameworks of empathy and literature for social justice, underlining the power of storytelling to counteract the manipulation of discourse through interrogation of dominant versions of "history" and identifying storytelling's role in enacting change in attitudes and behaviors. The Latina narratives of transnational migration included in *Ripped Apart* expose the exponential impact of the interconnected nodes of legal / structural, sociocultural, physical, and psychological violence of immigration policies and practices and, as such, function didactically to rectify distortions and omissions in the traditional K–12 curriculum and beyond. Via strategic use of a variety of techniques, Latina authors restore the humanity of individuals affected by transnational migration, emphasizing the interplay of the personal and the political, and both unsettling and compelling readers to become more informed and better equipped to engage with polemic issues of immigration and the family in their own communities.

CHAPTER 1
Historia(s) of Borderlands Violence: Telling the Tales of Historical and Contemporary Violence

The Power of Stories to Expose Violent Truths of History

"If every age has its symptoms, ours appears to be the age of trauma," Nancy K. Miller and Jason Tougaw (2002, 1) aver, describing the twentieth century literary "[turn] to narratives that record for public consumption the personal strain on the body and the mind produced by certain kinds of extreme suffering, from the annihilatory technologies of the Holocaust to the devastation of AIDS" (2), and American culture's apparent penchant for traumatic accounts. "In a culture of trauma," they contend, "accounts of extreme situations sell books" (2). This may explain, at least in part, the evident recent interest of independent and mainstream publishers alike in the proliferation and diversification of fiction and nonfiction that address the harrowing experiences of Mexican and Central American immigration. Whether they examine the circumstances compelling individuals or entire families to leave their homelands, the trials faced during and after the journey north, or the aftermath of separation due to detention or deportation, such narratives ultimately attempt to represent the unrepresentable or articulate the unspeakable violence (Guidotti-Hernández 2011; Morrison 1989). How, one might ask, can they accomplish this given the very limits of language and, moreover, do so in a way that engages, rather than alienates, a broad readership?

In the early 1990s, scholars like Cathy Caruth had already begun to undertake an interdisciplinary analysis of the nature of trauma, memory, identity, and representation, applying psychoanalytic and post-structuralist theories to literary studies. Although the contemporary contexts of individual and cultural trauma faced by Latinx families of migration undoubtedly diverge from those of victims of, for example, the Holocaust or the Rwandan genocide, the frameworks that historians and trauma scholars have proposed to understand trauma and its aftermath are useful in considering the nature of the violence and trauma associated with immigration and the Latinx experience in the United States from the mid-nineteenth century onward and the portrayal of such trauma in recent narratives of migration, as Marta Caminero-Santangelo (2016) has described. How and why are such texts effective means for exposing the historic deployment of violence in the borderlands? It is critical both to clarify the nature of the relationship between traumatic experience and representation and to define "empathy" in a literary sense before exploring the capacities (and limits) of specific narrative techniques to develop empathetic responses and perhaps enhance the potential for extratextual action from readers.

Based upon Freudian notions of fragmentation and repression of traumatic events and Lacanian repetition, Caruth's conceptualization of individual trauma posits the impossibility of locating or identifying a specific traumatic event, its impossible assimilation or understanding, and the return of elements surrounding such that continue to haunt the survivor later. The memory of trauma, "the story of a wound that cries out, that addresses us in the attempt to tell us of a reality or truth that is not otherwise available" (Caruth 1996, 4), emerges later in flashbacks and nightmares and defies understanding and therefore representation. "Instead of possessing the traumatic event as something to 'claim,' to narrativize and interpret—to work through—the Caruthian trauma victim is possessed by the trauma, which continues to haunt her in a vividness beyond comprehension," Emy Koopman notes (2010, 238). Taking a cue from post-structuralism, Caruth points to the incomprehensibility of trauma as well as the impossibility of its accurate artistic or textual representation. Yet, the enterprise of writing trauma is not a lost cause. In fact, LaCapra claims, "the literary (or even art in general) is a prime, if not the privileged, place for giving voice to trauma" (2001, 190), and its artistic representation is critical, but should begin from the stance of "not knowing" (Caruth 1996, 9), "rooted in the 'gap' or aporia, by language that defies referentiality" (Koopman 2010, 236).

To be sure, occurrences of trauma are uniquely individualized and difficult to categorize, and scholars like Stef Craps and Gert Buelens note the importance of "expand[ing] our understanding of trauma from sudden, unexpected catastrophic events" to encompass "the chronic psychic suffering produced by the structural violence of racial, gender, sexual, class, and other inequities" (2008, 3). This shift to consider overarching societal structures' contributions to ongoing stress—or "insidious trauma" (Root 1992, 240–41)—is appropriate in the case of individuals and the broader collectivity and is instrumental in understanding trauma as collective and chronic, particularly in the case of Latinx families affected by immigration. As Caminero-Santangelo rightly observes, "The move to conceptualize pervasive sociohistorical *conditions*, as well as events, as potentially traumatic constitutes a significant addition to trauma studies, with direct and obvious implications for an understanding of US Latino/a and Latin American communities impacted by large-scale migration north and by US policies that render that migration 'illegal'" (2016, 18).

Latina texts that broach the overlapping nodes of violence to which immigrants and their families are subject clearly depict the ripple effects of individual traumas of border crossing, detention, and/or deportation on their families and communities more broadly. The creation and dissemination of such texts, as Jeffrey C. Alexander and Neil J. Smelser have argued, contribute to a collective and cultural trauma that is not "inherent" (Alexander 2004, 8) but instead is constructed through its repetition and representation and thus "remembered, or made to be remembered" (Smelser 2004, 36). Although I would agree with Caminero-Santangelo's argument that "the narration of ongoing trauma simultaneously constitutes the community that is its subject" (2016, 102), and that transmission of stories enhances the potential for individual traumas to become collective or cultural, my focus in *Ripped Apart* is instead on the various strategies that Latinx authors utilize to communicate these traumas and foment narrative empathy with the texts' characters and situations.

Before delving into the potential for authors to manipulate narrative empathy, it is important to distinguish between narrative empathy and the broader emotional responses of both empathy and sympathy, and the potential relationships between them. Generally speaking, Keen describes empathy as "a vicarious, spontaneous sharing of affect, [which] can be provoked by witnessing another's emotional state, by hearing another's condition, or even by reading" (2007, 4). As opposed to empathy, sympathy has been conceptualized as a more distanced or disengaged emotional reaction, reflecting a concern or "an emotion felt for a target that relates to but does not match the target's feeling. ('I feel for you' rather than 'I feel with you.')" (Keen 2016, 17). While sympathy may entail a concern for another, it may also obstruct affective relationships, affinities, or actions through "implying difference from the discrete other who is the object of pity, charity, or condescension" (LaCapra 2001, 212).

On the negative repercussions of sympathetic (rather than empathetic) responses to depictions of suffering, for example, Susan Sontag comments, "So far as we feel sympathy, we feel we are not accomplices to what caused the suffering. Our sympathy proclaims our innocence as well as our impotence" (2003, 102). Alternatively, empathy enables "feeling your sorrow" rather than "feeling sorry for you" (Eagleton 2003, 156), and consequently accounts of the various traumas inflicted on Latinx families of migration that evoke empathetic responses may "[allow] us to feel for, or better: feel with, the other whom we do not know, may not understand, or even like" (Koopman 2010, 243), as opposed to merely provoking a response of sympathy or pity that enables readers simply to experience an emotional reaction without necessarily being compelled to identify with or consider how they have somehow been complicit in their previous disregard for the circumstances affecting the characters and the real-life individuals upon whom they are based.

Keen's theory of narrative empathy offers a useful framework for exploring how "empathy may be strategically employed in narrative for purposes of ideological manipulation" (2013, 5) in the context of contemporary Latinx narratives of migration to influence different audiences for distinct purposes. Defining narrative empathy as "the sharing of feeling and perspective-taking induced by reading, viewing, hearing, or imagining narratives of another's situation and condition . . . [that] overarches narratological categories, involving actants, narrative situation, matters of pace and duration, and storyworld features such as settings" (2013, 1), Keen describes the incorporation of empathy at the level of the author in its production, at the level of the reader in its reception and the alignment of "bodily sensations, moods, and motivations [that] match the character's" (2016, 18), and at the level of the text itself in "the mediation of fictional representations and narrative techniques" (2011a, 366). Often rooted in pursuit of social change or raising awareness, "Authors' efforts to use strategic narrative empathy show their ambition to reach target audiences with representations that sway the feelings of their readers" (Keen 2008, 478–80). Consequently, writers will develop three primary strategic uses of narrative empathy: "Bounded strategic empathy addresses members of in-groups. Ambassadorial strategic empathy addresses members of more temporally, spatially, or culturally remote audiences. Broadcast strategic empathy calls upon all readers to experience emotional fusion through empathetic representations of universal human experiences and generalizable responses to particular situations" (Keen 2008; 2013, 6). I argue throughout *Ripped Apart* that Latina authors employ a combination of bounded, ambassadorial, and broadcast strategic empathy in fiction and nonfiction texts alike with distinct motivations.

Latina authors whose works are included in *Ripped Apart* have often described their explicit objective of creating texts with which other Latinx individuals can identify and that document the histories and experiences that have traditionally been omitted or distorted in mainstream representation. It stands to reason, then, that these authors incorporate bounded strategic empathy, which "addresses the maker's in-group, close-by in time and space, and aspects of identity [and] relies on mutual experiences to stimulate readers' feeling for familiar others" (Keen 2015, 20). Nevertheless, the authors' aim extends beyond the in-group (i.e., fellow Latinx readers with potentially similar histories and experiences) to exemplify tactics of ambassadorial strategic empathy that "addresses targeted audiences with the aim of cultivating their empathy for the needy, the disenfranchised, or the misunderstood, often with a specific appeal for recognition, assistance or justice" (Keen 2015, 156–57).

Appealing to mainstream English-dominant US audiences of all ethnic and racial backgrounds, these narratives of the violence(s) of transnational migration function as ambassadorial texts that "[go] out into the world to recruit readers/viewers/ audiences by means of emotional fusion with current causes" (Keen 2015, 156–57). As opposed to broadcast strategic empathy, which focuses on universals of the human experience and can potentially connect present and future readers with characters and their experiences, "Ambassadorial strategic empathy is time-sensitive, context- and issue-dependent: it has a sell-by date, after which it remains historically interesting" (Keen 2015, 156–57). Given the attention to immigration and the plight of immigrant families in recent years, it is logical that authors would utilize their texts to expose the horrors that Latinxs have faced, thereby cultivating awareness and empathy among a broad audience in the name of social justice and change. This ambassadorial strategic empathy, then, aligns with notions of developing transborder solidarities.

Taken together, a variety of narrative elements and techniques may evoke an empathetic response to literary representations among readers, as is to be expected when texts incorporate the narrative affects of curiosity, suspense, and surprise that are part and parcel of storytelling (Keen 2015, 152). Moreover, various scholars of ethics, psychology, art, literature, and empathy studies have investigated relationships between reader response and identification with characters within and across group boundaries, as well as the influence of manipulation of perspective, point of view, imagery detail, conventions of genres that may affect reader reaction like serial delivery, length(iness), repetition, spatial and temporal fragmentation, metanarrative interjections, or commentary and more.[6] As it turns out, even paratexts of fictionality—that is, indicators of a text's categorization as fiction versus nonfiction—may be more likely to elicit an empathetic response (Keen 2007, 88–89). Keen privileges the fictive realm's potential for narrative empathy, suggesting, "some readers find it easier to share feelings with fictional characters than with real-life individuals, in part because our fiction reading doesn't demand anything of us. We can let our caution and skepticism relax when we read fiction: it doesn't matter if we are fooled by it because we go into the experience knowing that it is unreal" (Keen 2007, 168; 2016, 15).

Significantly, she notes the tenuous relationship between empathetic reader responses and extratextual social or altruistic action, as well as the tremendous influence of uncontrollable variables that each reader brings to the textual experience. Much like the sympathetic bystander that Sontag cautions against, Keen explains, "I have hypothesized that the 'no strings attached' expectation invoked by the paratextual label 'fiction' releases the readers to make empathetic connections without fear that they will be required to reciprocate, make commitments, or act in the real world" (2016, 15). Ironically, this suggests that the readers' awareness that the text is fictitious and thus that they will not be socially or ethically bound to engage with the relevant issues extratextually is what subconsciously permits them to be absorbed in the story and therefore be more inclined to display empathetic reactions to the characters and their situations. After all, "The combination of our actual distance and the aestheticized vividness of the representation may make it easier for us to feel for others made of ink and paper than for others made of flesh and bone (cf. Keen 2007)" (Koopman 2010, 235). This would imply a simultaneous connection or identification with the characters and yet a disassociation or disidentification, although perhaps to varying degrees depending on a variety of factors beyond the text itself.

Paratextual labels aside, once readers have experienced trauma alongside the characters and have gained access to previously unknown historical details that contextualize and accentuate characters' suffering, surely many readers will be less inclined to discard or dismiss that emotional experience upon physically closing the text and putting it down. Although Keen is reluctant to draw any conclusions about consistent causal relationships between narrative empathy and the altruism and "good world citizenship" that Martha Nussbaum proposes, we mustn't disregard the potential for literary production to effect change. As Koopman comments, "That literature constitutes a domain of its own does not cut it loose from the real world. On the contrary, precisely by relating to the real world[,] literary texts can disrupt conventional notions and confront us with what we would rather not look at in everyday life" (2010, 250). Perhaps the key to understanding how texts may function as tools for social justice is identifying that the amalgamation of narrative strategies that constitutes such a compelling story is what engages readers sufficiently to experience an empathetic response. I am inclined to think LaCapra's notion of empathic unsettlement may be the trick to understanding how—when the conditions are right—readers can be sufficiently drawn into texts and perhaps moved to action, even if said action is limited to "challenging normative ways of thinking and being" (Koopman 2010, 240), all the while protecting against both the under-identification *and* the over-identification with the victims of individual and/or collective cultural trauma.

Writing in the context of history and Holocaust studies, LaCapra highlights the need to "work through" rather than "act out" trauma in writing (on) trauma, and cautions against the potentially problematic relationships between victims and (secondary) witnesses of trauma derived from over- or under-identification with the victims on the part of the author and the reader. He notes that while "[i]t is dubious to identify with the victim to the point of making oneself a surrogate victim who has a right to the victim's voice or subject position" (2001, 78), at the other extreme is the propensity for complete detachment from, or disidentification with, the sympathized or pitied "discrete other" (212). LaCapra posits the importance of written representation of suffering and trauma embodying "empathic unsettlement," facilitating the development of "an affective relation, rapport, or bond with the other recognized and respected as other" (212–13). "Responsive to the traumatic experience of others" (41), writers—and by extension, readers—do not "seek facile uplift, harmonization, or closure" (78), but instead engage with the trauma of the other in "a kind of virtual experience through which one puts oneself in the other's position while recognizing the difference of that position and hence not taking the other's place" (78). In the context of narratives that broach intersecting experiences of violence and trauma related to migration, then,

26

I propose LaCapra's "empathic unsettlement" as a useful concept to understand how Latinx authors elicit a reader response via bounded and ambassadorial empathy strategies while safeguarding against the appropriation of the trauma or the minimization or diminishing of the trauma through its narrativization.

These dangers of the appropriation or trivialization of trauma via its textual or artistic representation have been the subject of much scholarly discussion surrounding ethics and arts. For, as Jill Bennett observes, "If art purports to register the true experience of violence or devastating loss—to be about a particular event—then it lays claim to an experience that is fundamentally owned by someone. Moreover, it invites a wider audience to partake of this experience in some way" (2005, 3). Thus, in addition to the post-structuralist concern about the inadequacy of language to convey trauma, the artistic or textual representation of trauma may capitalize on the experience that does not inherently "belong" to the creator of that representation. Moreover, in its narrativization, any inadequacy or inconsistency "can be felt as a betrayal, a sacrilege, or a renewed act of violence" (Roth 2012, 83), particularly in the transformation of historical events and/or memories inherent in their representation. "Narrative memory, which is at the core of historical representation on paper or on film," Roth asserts, "transforms the past as a condition of retaining it" (85). In a sense, the Latina authors who write about the traumas endured by Latinx families affected by migration are not just transforming the past through ensuring the memory and retention of it. Rather, they are unsettling the very historical representations of such traumas by inscribing them in literature and, vis-à-vis empathetic narrative techniques, compelling readers to engage with these traumas within and beyond the text.

Through repeated engagement with diverse narrative depictions of the intersecting layers of violence and trauma that permeate the lives of Latinx migrants and their families, readers may reflect metacognitively on their own preconceived notions of individual and collective migrant experiences, or at least take note of the disparity between their assumptions about Latinxs affected by immigration and their textual representation(s). As Keen observes in reference to English author Thomas Hardy's works, for example, "His novels and stories provide readers with proxy visits with their countrymen and women, offering a route to the familiarity that would disabuse readers of set views about laborers' uncouth speech, uncleanliness, misery, and laziness" (Keen 2011a, 373). Readers' access to descriptions that go beyond the stereotypical representations of marginalized groups and emphasize the "economic realities that shaped their lives" (Keen 2011a, 374) has the potential to counteract readers' negatively biased mental schemas that are based on essentialist notions of individuals as homogeneous and immutable and tend to ignore how environment and circumstances affect choices and life outcomes.

Along these same lines, Bracher proposes in *Literature and Social Justice: Protest Novels, Cognitive Politics, and Schema Criticism* an innovative and interdisciplinary model that explains how protest novels (like Upton Sinclair's *The Jungle* or John Steinbeck's *The Grapes of Wrath*) function as part of a broader "radical cognitive politics: a strategy of intervention that corrects not just faulty propositional knowledge but also the multiple faulty nonpropositional forms of knowledge that constitute the roots of false and unjust perceptions, judgments, feelings, actions, and policies concerning other people" (2013, 12–13). He notes that the mere presentation of data and/or sound arguments is unlikely to effectively alter others' perspectives because of how deeply embedded the erroneous beliefs or assumptions are in "faulty cognitive apparatuses" (10). Thus, it is critical to modify four types of knowledge: (1) *exemplars*, or specific examples of individuals; (2) *prototypes*, or templates that constitute a composite description of general types of individuals and often manifest as stereotypes; (3) *information-processing routines* that a given exemplar or prototype activates, resulting in certain emotional responses and/or actions; and (4) *propositional knowledge*, or metacognition, that permits awareness of one's information processing with attention to whether, for example, they take into consideration circumstances or context when judging another's actions (Bracher 2013, 13, 26–27). As Bracher notes, literature is well positioned to enhance the cache of cognitive exemplars and prototypes—albeit second-hand—and, through these additional and corrective exemplars and prototypes, alter the perceptions of such individuals within one's mental schemas that ultimately lead to decision-making and action. Complementing Keen's notions of bounded and ambassadorial empathy strategies, the application of Bracher's schema criticism methodology may help to explain how and why Latina narratives of transnational migration that document the interconnected layers of trauma are potentially powerful vehicles for social change.

Of utmost importance are readers' "repeated encounters with, and encoding in memory of, corrective exemplars, and repeated rehearsals of corrective information-processing routines" (Bracher 2013, 295). As Bracher notes, protest novels have the potential to effect extratextual change via cognitive training, so to speak:

> The novels we will examine work to correct readers' deficient general knowledge of persons in a similar, but much more systematic and thus presumably more powerful, way: by providing multiple new exemplars that embody crucial information that many readers' current exemplars and prototypes omit. In addition, by

repeatedly engaging readers in processing numerous emotionally powerful exemplars representing a more adequate understanding of persons, these novels promote the gradual construction of new, more adequate general person-prototypes incorporating the recognition that individuals are situated rather than purely autonomous, malleable rather than immutable, in fundamental solidarity with each other rather than in unmitigated opposition, and internally heterogeneous rather than homogeneous. (28)

By extension, then, a larger and richer collection of adequate exemplars in episodic memory—from textual and extratextual experiences connected with Latinx migrants and their families, for example—will contribute to the construction of more adequate prototypes in semantic memory. Subsequent extratextual encounters with Latinxs and/or immigrants are then more likely to trigger information-processing mechanisms that will ultimately produce (more) appropriate emotions and actions based on the activation of the memory of the more comprehensive set of cognitive exemplars and prototypes, literary or otherwise.

Moreover, the narratives analyzed in *Ripped Apart* tend to highlight the unique and specific circumstances of Latinx migrants and their families within frameworks or systems that largely determine individuals' courses of action. As Bracher comments, "As in *The Jungle*, *The Grapes of Wrath*'s foregrounding of the circumstantial causes of characters' behaviors and life outcomes evokes sympathy[7] for the characters and anger at the system that produces these circumstances, and readers' repeated experience of these emotions in relation to their respective objects increases their inclination to experience the same emotions toward similar extratextual objects" (200). Similarly, the narrative portrayal of the various traumas endured by Latinx migrants, their families, and their broader communities fosters a greater degree of understanding of characters' handling of their unique and often unjust situations, and simultaneously condemns the overarching institutions and social, political, and economic global forces that shaped their individual actions and behaviors.

Accordingly, Bracher remarks, "[T]o the extent that these circumstances [beyond individuals' control] are a product of human institutions and systems . . . efforts to prevent harm and injustice should be directed toward changing the institutions and systems" (204). Indeed, he adds, collaborative action to effect this degree of social change will also inherently involve cognitive retraining to privilege the solidarity schema—the concept of "individual welfare and life outcomes as inextricably interwoven with those of other" (291)—rather than the atomism schema that "obscures one's inherent sameness and interconnectedness with all other human beings and supports the view that individuals are fundamentally separate and isolated from each other, that life is a war of each against all, and . . . potentiates the infrahumanization and dehumanization of the other" (15). With the cognitive shift from atomism to solidarity, readers will be more apt to adopt the stance that "we are all responsible for each other and to each other and must exercise this responsibility through collective actions in the form of policies, institutions, systems, and structures that take our situatedness, malleability, and solidarity into account" (Bracher 2013, 291).

With this framework in mind, I contend that Latina narratives of transnational migration not only document the layered traumas to which immigrants and their families have historically been subject but effectively utilize narrative techniques that enhance the potential for empathetic reactions among readers, and—through their contributions to diverse exemplars of the Latinx immigrant experience—may impact extratextual actions. With repeated exposure to corrective exemplars that shift the default from an assumption of migrant characters' autonomy and immutability to their situatedness and malleability, readers may accordingly shift toward a schema of solidarity (rather than atomism) and thus be more compelled to take action to change harmful policies and practices related to immigration. Nevertheless, it is imperative to note the unlikelihood of fully embracing this cognitive schema of solidarity and, following LaCapra, that doing so could potentially result in over-identification with characters (and, by extension, those whose experiences they portray). Thus, I maintain that Latina narratives of the intersecting violences of transnational migration "unsettle" both the historical representations of immigrant experiences and the readers themselves through implementation of narrative strategies to produce mediated empathetic responses, all the while providing sufficient narrative distance via readers' awareness of their own positionalities and/or privilege to prevent the potential appropriation of trauma.

Intersecting Nodes of Violence in Latina Literary Production

The specific intersectional nature of experienced traumas is unique to each individual affected by transnational migration, and the various permutations of such within Latina narratives reflect this circumstance. Nonetheless, one can typically identify four overarching categories, although they are largely difficult to disentangle from one another. Perhaps the most obvious category is that of physical violence, primarily evident in narrative depictions of bodily assault but also in representations of physical discomfort related to, for example, hunger, thirst, or exposure that can be experienced before, during, and after the migratory journey. Physical violence may entail feminized or gender-based permutations of violent assault like rape or the distinct implications of hunger and starvation of one's children, as well as experiences of broader vulnerability, particularly for women and/or children who have been left behind. Nevertheless, the risk of physical violence is high for any unauthorized migrants outside of their countries of origin because of the likelihood that they will be subject to heightened levels of policing and the physical implications of such.

Closely connected to physical violence—and in some cases borne out of physical trauma(s)—is psychological violence. Within the realm of this category, individuals who remain in their countries of origin may experience a sense of abandonment and fear for the well-being of loved ones who have embarked on the migrant journey. The uncertainty about their loved ones' whereabouts and their own future economic, social, and familial stability will undoubtedly affect their emotional well-being. Those who have experienced physical violence in the wake of a loved one's departure, during their own trek, or thereafter are apt to suffer from post-traumatic stress disorder, anxiety, and depression. For unauthorized and mixed-status families, the fear of apprehension even long after crossing the border and establishing a life in the US—and the consequent experience of living in the shadows and the consistent uncertainty that entails—contributes to their ongoing psychological distress. In the event of physical arrest and detention, the psychological trauma becomes even more profound. In addition to the physically deleterious conditions and dehumanizing and isolating experiences of detention itself, detainees further struggle to cope with their inability to support family members economically and emotionally and the uncertainty of their future, particularly if they will be deported. Family members of (potential) detainees similarly face this insidious and ongoing trauma due to their forced separation related to detention and/or deportation.[8]

As noted above, trauma studies scholars have begun to consider the role of sociocultural structures, conditions, and institutions in engendering and perpetuating chronic psychological distress, in addition to perhaps more obvious examples of discrete traumatic events. Accordingly, I identify various manifestations of sociocultural violence that surface in texts written by Latina authors with attention to overarching xenophobia, ethnocentrism, racism, and discrimination that affect broader Latinx and/or immigrant communities and how these are inherently linked to physical and psychological traumas. The sociocultural node of violence also encompasses gender-based vulnerabilities tied to patriarchal cultural norms and historical patterns of migration and separation, as well as the repercussions of non-compliance with societal norms.

Finally, narratives featured in *Ripped Apart* often address the cascading physical, psychological, and, to an extent, sociocultural effects that are rooted in legal / structural violence. I thus draw on Cecilia Menjívar and Leisy J. Abrego's notion of intersecting legal, physical, structural, and symbolic violence. As they explain:

> The concept of legal violence incorporates the various, mutually reinforcing forms of violence that the law makes possible and amplifies. This lens allows us to capture the aggravation of otherwise "normal" or "regular" effects of the law, such as the immigrants' predicament that results from indefinite family separations due to increased deportations; the intensification in the exploitation of immigrant workers and new violations of their rights; and the exclusion and further barring of immigrants from education and other forms of socioeconomic resources necessary for mobility and incorporation. (Menjívar and Abrego 2012, 1384)

Taking a cue from Menjívar and Abrego's understanding of the various types of violence as "linked and mutually constitutive" (1385), my conceptualization of legal / structural violence expands the category to include the ongoing traumas embedded in the implications of exploitative labor institutions and practices; inadequate access to resources related to education, healthcare, and social services; migrants' "legal liminality" (Menjívar 2002); and, most important, specific immigration policies that have resulted in the forcible separation of families. The traumas of loss and long-term separation have stemmed from government initiatives like the Bracero Program and various enforcement operations, in addition to the inherent inequalities based on gender and (il)legality in US immigration laws that, according to Abrego, have not only "limited migration in multiple ways, but . . . also make life unbearable for immigrants already in receiving countries, blocking routes to obtain legal residency and diminishing the possibility for family reunification" (2014, 196). Likewise, even transnational family members who are eligible for reunification endure exacerbated physical, psychological, and sociocultural violences because of the legal and structural mechanisms that stall the process.

The Racialization and Policing of Immigration

A glimpse at the history of US immigration and naturalization laws brings to light how policies have contributed to the construction of race and the racialization of ethnicities and nationalities, as described by Ian Haney López in *White By Law: The Legal Construction of Race* (2006), and further, how notions of whiteness and illegality have been instrumental in shaping the economic, social, and broader legal structures in what has been termed by Aristide Zolberg "a nation by design" (2008). By and large, laws have codified a hierarchical (and, following Barrera (1979), colonial) racial system that benefits capitalist interests through the creation, exploitation, and oppression of a disposable labor force that, even despite assurances of citizenship and

35

its associated rights, is never considered to be wholly "American." The Naturalization Act of 1790 considered only "free white persons" to be eligible for US citizenship (Molina 2014, 24), defining whiteness in connection with citizenship in opposition to slaves and indigenous peoples. Nevertheless, with shifting demographics due to an influx of immigrants from around the globe, determining who would count as legally and socially "white" became complicated, and the racial classification of Mexicans morphed depending on the historical context.

Ending the Mexican–American War, the 1848 Treaty of Guadalupe Hidalgo pushed Mexico's northern geopolitical border further southward to its current location and guaranteed US citizenship and land rights to an estimated 80,000 Mexican and/or Spanish inhabitants of the considerable portions of northern Mexico that essentially became a part of the US overnight (Rumbaut 2003, 94). However, Anglo-Saxon Americans—particularly those who stood to benefit from the land or other capital of Mexicans now living in the US—would utilize racial scripts that applied to other groups like Native Americans, Asians, and blacks to contend that Mexicans were, in fact, culturally and socially nonwhite and should thus be treated as such (Molina 2014). Although, as Molina notes, these other groups "were written out of whiteness and, at different points of history, citizenship, in absolute terms" (23), the framework—or racial script—that institutionalized discriminatory and racist treatment of these groups as inferior could rather easily be applied to Mexicans. While not initially subject to dispossession, displacement, and prohibition from entering the US to the same degree as were Native Americans (with the Indian Removal Act of 1830) and Asians (as per the Naturalization Act of 1870, the Chinese Exclusion Act of 1882, the 1907–1908 Gentlemen's Agreements limiting Japanese immigration, and the Immigration Act of 1917 that created the Asiatic Barred Zone), individuals of Mexican descent would contend with policy changes rooted in nativist sentiment, likely as a reflection of the shifting—and, to the socio-economically dominant classes, threatening—demographics.

During the first decade of the twentieth century, immigrants constituted a larger portion of the US population than ever before (Sampaio 2015, 38), and as World War I began, the US began to target immigrants who were considered subversive. Sampaio remarks that Mexicans were largely exempt from scrutiny or immigration quotas at the time because they provided necessary support for US agricultural and industrial needs and many were considered to be merely "birds of passage," or seasonal workers, thereby demonstrating how "[c]apitalist needs eclipsed desires for a racially and culturally homogenous nation" (21). Perhaps coinciding with massive migration of approximately one million Mexicans in the wake of the Mexican Revolution (Rumbaut 2003, 95), ethnic tensions began to escalate during the 1910s and 1920s, evident in the increased hostility toward Mexicans, especially on the part of the Texas Rangers and other vigilante groups, that functions as the backdrop of some of the Latina narratives included in *Ripped Apart*. Mae M. Ngai notes, "During the 1920s, immigration policy rearticulated the US-Mexico border as a cultural and racial boundary, as a creator of illegal immigration" (2014, 67), through its implementation of mandatory baths, delousing, and medical-line inspections in addition to literacy tests (68). Notably, these dehumanizing and degrading procedures were not required for all immigrants, or even for all Mexican immigrants. Rather, Europeans and those Mexicans who arrived as first-class railroad passengers were exempt, suggesting that "[r]acial presumptions about Mexican laborers, not law, dictated the procedures at the Mexican Border" (Ngai 2014, 68).

Despite Mexicans' continued exemption from the exclusions or quota system stipulated in the Immigration Act of 1924—or perhaps because of it—popular sentiment toward Mexican immigrants had changed. Sampaio suggests that this was due in part to their increased presence (from just 10.9 percent of all legally admitted immigrants a couple of years prior to the 1924 act to 16.1 percent, and second only to German-origin immigrants by 1927) and their movement toward interior regions (2015, 21). The Immigration Act of 1924 also authorized the creation of the Border Patrol, primarily to monitor and prevent the entry of Asian immigrants as well as contraband like alcohol (it was Prohibition, after all). Ngai points to this legislation as critical in paradoxically cementing the notion of the interconnectedness of race and illegality of Mexicans:

> It was ironic that Mexicans became so associated with illegal immigration because, unlike Europeans, they were not subject to numerical quotas and, unlike Asiatics, they were not excluded as racially ineligible to citizenship. But as numerical restriction assumed primacy in immigration policy, its enforcement aspects—inspection procedures, deportation, the Border Patrol, criminal prosecution, and irregular categories of immigration—created many thousands of illegal Mexican immigrants. The undocumented Mexican laborer who crossed the border to work in the burgeoning industry of commercial agriculture emerged as the prototypical illegal alien. (2014, 71)

Kelly Lytle Hernández similarly identifies the role of Border Patrol surveillance in contributing to the connection between Mexicans, as members of a racialized category, and illegality (2010, 57–58). Not coincidentally, it is during this period that stereotypes of Mexicans as "illegal," criminal, and diseased[9] emerged with more regularity.

At the time, there was also a concerted effort to police "women and their reproductive capabilities" in connection with citizenship. Beyond proposed legislation to limit the potential for children born abroad to American-born women to inherit their citizenship (Sampaio 2015, 69), some politicians argued for limiting Mexican women's immigration on the basis of inordinately high birth rates and the likelihood that their children would become public charges or otherwise need governmental support (Sampaio 2015, 82). Perhaps not surprisingly, after the Great Depression devastated the US economy, Mexicans were scapegoated as the culprits who were draining resources and/or stealing jobs from more deserving Anglo Americans. A massive deportation program ensued nationally, during which over one million Mexicans and Mexican Americans,[10] approximately 60 percent of whom were US citizens, were rounded up and forcibly removed during the so-called Mexican Repatriation (1929–1936) (Balderrama and Rodríguez 2006). The unconstitutional and unethical practice of forced displacement emerged again the following decade when Franklin Roosevelt signed Executive Order 9066, resulting in the internment of 112,000 Japanese and Japanese American individuals (approximately 70,000 of whom were US citizens) from 1942 to 1945 in the name of protecting national security during World War II (Sampaio 2015, 45; "Japanese-American Internment"). Despite the fact that the Mexican (American) community had established a long-standing presence in the US by the 1940s, they, like their Japanese (American) counterparts, "continued to be seen as outsiders . . . as not full citizens" (Molina 2014, 15), embodying Raymond Rocco's concept of "exclusionary inclusion" (2014, 29).

Although "Okies" and other migrants filled some of the gaps created by the massive deportations of Mexican agricultural workers in the 1930s, growers were concerned about labor shortages brought on by the deployment of US soldiers to fight in WWII and thus pushed for arrangements to recruit temporary guest workers. Bilateral agreements between Mexico and the US established the Bracero Program (1942–1964), facilitating the immigration of approximately 5 million Mexican contract laborers primarily to maintain the US agricultural industry (Rumbaut 2003, 95). Although one of the intentions of the program may have been to curb unauthorized immigration, Mexicans continued to migrate illegally in even greater numbers (Goodman 2018, 44). Deportations continued, particularly in the tense political context of the Cold War and the approval of the Internal Security Act in 1950, authorizing the deportation and expulsion of "politically dangerous" non-US citizens. This legislation also served as a pretext for the 1954 implementation of Operation Wetback, an immense and aggressive deportation effort that aimed to expel at least a million undocumented immigrants (Molina 2014, 112).

Indeed, the various raids and roundups resulted in the deportation without hearings of approximately one million individuals, including US citizens. Even the use of the term "wetback" signals the conflation of illegal entry, criminality, and the racialization of Mexicans and Mexican Americans. The approval of the Hart-Celler Act of 1965 has also been identified as a critical moment in the creation of illegality (A. Chomsky 2014, 35–36), particularly as pertains to Mexican immigrants. By abolishing the previous national quota system and imposing a cap on visas for immigrants from the Western Hemisphere—and thus Latin America—for the first time the year after the termination of the Bracero Program, the legislation ultimately criminalized any entry above and beyond the annual limit of 120,000. Such a cap would be insufficient to deter migration, given the history of the recruitment of Mexicans as a reserve labor force.

What, then, would serve as an effective deterrent? Decades later,[11] Immigration and Naturalization Service (INS) would continue its tactics of conducting sweeps, as in the case of Operation Restoration, the 5-day raid known as the "Chandler Roundup" that resulted in the arrest of hundreds of individuals suspected of being unauthorized and unable to present immediate proof of lawful status. However, the Border Patrol would largely change its focus in the 1990s from apprehending immigrants after they crossed the border to increasing surveillance of the major ports of entry, thereby pushing border crossing to rural zones that would be easier to monitor and be less visible to the general public (De León 2019, 23). Soon thereafter, the US Border Patrol Strategic Plan announced its Prevention Through Deterrence (PTD) strategy, which capitalized on the dangerous terrain of the natural environment of the borderlands as a primary deterrent. The report explains, for example, "Illegal entrants crossing through remote, uninhabitable expanses of land and sea along the border can find themselves in mortal danger" (US Border Patrol 1994, 2).

As Jason De León deduces from governmental reports about the assessment of the strategy's effectiveness, any insinuation that an increase in migrant fatalities is an "unintended consequence" of PTD blatantly contradicts the Government Accountability Office's (1997) report that predicts that "deaths may increase (as enforcement in urban areas forces aliens to attempt mountain or desert crossings)" (2019, 84). By militarizing the El Paso, San Diego, and Tucson sectors and fortifying the border between Mexico and Texas and New Mexico via Operation Blockade (and Operation Hold the Line), Operation Gatekeeper, Operation Safeguard, and Operation Rio Grande respectively, US policy only further contributed to the imminent traumas that migrants crossing the US-Mexico border will face. Moreover, that tracking migrant fatalities is included as a means to evaluate PTD's effectiveness lays bare the organization's underlying view of migrants as expendable and lacking humanity. It is not surprising, then, that the plots of various Latina narratives of transnational migration develop within the context of PTD, drawing attention to the concomitant interconnected physical, psychological, sociocultural, and legal / structural violences of such policies and operations.

Coinciding with the rollout of the PTD operations, the approval of new laws in the mid-1990s led to marked increases in detention and deportation. The 1996 Illegal Immigration Reform and Immigrant Responsibility Act (IIRIRA), and to a lesser extent the 1996 Antiterrorism and Effective Death Penalty Act (AEDPA), were detrimental because they authorized additional funding for staffing and enhanced militarization of the border to support PTD operations and established new grounds for inadmissibility (including suspicion of terrorism and not demonstrating evidence of certain vaccinations, among others) (Sampaio 2015, 53–54). More important, though, they stipulated mandatory deportation requirements for a broadened category of aggravated felonies that had previously allowed for judicial discretion / review, applied laws retroactively, implemented bars on (re)entry, and subjected individuals who had unlawfully entered the US twice to a possible federal prison sentence (Golash-Boza 2012, 27). More specifically, IIRIRA created a category of individuals as "unlawfully present" and stipulated penalties corresponding to the length of time during which one fell within this category, after unauthorized entry or overstaying a visa, for example. If an individual had been unlawfully present for over a year, then they would be deported and denied the possibility of legal entry for a minimum of ten years. If the same individual (who had been unlawfully present for over a year) attempted to reenter the US illegally prior to the end of the 10-year period, they would then face a permanent bar, essentially precluding any possibility for legal immigration, even for spouses or parents of US citizens or lawful permanent residents (Golash-Boza 2012, 34).

Connections between immigration enforcement and criminal law intensified through these additions of criminal violations that could potentially impact immigrants' status—even retroactively after having already served time for said violation(s)—and the increase in immigration violations that could result in criminal charges (Martin 2018, 152), and exemplify the intersection that Juliet Stumpf (2000) has described as "crimmigration." This again feeds into the notions of the undocumented or "alien Other" as criminal or aberrant that had already emerged in the law and popular sentiment. The stipulations of IIRIRA have largely remained intact, further enhanced after 9/11 in the name of winning the War on Terror. The 2001 USA PATRIOT Act and 2002 Homeland Security Act provided additional funding for surveillance and deportation, authorized certain circumstances in which noncitizens could be deported without due process, and established the Department of Homeland Security, dismantling the Immigration and Naturalization Service and reorganizing into U.S. Citizenship and Immigration Services (USCIS), U.S. Customs and Border Protection (CBP), and U.S. Immigration and Customs Enforcement (ICE).

Complementing the anti-terrorism legislation, ICE carried out a variety of post–9/11 enforcement and removal operations to target suspected terrorists or other national security threats, inevitably also apprehending, detaining, and deporting hundreds of thousands of non-terrorists. Operation Endgame (2003), Operation Frontline (2004), and Operation Return to Sender (2006–2007) are just a few examples of the sweeps and raids that stoked fear in immigrant communities across the nation and reinforced the concept of immigrants as terrorists in the national imaginary (Massey and Pren 2012, 10–11). During the same decade, the Department of Homeland Security and Department of Justice jointly launched Operation Streamline (2005), which mandated criminal charges for unauthorized entry, even for first-time offenders, and is notorious for its mass hearings. This "zero-tolerance" initiative further muddied the already murky waters between the civil immigration system and the criminal justice system by diverting nonviolent unauthorized immigrants from civil deportation proceedings to face federal prosecution and potentially serve time in federal prisons. Compared with a daily average of 2,370 detainees awaiting civil proceedings or deportation (not serving time for criminal convictions) in 1973 and 5,532 in 1994, the average daily rate of immigration detention jumped to 20,000 in 2001 and steadily increased to 33,400 in 2008 (Golash-Boza 2012, 3). All told, over two million people were deported between 1998 and 2007, and 100,000 of these individuals were parents of US-citizen children (Department of Homeland Security 2009, 5).

Thus, the mandatory detention, deportation, and potentially permanent prohibition that indisputably embedded familial separation into the law as punitive measures continue to worsen the scope and degree of trauma(s) faced by the growing number of immigrants, their families, and their broader communities. In 2017, these US communities included 10.5 million unauthorized immigrants, up from 3.5 million in 1990, who are likely to have lived in the US for at least ten years (Passel and Cohn 2019; Radford 2019). Moreover, recent figures indicate that approximately 5 million US-born minor children lived with at least one unauthorized immigrant in 2016 (Passel et al. 2018). A broader view of the 2012–2016 period suggests that roughly 5.1 million children under age eighteen were living with an undocumented parent, 80 percent (or 4.1 million) of whom were US citizens,

16 percent (809,000) who were undocumented themselves, and 3 percent (167,000) who were legal permanent residents or held temporary visas (Batalova et al. 2020).

Families continue to be ripped apart by policies and practices that police their very presence and, in many cases, they become targets simply because of assumptions based on their appearance, language, neighborhood of residence, etc., regardless of legal status. As Sampaio observes, "Immigrants who were already marked by race, ethnicity, or religion as 'foreign' were easily positioned as 'enemies' or 'threats'" (2015, 17), as opposed to newcomers who would—or could—potentially integrate, assimilate, or become "Americanized." In a sense, anyone somehow marked as "Other" was further pushed to the fringes of American belonging and became collateral damage. "While the image of detainees cultivated in raids and round-ups was often that of Latino and Arab men, Latinas were apprehended with greater frequency as the raids expanded, and reports of gendered violence increased as these women were held in or transferred to immigration detention centers" (Sampaio 2015, 97), with obviously negative repercussions for families.

Although a common assumption is that deportations are deployed as tactic of control and enforcement more regularly under the directives of Republican administrations (like that of Ronald Reagan or George W. Bush), the reality is that deportations reached a peak number during the Obama administration. During President Obama's two terms, 3,066,457 individuals were deported (Nowrasteh 2019), a figure that exceeds the sum of the removals during the administrations of all other presidential administrations during the twentieth century combined (Marshall 2016). This steep increase is likely a result of the combination of more stringent federal policies, joint efforts with local law enforcement, and the development of state-level legislation. The federal Secure Communities program implemented nationally in 2008, for example, permitted local law enforcement to check the immigration status of all individuals booked into a county or local jail through comparison of fingerprints with those in Department of Homeland Security databases (Preston 2010).

One of the most noteworthy state bills to surface during this time is Arizona's Support Our Law Enforcement and Safe Neighborhoods Act, otherwise known as Senate Bill 1070, which was passed in April 2010. Upon signing SB 1070 with its "show me your papers" provision into law, Governor Jan Brewer aimed to criminalize presence in the country without appropriate immigration documents through granting police the power to detain anyone suspected of being in the United States illegally, essentially legalizing racial profiling (and reminiscent of the intent behind the 1997 Chandler Roundup). Blocking three of the four provisions of SB 1070, the federal Supreme Court ultimately upheld the provision that requires the determination of arrested or detained individuals' immigration status if there is "reasonable suspicion" that they are not legally in the US and consequent action, like deportation. A June 2012 hearing specified that state police may not detain individuals for prolonged periods for not carrying documents that prove legal immigration status, and that cases involving allegations of racial profiling would be permitted to proceed through the courts should they arise. The American Civil Liberties Union filed the first such legal challenge in November 2013 (ACLU, n.d.).

Prior to the US Supreme Court's ruling on the constitutionality of Arizona SB 1070, twenty-five other states introduced copycat legislation in 2011, with only five—Utah, Indiana, Georgia, South Carolina, and Alabama—ultimately passing anti-immigrant laws. Lower courts struck down the implementation of the primary components of this legislation before the laws could take effect in all of these states except Alabama (National Immigration Law Center 2014). Ultimately, though, Alabama House Bill 56, signed into law by Governor Robert Bentley in June 2011, would also face considerable obstacles. Even more stringent than Arizona SB 1070, Alabama HB 56 would require public schools to determine the immigration status of students in kindergarten through 12th grade, require police officers to stop anybody suspected of being an undocumented or "illegal" immigrant, criminalize employing or leasing property to undocumented immigrants, and even go so far as to make it a crime to give a ride to an individual without documents (CNN 2011; Preston 2011). Thus, HB 56 recruited Alabama police officers, teachers, school administrators, and landlords to work alongside Immigration and Customs Enforcement authorities in the name of deterring and eradicating illegal immigration. Judges eventually blocked the most restrictive provisions in October 2013 (Peterson Beadle 2014).

The deleterious ramifications of the implementation, and even the consideration, of the 164 anti-immigrant laws proposed by state legislatures from 2010 to spring 2012 (Molina 2014, 145) inevitably extend to the families of transnational migration. Between July 2010 and September 2012, 204,810 undocumented parents with at least one child who was a US citizen were deported, constituting 23 percent of the total deportations during that time (Freed Wessler 2012). ICE reports that were sent to the Senate Appropriations Committee and the Senate Judiciary Committee in April 2014 indicate that 72,410 parents of one or more US-born children were removed in 2013; about 10,700 of these immigrants had no criminal convictions (Foley 2014). More recently, ICE deported 87,351 parents of at least one US-citizen child between 2015 and the end of 2017 (Buiano 2018).

Scholars have thus begun to direct attention to the monumental consequences for US-born children whose undocumented parents were among the deported (or could be) and to attempt to comprehend more fully how the global phenomenon of migration and the legislative consequences of fluctuations in such impact migrant families. Their work builds upon a sizeable interdisciplinary body of research that explores the implications of historical patterns of gendered migration and the separation of families caused by parents' migration as well as that caused by the migration of unaccompanied minors, all of which helps to contextualize the ways that transnational migration has inherently altered familial structures and roles. A better understanding of how the experience of family separation leads not only to hardship and exposure to various types of trauma but also to developing agency will be helpful in informing the portrayal of simultaneous vulnerability and empowerment in Latina narratives of migration.

Families Divided by Borders

US policies and programs not only fostered immigration at large but did so in a manner that promoted gendered patterns of movement (Segura and Zavella 2007, 6). The Bracero Program, for example, afforded an opportunity for men to fulfill economic obligations as breadwinners, "in effect legislatively mandat[ing] Mexican 'absentee fathers' who came to work as contracted agricultural laborers in the United States" (Hondagneu-Sotelo and Avila 2007, 392). Although women (and their children) endured physical, emotional, financial, and social hardships due to the government-sanctioned migration of the men, "For these women, the Bracero Program was a source of both stress *and* empowerment, a decisive factor leading them to shoulder new responsibilities and to express to their Mexican immigrant male relatives their aspirations, fears, and hopes" (Rosas 2014, 4). Ana Elizabeth Rosas details the adaptations that women left behind made to single-handedly raise their children while also becoming the financial head of household, sometimes renting and operating business lots in town centers when middle-class families created growth for investment in local marketplaces (2014, 211). Many women, however, were subject to exploitative labor conditions, as were children of *braceros* and undocumented Mexican immigrant men in the US.

In order to preserve their middle-class status, the wives of more affluent *bracero* families would hire these children to complete the tasks that had previously been performed by their male relatives who had since immigrated, and "children were expected to meet and exceed the middle-class families' expectations without complaint" (Rosas 2014, 191). Rosas describes these "exemplary [Mexican] children . . . who labored as if they were adults, in the place of or alongside adults [and] . . . were entrusted to undertake any task with the utmost attention to completing it perfectly" (186). Moreover, one's "attitude and actions would be seen as a reflection of his family upbringing and would be used to judge his and his entire family's moral character" (186). Rosas points to the "insurmountable pressures" (186) placed on children by the Bracero Program, who "had very little opportunity to experience life as children" (186) due to the expectations that they would toil instead of, or alongside, their parents, that they would largely be independent and care for themselves while working and at home, and that their actions and behaviors would be monitored with repercussions for the entire family's prestige and further socioeconomic opportunities.

As opposed to the perspective of the "one-sided" negative impact on Mexican children of *bracero* families (Goodman

2018, 45), Rosas interprets these shifting roles as also a source of independence and empowerment. Her study of the various ramifications of the Bracero Program for (newly) transnational families aligns with Yolanda Chávez Leyva's take on how "[w]riting children into history transforms the way we look at the US-Mexico border as well as Mexican American history. At the most basic level, it allows us to understand the day-to-day lives of the majority of the Mexican population on the border. But centering children's experiences and representations does more," she declares, elaborating, "It also enables us to realize more clearly the obstacles faced by the Mexican community and the strategies employed by adults and children to assert agency" (Chávez Leyva 2008, 72), particularly in the context of familial separation.

Braceros would have to work for multiple seasons with a specific grower with the hope that the grower might eventually help them get legal status and thus be able to bring their families to the US. When the Immigration Reform and Control Act (IRCA) was passed in 1986, a provision of which made any immigrant who had entered the US before 1982 eligible for amnesty, the potential for legalizing status—and thus being able to petition for family to come to the US legally—arose. However, it proved more advantageous to those migrants who could document their residency and employment (Segura and Zavella 2007, 6–7). Along with many migrant agricultural workers and construction day laborers, migrant women who traditionally worked within an informal or domestic sector were, therefore, largely ineligible for the amnesty offered under this legislation, once again illustrating legal and gendered inequities that inevitably affect the well-being of transnational families (Abrego 2014, 159). Regardless of whether they held appropriate documentation to do so, the wives of migrants who had been left behind began to join the migrant stream in larger numbers, gaining increased social mobility and contesting their characterization as passive agents awaiting their spouses' return.

One would err in supposing that Mexican women only recently began to participate in northward migration. Chávez Leyva describes how social and political circumstances in Mexico have affected its men and women in divergent ways. Whereas men's migration in the 1910s accelerated due to a burgeoning economy in the US Southwest, women and girls similarly crossed the border in greater numbers but did so to flee the violence and destruction left in the wake of the Mexican Revolution (Chávez Leyva 2008, 77). More specifically, "In those years thousands of women and children crossed into the United States, both temporarily and permanently, fleeing rape, abduction, and other forms of gendered violence by entering the United States" (77). Chávez Leyva continues, "With few other options available to them, Mexican women and children, understanding the safety afforded them, took advantage of the international boundary to seek sanctuary" (77).

The physical act of crossing the border from Mexico into the United States was remarkably simple in those years and, consequently, thousands of children walked across the border without documentation (Chávez Leyva 2008, 79). That circumstance would change initially, however, with the passage of the Immigration Act of 1917, which targeted women and children in the name of protecting US borders. Chávez Leyva notes, "Women and children became central to this new system of control and exclusion, since both represented threats to the sovereignty and maintenance of the nation-state" (2008, 79). Aside from the US government's concern that the women and children would become "'public charges' because of their prevalent poverty and lack of education" (Chávez Leyva 2008, 79) while separated from the male head of household, "Mexican women, as bearers of children and culture, and children, symbolic of the future, were threatening to the U.S. racial hierarchy" (79). Those government officials would surely be distressed to discover that Mexican (and Central American) women have continued to migrate in high numbers, particularly since 1970.

While initial migratory patterns typically promoted the income-earning travels of the husband while reinforcing women's roles in the home (Ashbee et al. 2007, 40) long before the implementation of the Bracero Program, a lack of savings or remittances obligated women to contribute to the household's economic sustenance. Thus, many Mexican women entered the labor markets of agriculture and crafts, combining their child-rearing responsibilities with their new economic activities (Hondagneu-Sotelo 1994, 62–63). With the expansion of their skills, women began to develop identities that reflected increasing independence from their husbands and mechanisms of patriarchal power in general (Hondagneu-Sotelo 1994, 66). Nevertheless, "Earning and administering an autonomous income without the added burden of having to tend to their husbands' daily needs did not automatically translate into a better life for these women" (66), as Pierrette Hondagneu-Sotelo comments. Rather, "Over time, many of these women developed a sense of indignation toward their husband's prolonged sojourns, and this anger shaped their own migration motives. Some women believed their husbands were shirking their responsibilities as fathers, and . . . this belief served as an impetus for migration" (67), provoking wives to seek their husbands north of the border out of a sense of abandonment or suspected infidelity. At this stage, then, it was primarily with the hopes of family reunification that women contributed to a "feminization of migration from Mexico" (Segura and Zavella 2007, 7), with undeniable consequences for the labor market, family, and culture.

Despite the additional gender-based physical dangers that women face in crossing the US-Mexico border without papers (Amnesty International 1998), "Today . . . mothers who migrate without their children are increasingly common, suggesting a major shift in the ways families around the world fulfill individual and household needs" (Dreby 2010, 5–6). Although familial separation was common in the context of, for example, Chinese, Polish, Italian, and Jewish immigration a century ago, such a division was primarily a result of men's migration. Transnational families—that is, "individual families who are divided by international borders and who maintain significant emotional and economic ties in two countries" (Dreby 2010, 5)—are thus in no way a new phenomenon. These ties extend beyond economic duty or familial relationships to encompass migrants' concepts of their individual and national identity when maintaining strong connections with their country of origin while in the so-called host country.

In the post-millennial context, more families are divided by borders as a result of migration from less wealthy or less developed home countries to more affluent host nations (Dreby 2010, 5) by one or both parents. As Dreby describes, "[Migrant mothers and fathers] weigh the economic opportunities available in the United States, as well as the personal benefits they may gain from migration, with the costs of bringing children with them. But mothers and fathers arrive at the decision to leave their children in different ways" (29). Whereas men consider their paternal roles to be fulfilled economically north of the border, "For mothers, the decision to migrate arises out of a combination of economic and family considerations" (29). For women, the prospect of "a busy work schedule, the border crossing, and the insecurity of living in the United States without legal documents" (29) discourages them from bringing children along *al otro lado*.

Indeed, as a result of financial necessity within a context of global capitalism, increasing numbers of Latin American immigrant women are developing new strategies to reconcile economic demands and maternal responsibilities, either as the primary income earners in the United States or left behind as heads of the household as a result of men's migration. One consequence is the construction of alternative maternal relationships, like when Latin American immigrant women work and reside in the US, Canada, Europe, or elsewhere while their children remain in their countries of origin in the care of "other mothers" (Hondagneu-Sotelo and Avila 2007, 400), primarily the migrants' own mothers, *comadres*, sisters, aunts, or other female relatives. Although the collectivist approach to mothering is common in Latin American cultures, it doesn't mitigate the profound psychological traumas associated with the separation from their children, never mind those brought on by experiences on the migrant journey itself.

Mexican and Central American women's desperate circumstances and identification of their financial role as parents—to feed, clothe, and provide shelter for their children—are often the only motivation necessary to drive them to undertake the perilous journey across the border without their children. Especially in the post-9/11 environment of anxiety regarding border security, there exists no means for many parents to migrate, with or without their children, legally in an expedient manner. Consequently, they face grave danger and great expense in order to cross the border. One supposes then, as Douglas Massey, Jorge Durand, and Nolan Malone aver, "Although United States immigration policies are intended to deter Mexicans from

working in the United States illegally, they have had the oppo-
site effect. Mexicans continue to come north, and they are
not returning home, as they used to" (2002, 8), reflecting the
recent decline of circular Mexican migration for the first time
over the past twenty-five years (Dreby 2010; Massey, Durand,
and Malone 2002). The increased militarization of the border
has resulted not only in a more expensive crossing but also an
alarming rise in death rates which, taken together, certainly
contribute to migrants' inclinations to make their stays in the
United States more permanent. Wayne Cornelius (2001; 2004)
reports that the average cost to cross the border without documents tripled between 1995 and 2001 during the same time in
which deaths among undocumented migrants in Arizona rose
by 1,186 percent. It has only increased in the decades since then.

The danger and expense of crossing the border with children
are even greater; thus, many parents opt to leave their children
behind in Mexico or other Latin American countries while they
temporarily work in the United States. The temporary separation, however, almost inevitably becomes permanent as a result
of increased militarization of the border, which simultaneously
discourages migrants already working in the US to risk another
crossing and makes the journey for unaccompanied children
even more hazardous and costly (Adler 2004; Dreby 2010;
Nazario 2006; G. Thompson 2003). Much like those for adults,
"Risks for children at the border include experiencing human
rights abuses, getting lost, sustaining injury or death, and being
caught by officials. Indeed, border enforcement policies have
made the crossing even riskier for minor children, with the
number of children returned to Mexico by border officials sky-
rocketing over the past few years" (Dreby 2010, 28). After the
publication of Dreby's text, the numbers would escalate in an
even more astonishing fashion.

While much of the migration of unaccompanied minors was motivated by a desire to reunify with parents already in the US or to seek economic opportunities in the 1990s and early 2000s, the tremendous levels of violence and crime associated with gangs and cartels in the "Northern Triangle" (El Salvador, Honduras, and Guatemala) have been the primary motive[12] for youth migration in more recent years (Carlson and Gallagher 2015; Chishti and Hipsman 2015; Clemens 2017; Lorenzen 2017; UNHCR 2014), and minors from this region outnumbered their counterparts from Mexico for the first time in 2013 (Clemens 2017, 5). Particularly during the years immediately following Mexican president Felipe Calderón's 2006 declaration of a war on drugs, many of the trafficking enterprises were pushed southward to the Northern Triangle, increasing the violence and insecurity associated with drug trafficking, which was further enhanced by the availability of firearms, relatively weak criminal justice institutions, and gang activity (Clemens 2017, 5). Notably, the activities related to the *maras*[13] (including the MS-18 and 18th Street gangs) extend beyond the usual drug trafficking, and regularly involve extortion, armed robbery, kidnapping, and forced recruitment (Lorenzen 2017, 747). Homicide rates in Honduras nearly doubled between 2005 and 2010, and Honduras and El Salvador had the highest intentional homicide rates worldwide in the years leading up to the 2014 "surge" of unaccompanied youth (UNODC 2019). During 2011, for example, the homicide rates were 85.1, 70.6, and 38 per 100,000 people in Honduras, El Salvador, and Guatemala respectively. Those figures stand in stark contrast to the US rate of just 4.7 for that same year.[14]

These statistics alone suggest a feasible explanation for the increasing number of unaccompanied alien children (UACs) apprehended at the Southwest border leading up to the spike of arrivals in 2014. Taken as a whole, Border Patrol figures demonstrate a steady upward tick of apprehensions from 15,949 in FY2011 to 24,403 in FY2012 and 38,759 in FY2013. A sizeable jump ensued in FY2014, with a record 68,541 UAC apprehensions (U.S. Customs and Border Protection 2019). A closer look at the breakdown based on country of origin similarly shows a steady increase from FY2011 to FY2013 and then a steep increase in FY2014 statistics for youth from El Salvador (1394, 3314, 5990, and then 16,404), Honduras (974, 2997, 6747, and then 18,244), and Guatemala (1565, 3835, 8068, and then 17,057). In contrast, the apprehension of Mexican youth increased more incrementally (11,768 to 13,974 and 17,240, and then decreased from FY 2013 to FY 2014 (15,634) (U.S. Customs and Border Protection 2016). It seems, then, that in this contemporary context of transnational migration, a great deal of familial separation derives from children who are now the ones leaving their families behind in order to survive.

For that reason, the surge of unaccompanied minors was considered a humanitarian crisis. Overwhelmed by the sheer number of minors in custody, makeshift detention centers were constructed on military bases to house youth temporarily before their transfer to the custody of the Office of Refugee Resettlement, a division of Health and Human Services. Per adherence to the dictates of the 1997 Flores Agreement that limits the length of minors' detention, the children would remain in a shelter until an appropriate sponsor was located or potentially placed in long-term foster care while awaiting their immigration proceedings. The general reaction to the plight of these young migrants tended to highlight their vulnerability. Simultaneously, though, the huge influx of youth also raised alarm and, transferring the already cemented connection between immigrants and criminality, turned public (and political) attention to the policing of children.

The Obama administration's response to the 2014 crisis was the expansion of border militarization, expanded capacity for family detention and immigration detention more broadly, and an increase in adults' deportation. In the name of protecting migrants, the US government established the Central American Minors (CAM) Program, which facilitated in-country refugee / parole processing for minors in Honduras, El Salvador, and Guatemala. It also invested millions of dollars in the Southern Border Plan (*Programa Frontera Sur*), an initiative that the Obama administration pressured Mexican president Peña Nieto to implement both to protect immigrants and to apprehend and deport US-bound migrants at Mexico's southern border (Wilson and Valenzuela 2014, 1–3). Although the number of unaccompanied minors apprehended at the US-Mexico border dropped substantially in FY2015, by the following year, figures again generally increased steadily and reached a new high of 76,020 UAC apprehensions in FY 2019 (Gramlich and Noe-Bustamante 2019). Violence in the Northern Triangle countries of origin (as indicated by homicide rates) has decreased; however, the rates remain alarmingly high in comparison to those of other regions around the world. Thus, the displacement of Central American youth is likely to continue, as will the policing of their movement.

While public attention to the transnational migration of children and teenagers is relatively new, unaccompanied children were journeying northward at the turn of the twentieth century, although in much smaller numbers and primarily from Mexico. Chávez Leyva points to the policing of youth even back then, describing a 1907 act that specified "children unaccompanied by their parents" as one target of exclusion from the US (2008, 79–80), and further noting the manner in which, "[e]fforts to demarcate the [border] line geographically were followed by attempts to demarcate the line socially and culturally.

The migration of children threatened these intentions, making Mexican children lightning rods of controversy" (72).

Past and present policies and practices related to Mexican and Central American migrant youth and women point to the US government's continued vigilance of this population's movement, perhaps also reflecting public perception of the social and cultural threat they presumably still pose to the fabric of American life. Nevertheless, exposure of the stories of their transnational migration and the various traumas that they endure—before, during, and after their journeys—both undermines the government's efforts to criminalize them and draws attention to the overarching systems and structures that have created the need for migration in the first place. Furthermore, they contest the past and present discourse that positions Latinx migrants and their families as indelibly marked by their lack of "Americanness" and consequently perceived as threatening and criminal. As Bill Ong Hing asserts:

> De-Americanization is a process that involves racism, but unlike the racism directed at African Americans, with its foundations in the historically held beliefs of inferiority, de-Americanizers based their assault on loyalty and foreignness. . . . Their victims are *immigrants* or *foreigners* even though they may in fact be citizens by birth or through naturalization. Irrespective of the victim community's possible long-standing status in the country, its members are regarded as perpetual foreigners. (2004, 260)

In developing narrative empathy and providing diverse and positive exemplars of individual migrants, their families, and their traumatic experiences associated with transnational migration, the Latina texts in *Ripped Apart* function as a counter-discourse to the political rhetoric and explosion of images in popular culture and the media that anthropologist Leo Chávez (2001, 2008) describes as manipulating public opinion so that immigrants and immigration are considered a threat to citizens' liberties and resources. Incorporating various elements and techniques based on their specific literary genre, the narratives analyzed here capture the intersecting layers of violence that both women and children uniquely experience when, due to untenable situations, they must adapt to their circumstances. Although the texts certainly reveal the vulnerabilities and victimization of their characters, they also ultimately demonstrate how the various violences inherent in transnational migration force independence and agency on women and on children, rupturing gender- and age-based norms of dependency that are traditionally cultivated in Latinx familial structures.

CHAPTER 2
Coming of Age amid Revolutions and Roundups

I n recent years, the area of young adult (YA) literature has evolved toward "more expansive interpretations of . . . inclusivity [that] . . . are positioning the conversation toward empathy through texts and socially responsible literacies that speak to various identities and perspectives" (R. Rodríguez 2019b, xiv). It is perhaps not surprising, then, that more and more literary works directed toward upper-elementary and middle-school students incorporate narrative techniques to foster more active reader engagement and specific thematics that introduce relevant topics and offer positive and diverse exemplars rather than stereotypical characters. To be sure, YA fiction that addresses displacement and migration in the US-Mexico borderlands embeds what R. Joseph Rodríguez identifies as "the signposts to note for critical literacy with culturally responsive and sustaining pedagogies for inclusive YA literature . . . : (a) counternarrative inquiry, (b) cultural literacy, and (c) self and social responsibility" (2019b, xiv). Various coming-of-age novels by

Chicana authors, in particular, challenge hegemonic conceptualizations of the history of cultural conflict in the border region
and the so-called immigrant experience and point to the interconnected layers of violence inflicted on individuals of Mexican
descent. Fictional narratives like Beltrán Hernández's *Across
the Great River*, García McCall's *Shame the Stars* and *All the Stars
Denied*, and Muñoz Ryan's *Esperanza Rising* depict family separation in the context of the Mexican Revolution and its aftermath—including the violent period of Texas history known as
"La Matanza"—and mass deportations of individuals of Mexican
origin in the 1930s. Taken together, these novels contest traditional representations of immigration through a focus on
women and youth with whom readers may develop an affective
connection and the exposure of the often omitted or distorted
histories of marginalized communities. One would suppose
that, equipped with these alternate perspectives and newfound
information regarding injustices and trauma, readers would be
moved to reflect on individual and collective ethical responsibilities and potentially engage in extratextual, pro-social action.

The Evolution and Regression of a Young Migrant in the Wake of Trauma

In Irene Beltrán Hernández's YA novel, *Across the Great River*,
the young narrator linearly chronicles her family's migratory
experience from an unnamed Mexican border town to Eagle
Pass, Texas. From the first scene of the text, it is clear that
the decision to uproot the family lies entirely in the hands of
Papa. "'Kata,'" Mama says to the daughter, "'I wish we weren't
going anywhere, but . . . '" (1989, 5), she abruptly interrupts herself. Her rational objections to the journey are met with anger:
"'Silence! I will hear no more!' [Papa] commands as he walks on
even faster" (6). Upon regaining composure, Kata's father gently

comforts his fearful wife, "'Do not fear, my love. All is ready and a new life across the border awaits us. . . . Come, we do this for the children's sake'" (8), he reminds her. Not much later into the narration, however, Mama becomes seriously injured and Papa disappears when the family attempts to cross the Río Grande illegally. Glossing over the details of the physical dangers of crossing the border, the novel instead focuses upon the challenges that Mama, Kata, and baby Pablito face thereafter while enduring the geographic and cultural displacement upon which Papa has insisted. Having left the only home the family has known, Mama must put her worries regarding her missing husband aside and, once she heals, seek economic stability as the sole breadwinner of the family.

Fortuitously, the coyotes (people who smuggle immigrants into the US illegally) with whom the family has traveled seek the aid of Doña Anita, a local *curandera*, to heal the narrator's mother once they have arrived in the United States. As Mama recovers, Doña Anita—a resourceful and caring character—becomes the physical and emotional caretaker of the family. As the primary caregiver, Doña Anita modifies the familial structure and provides an alternative model of motherhood for the narrator.

Once Mama has fully recuperated, she must seek employment away from Doña Anita's *ranchito* as the new head of her family. Initially, Kata's mother entrusts the narrator to Doña Anita's care, and mother and daughter must endure a temporary separation. Kata, however, will later join her mother in the city to care for her baby brother while Mama works. Fortunately, Doña Anita takes advantage of her mysterious gift, akin to clairvoyance, to arrive in town in order to protect Kata and her family from the physical threat posed by the coyote, who has seen gold in the family's possession and knows them to be unprotected—by a man, that is. Despite her efforts, Doña Anita is unable to prevent the attack on Mama that leaves her "limp as a doll" (63). As the narrative voice describes, "The front of Mama's blouse is ripped apart, as is her skirt. Her legs are bruised with deep patches of purple and red running along the inside. Deep welts along her arms lead to a bruise the size of my fist upon her cheek. Blood trickles from her mouth and onto her neck" (63). This example of physical—and implicitly sexual—victimization as a consequence of crossing the border also carries additional implications for the familial structure.

Once again, Mama finds herself incapacitated, this time due to the inherently gender-based violence she endures; not only is she unable to work due to her hospitalization, she is also incapable of caring for her children. Kata, a young girl who had asked to bring a doll along for the journey across the river, must mature quickly, and consequently the relationship she shares with her mother evolves throughout the novel. "'Don't worry about a thing, Mama. I'm right here and I will take care of you'" (117), the narrator reassures her mother. Somewhat surprised, Mama responds, "'You sound sure of yourself, my little Kata. How you've grown since we left the village. You're not a little girl anymore'" (117). As a result of the circumstances surrounding the frustrated family migration, the narrator must take on new responsibilities that translate into a great deal of individual growth and maturity. In a certain sense, Kata views her new identity in opposition to Mama's, declaring, "Sometimes I wish [Mama] would grow up and behave like a strong woman, instead of like a little girl who is lost in the woods" (133). Evidently, Mama's identity has not evolved much after the tragic disappearance of her husband despite having to work outside the home. The new roles forced upon Kata, however, contribute to her maturity and the redefinition of her identity.

Typical of the *Bildungsroman*, the narration of Kata's (mis)adventures conveys her personal growth as she seemingly progresses toward the attainment of knowledge and the fulfillment of her identity. As a border subject, her experiences further convey the necessarily metamorphosing identity imposed upon her as a result of displacement. Sophia Emmanouilidou goes so far as to claim that Kata exemplifies a case of "non-identity" (2005, 165) before a symbolic birth and/or baptism while crossing the Río Grande into the United States. The critic elaborates, "While waiting on one side of the border, Kata is in an identity-limbo, not knowing where she is going and why she is abandoning her homeland. In Mexico, Kata was a cultural embryo, which was kept well-protected from the outside world. The Mexican home was the womb, but now she experiences a symbolic birth" (165). "Baptized" in the river, Kata will presumably adopt the hybridity of the border crosser's identity, an identity that will be revised as she negotiates multiple cultures. Nevertheless, despite her presence in a cultural contact zone, I would argue that the negotiation of Kata's new identity has little or nothing to do with cultural or national affiliations. Rather than acting upon a conscientious decision to retain her cultural heritage while in the United States, the young girl remains in a cultural comfort zone of her family's own making, largely unaware of her cultural and psychological displacement.

Despite the journey from one nation to another, the narrator comments, "'Sometimes I forget that I'm no longer in Mexico'" (Beltrán Hernández 1989, 58). Once she is in "the land of good opportunity" (13), her experiences in the small American town are not much different from those of her native *pueblito*. Indeed, Doña Anita must explain to her, "'You see, the people here are mostly Mexicans, but they are born on this side of the river and that makes them Mexican Americans. You were born on the other side of the river and that makes you a native Mexican'" (58). She continues, "'Language has nothing to do with it. There is a government that runs Mexico and there is a different government that runs the United States'" (58). Perhaps as a result of her youth and naiveté, Kata does not appear to suffer the psychological and emotional turmoil that typically results from the migrant's geographic dislocation. She is in the care of a loving individual who protects her from physical dangers while also teaching her about her way of life as a *curandera*.

Although the border is often offered as a trope to reflect the inevitable encounter and potential conflict with the cultural Other(s) and the subsequent negotiation of a hybrid borderlands culture, the Mexican protagonist of *Across the Great River* further embraces her cultural heritage once she has relocated to the United States. The young girl resorts to her prior experiences in her homeland to interpret and better understand the activities and behaviors she observes in her new location. Constantly drawing comparisons between life in the American town and her Mexican *pueblito*, Kata defines and affirms her own identity through always positioning herself relative to the cultural Other. She ponders the identities and lives of the individuals whom she encounters in her new urban environment, although from afar. "Often we sit on the steps and watch people pass. I study them silently," she explains. "Is he a farmer? Or does he work in a laundry? How many children does she have? It's a game I play with myself because I never speak to these people" (Beltrán Hernández 1989, 50). She wonders about their existences but isolates herself within her new social context. Furthermore, the protagonist maintains a link to her homeland as she matures through her protection of physical "tokens of cultural inheritance" (Emmanouilidou 2005, 165).

Describing these artifacts in more conflictive terms, Emmanouilidou specifically identifies the doll and pouch that Kata carries with her as "the items of a cultural smuggling" (2005, 166). The protagonist herself voices the significance of the latter, commenting, "My hand reaches to the pouch on my waist as if it were the only thing left from my previous life" (Beltrán Hernández 1989, 88). Retaining these items that originated in Mexico enables Kata to maintain a connection, albeit tenuous, to her *patria*. According to Emmanouilidou, the protagonist consequently embodies an attitude of cultural resistance since these mementos from home symbolize her refusal to totally integrate within American society. Furthermore, she purports that Kata takes advantage of her cultural awareness to manipulate cultural discourse effectively in order to align herself with the American "us" versus the immigrant "them" while responding to the police sergeant's questions following the violent attack on her mother. She cites, "'That man probably crossed the border illegally. Perhaps he's a wetback who doesn't have papers or identification. We get men like that here all the time'" (Beltrán Hernández 1989, 80). Unfortunately for her case, though, Emmanouilidou erroneously attributes these comments to the protagonist when, in fact, the sergeant is the one who makes these declarations. Nevertheless, the argument that Kata fails to integrate wholly within American society still holds. Rather than exemplifying effective cultural maneuvering, however, I contend that Kata's behavior simply stems from the fear that her undocumented status will be discovered by the Anglo authorities, and I suspect that the portrayal of her attachment to personal items like her doll may be rooted more in childhood nostalgia than cultural resistance per se.

Since Doña Anita has explained to her that she entered the country illegally and the ramifications of such, Kata largely remains silent during the questioning, "[her] heart rac[ing] at the sound of the word 'papers'" (Beltrán Hernández 1989, 80). Out of fear, she merely expresses her opinion about the attacker's fate, responding, "'Well, he deserved to die because he hurt Mama and Anita'" (80). Although she omits the entire truth of her origins by explaining to the sergeant, "'We just came from Anita's *ranchito*'" (79), rather than delving into details about her family's illegal border crossing that preceded the stay with Doña Anita, this in and of itself does not constitute an act of subversion.

Perhaps the true subversive nature of the protagonist's behavior lies in the apparent obliteration of traditional cultural norms with respect to gender and generational responsibilities while she is in the United States. Due to the circumstances surrounding her family's frustrated attempt at migration, Kata embarks upon a journey that reflects what Mary Pat Brady would term "subjectivity-in-process" (2002, 52), reflecting her dynamic, rather than fixed or static, identity within newly imagined familial and cultural contexts. The emergence of such subjectivity as a process of individual growth and maturity is typical fodder for the narrative genre of the *Bildungsroman*. In what superficially appears to be a rather traditional coming-of-age novel, Kata shapes her identity while overcoming a series of trials, particularly with the help of Doña Anita. Elizabeth Coonrod Martínez and Annie Eysturoy astutely note the manner in which the heroine's quest subverts the traditional *Bildungsroman* form, which narrates the coming-of-age of a male protagonist. As opposed to the "happy" ending of social or cultural integration typical of the male *Bildungsroman*, they argue that the heroine's journey satisfactorily results in some form of rebellion, particularly against patriarchal norms (Coonrod Martínez 2000, 364; Eysturoy 1996, 58).

Although Kata adapts to her circumstances by adopting roles that conflict with typical generational and gender norms implicit within Mexican culture, her actions do not constitute such a rebellion. Rather, her circular physical journey mirrors the simultaneous return to innocence and her comfortable reintegration within the patriarchal expectations of Mexican society. While one may question, then, whether *Across the Great River* can, indeed, be considered a feminine version of the *Bildungsroman* as described by Coonrod Martínez and Eysturoy, I would suggest that Beltrán Hernández offers her readers yet another permutation of the typical *Bildungsroman*, further capturing the complexity of feminine transnationalism decades before sociological scholars and literary critics turned their attention to the unique experiences of Mexican women and/or youth affected by migration.

As previously mentioned, Kata's journey northward begins in the company of her beloved doll, Anna. At the moment of departure, the second of the aforementioned "tokens of cultural inheritance" (Emmanouilidou 2005, 165)—the pouch holding what the reader later learns to be a gold nugget—is in her mother's possession. Coinciding with Mama's initial injuries sustained during the river crossing and the consequent responsibilities that Kata adopts, the protagonist discovers the pouch and takes it upon herself to protect it, despite her ignorance as to its contents. Soon thereafter, when Kata moves from Doña Anita's *ranchito* to the city, her doll goes missing. Not coincidentally, it is at this point in the narration that Kata simultaneously parts with her childhood.

Despite the apparent process of maturing, Kata's personal transformation comes to a screeching halt once Mama recuperates from her second round of injuries and is ready to join her family at Doña Anita's ranch. Although Kata has behaved as an independent young girl, even when she is in the care of an American nurse and doctor in the city's orphanage during her mother's recovery period, she exhibits an emotional regression as soon as she returns to Doña Anita, apparently aware that she no longer bears the burden of familial responsibility. Content to be free of the pouch and its implications of duty, Kata explains, "'Anyway, I'm glad that I do not have to wear that old thing any longer. It scratches me'" (Beltrán Hernández 1989, 124). In a more emotional outburst, her stolid countenance breaks, and Kata wails, "'I really want to go home. I've even lost my Anna and I don't now [*sic*] where'" (123). At that moment, Doña Anita returns her doll and, as the protagonist describes, "I scream as I reach her and I crush her to my chest, then hold her at a distance to examine her dress, which is wrinkled but not torn. 'Anna, you're home, too'" (123).

Whereas Kata's mother had previously complimented this young woman on her maturity, circumstances have changed, and she now states, "'Ah, Kata. What a child you are'" (121). In response to this assertion, Kata complains, "'Yesterday you called me all grown up. Today I am a child again. I think you older people are the ones that are all mixed up!'" (121). Perhaps this complaint is right on target for capturing Kata's personal evolution of emotional maturity and subsequent regression throughout the text. As the novel nears its resolution and Mama and her children return to Mexico, even the border guard identifies Kata's juvenile attachment to her doll. "'It's all right, little girl. You don't have to part with your doll. Just run along with the señora'" (132), he assures her, in no way sensing the tremendous responsibility and maelstrom of emotions she has endured while north of the border.

As a result of her youth or, more likely, the limited duration of her stay in the US before returning to Mexico and the similar demographic makeup of both towns, Kata expresses a feeling of discomfort within, but not a confrontational exclusion from, American culture. Prior to the return to her family's homeland, Kata remarks, "I will miss the Doctor as I miss the gift of quietness that Anita's place offers. But for me, our little village in Mexico will always be home, no matter where I go or whom I meet" (Beltrán Hernández 1989, 120). She will reintegrate within Mexican society and culture as a young girl with this knowledge that she has attained during her experiences north of the border. Her mother echoes this sentiment, explaining to Doña Anita, "'It's just that we are so unfamiliar with the American ways and customs. In Mexico, our village life was so simple and happier'" (123). They eagerly anticipate their return to this comfortable and familiar lifestyle as they embark upon their journey southward.

The homeward trek begins in the urban American environment, passes through Doña Anita's ranch, and concludes in rural Mexico, where the family reunites with Papa, lost during his attempt to cross the river with the family and later incarcerated in a Mexican jail for unexplained reasons. Unbeknownst to Papa, thanks to Doña Anita's previous healing of his daughter, "'The Commandante [sic] did not ask questions, but simply ordered my release and drove me out here himself'" (Beltrán Hernández 1989, 134), Papa explains. In addition to the image of a simple and happy Mexican life that Mama describes, the family's reunification lends itself to an interpretation of a return to an idyllic existence.

Not coincidentally, this village is also the origin of the shining gold nugget that ultimately results in the family's redemption. Representative of the value of their homeland, the gold protected in the pouch serves as the family's only means of survival after risking and losing nearly all during its migration.

Further emphasizing the bounty that Mexico offers—as opposed to the violence and limited opportunities to the north—Papa is amused by the abundance of gold and the implications of such for his family once he recognizes its true worth. He tells Doña Anita, "'But, señora. There are many more of those stones in that boulder. All I need to do is pick them!'" (Beltrán Hernández 1989, 135), thereby assuring his family's well-being. Regardless of whether one interprets Mexico's plentitude as economic stability—in this case exemplified by the *pueblo's* ample gold nuggets—or cultural comfort and security, there remains no doubt that the novel portrays the migratory experience in a negative light, primarily through its depiction of the physical and psychological traumas that result from migration and familial separation.

Although cultural conflict between the Mexican and Anglo populations is less evident in this novel than in more recent publications like García McCall's *Shame the Stars* and *All the Stars Denied*, the migrant experience of displacement and disillusionment is one and the same. After consideration of the family's suffering as a result of its dislocation, Doña Anita chastises and admonishes Papa. "'Señor . . . you should stop all that foolish dreaming and provide for your family. They have been through much pain and heart-ache, which will take many years to forget'" (Beltrán Hernández 1989, 134). Papa's delusions of a better life north of the border result in the entire family's migration, which separates the family and ultimately empowers the female characters to varying degrees. Not only does Papa demand that the family oblige when he dreams of riches in the United States, he fails to support and care for his family once he disappears for what seems to be a matter of months. In one sense, the narrative voice vilifies Papa as the catalyst for the varied encounters with violence, although to a lesser degree than other principal male characters in the novel. In particular, the narrator characterizes the tattooed coyote as an evil perpetrator of violence against women and as a greedy manipulator of the victims of the socioeconomic phenomenon of transnational migration. In the end, though, justice is served as this villain dies at the hands of a vengeful mob after his attack on Mama becomes public. Beyond this, Papa apparently sees the errors of his ways.

Coinciding with the 1980s "boom" of Chicana literature (Lomelí 1993; Lomelí et al. 2000), the publication of *Across the Great River* challenged the predominantly masculine renderings of the Chicano and/or migrant experiences available at that time, thus contributing to the development of a body of literature to reflect the diversity of the Chicano *and* Chicana experiences(s). This text, then, is among those that exemplify the emergence of the "Contemporary Chicana Generation" (Lomelí et al. 2000, 288) that extends the trend beginning in the 1970s of "utilizing technique to unveil a cross-sectional disclosure of multi-faceted experiences covering gender, class, psychological and social determinants" (Lomelí 1993, 102). In adding to and contesting the narratives reflecting the masculinist and nationalist ideologies of the early Chicano Movement, texts by Chicana authors like Beltrán Hernández endowed the until-then "virtually invisible" Chicana women (Eysturoy 1996, 60) with a resonant voice. Equipped with this voice, these authors successfully declare a progression from being objects of subjection to empowered agents of subjectivity (42) through capturing the feminine agency exercised by the characters in their texts, particularly in response to the interconnected layers of violence that they endure.

By inscribing women and children within the history of Mexican immigration, the early fictional account of transnational migration by Beltrán Hernández asserts an alternate voice that recuperates the roles and experiences both of women and of children, despite their overwhelming absence in male-centered migrant literary discourses. As such, *Across the Great River* generally relocates their stories from "individual oblivion to collective memory" (Chabram-Dernersesian 1993, 37), and it does so in a manner that facilitates the development of empathy. While Beltrán Hernández makes little use of innovative narrative techniques or robust character development, the first-person narration by a young female protagonist narrows the distance between the character and the reader, particularly if the reader identifies with Kata based on age, gender, ethnicity and/or experiences with migration. One of the first Chicana texts to narrate the journey of female and juvenile immigrants, *Across the Great River* is a precursor to contemporary narratives that reveal the unique traumatic experiences that migrant women and children face, and, more broadly, to inclusive young adult texts that incorporate engaging empathetic narrative techniques and characters who "dispel biases, myths, and stereotypes in coming of age through various experiences, perspectives, and portrayals connected to the lenses of adolescence, culture, gender, identity, language, sexuality, schooling, and education" (R. Rodríguez 2019b, xiii).

Overcoming Violence and Oppression in *Shame the Stars* and *Esperanza Rising*

Capturing the aftermath of the Mexican Revolution nearly thirty years after the publication of *Across the Great River*, *Shame the Stars* more explicitly broaches the ambience of physical violence and psychological trauma rooted in broader structural and sociocultural violence with the hope that "the book makes people aware of the need to excavate our historical truths, to bring to light that which has remained hidden far too long,[15] and to speak about the 'unspeakable things unspoken' like Toni Morrison (1989) says," explains García McCall. She adds, "It is only by shedding light on the 'unspeakable' that we can begin to dialogue, to heal those old wounds" (R. Rodríguez 2019a, 175). Presenting various perspectives of the 1915 culmination of La Matanza, a chapter of state-sanctioned disenfranchisement and lynching of Mexicans and Tejanos at the hands of the Texas Rangers and other Anglo vigilantes,[16] the YA historical novel relies heavily on intertextuality and interpolation of fragments of texts of varied genres—including poetry, personal letters, historical documents, authentic newspaper articles, and fictionalized articles to frame each of the chapters—to encourage reflection on counternarratives and the power of speaking the truth. The novel's title and the list of the "cast of characters" are a nod to Shakespeare's *Romeo and Juliet*, which contextualizes the wedge between the star-crossed lovers Joaquín del Toro and Dulceña Villa, albeit based on familial political stances in this rendering. Notably, the intercalated texts also provide an avenue for readers to identify more closely with the emotional response of these 18-year-old characters to their immediate sociohistorical context, be it through poems taken from Joaquín's fictional journal, secret notes exchanged, or the incorporation of news items.

Inspired by Christina Diaz Gonzalez's use of headlines to introduce chapters in *The Red Umbrella*, García McCall explains, "I wanted [readers] to see the actual articles that shaped the novel and the plot development, so I decided to have the news articles appear as epistolary matter, as newspaper pieces literally ripped from the pages of history. Not only did it lend drama to the novel, it imbued it with a sense of secrecy, urgency and danger that I felt was in keeping with the tone of this particular piece" (Barisich 2016). Stylistically, she accomplishes this through including a graphic reproduction of jagged fragments that look as though they were torn from a paper and adhered to Joaquín's journal. She describes further, "The artifacts for this book were carefully chosen to help me tell the story in the most creative, but also most authentic, most realistic way possible" (Barisich 2016). She continues, "All artifacts, whether fiction or nonfiction, are parts of the puzzle, like bricks on a wall, that help either clarify or shed light on the issues surrounding the conflicts in South Texas in the time period of 1915 to 1919" (Barisich 2016).

Indeed, the novel opens with the supposedly anonymous political poem "Tejano," published in the March 23, 1913, edition of *El Sureño*, the fictional newspaper owned and operated by Dulceña's family. Establishing the context of danger, disenfranchisement, conflict, and violence that affects even the wealthy and landed Tejanos of Monteseco, the poetic voice decries, "These are dangerous / times in South Texas, / times of trouble, / times of loss. . . . Never mind the injustice. / Your father's land is not your / own anymore. It has been sold, / passed hands, bought and paid / for. It's history. It's gone" (García McCall 2016, 1). The repeated refrain warns against speaking out or raising suspicions: "Close your ears, / mind your tongue, / let the Rangers do their job" (1–4). Throughout the text, though, the tone of the interpolated poems shifts toward an urgency to take action despite an awareness of the dangerous repercussions of doing so. This evolving tone parallels the shifting perspectives of Joaquín and his father, "a reserved man who preferred we stay away from politics and public life" (8) to tend instead to the 600 acres of Las Moras, the ranch held by the family since 1775, until ethnic tensions, injustices, and impunity continue to escalate with devastating effects for the del Toro family and surrounding community.

An initial heated conversation between the patriarchs of the del Toro and Villa families ensues when Don Acevedo del Toro accuses Don Rodrigo Villa of printing dangerously incendiary pieces, particularly in light of the revelation of the Plan de San Diego, an excerpt of which García McCall includes to offer historical context regarding the authentic document calling for insurrection in the name of pursuing the independence of the Republic of Texas (18). As a journalist, Don Rodrigo defends his position: "'These things need to be said. They need to be read and talked about, discussed by every member of our community'" (11), thus planting the initial seeds regarding the freedom of press and the power of speaking out in the name of truth and justice, a theme that is manifest throughout the novel. Joaquín chimes in, declaring publications' unique capacity "'[t]o get the people thinking and reacting. It's the only way to wake them up, to make them stand up for their rights, to call attention to their situation'" (12). Only then does he go on to admit that he is the author of the inflammatory poem, adding fuel to his father's rage and serving as the primary basis for the conflict between the families.

The plot unfolds, detailing the particularly complicated predicament of the Tejano community in South Texas, which faces dangers from a multitude of directions. "While Mexican bandits caught up in their own civil war were crossing over to the United States, pillaging small Texas towns and blowing up railroads, tejanos dealt with wrongful accusations, unlawful raids, and the hanging of relatives suspected of working with Mexican revolutionaries" (21–22). Moreover, "The turbulent time had created the tejano rebel, a new breed of outlaw, a Texas Mexican fighting to keep his land and his dignity in the place he had called home long before it became part of the United States. Until Mexican revolutionaries stopped trampling on

American soil and Rangers stopped accosting and killing innocent tejanos, my family wasn't safe and I couldn't leave" (22),
Joaquín declares. García McCall effectively depicts the overlapping nodes of violence within this framework, initially focusing on physical violence at the hand of bandits, rebels, and *los
Rinches*, and further emphasizing the intimidation tactics and
psychological trauma that undermine the traditional notions of
the Rangers as brave and glorious heroes.

Despite the primary use of first-person narration, the novel
interweaves the perspectives and experiences of violence
to which multiple characters have been subject. In this way,
García McCall deftly links individual instances of physical and
psychological trauma with the underlying atmosphere of constant fear and sociocultural violence—evident in explicit acts of
discriminatory actions and behaviors—as well as legal or structural violence that sanctions robbing lawful landowners of their
possessions and fundamental human rights. Anybody who is
perceived as being of Mexican origin is an automatic target, and
even priests like Joaquín's brother Tomás are not immune. When
Captain Munro accuses Gerardo, a young ranch hand from Las
Moras, of involvement with rebel action, arresting him without
cause and illegally denying his bail, Doña Flora beseeches Don
Acevedo to intervene. "'You have to do something. They're going
to kill him like they did his father! Please, Patrón. You have to
help him!'" (34). Unfortunately, Gerardo suffers the fate Doña
Flora anticipated: "'They strung him up. Left him up there on
an old oak tree, hanging on the side of the road for everyone to
see'" (121). Other secondary characters share similar stories of
horrors of physical, psychological, and structural violence on
the part of the Rangers. Tejano rebel leader Carlos explains:

> "Without those documents, my wife and I had no way of proving
> the land was ours. No one would help us. Lawyers refused to take

our case. County officials wanted United States paperwork, when the only paperwork we had before the fire was from Mexico, a hundred years ago when our ancestors were granted the land. And then the Rangers made sure my wife and I moved out." He paused, a memory he obviously didn't want to relive coming to the surface. "They hung my sixteen-year-old son in our own back-yard." (129)

Carlos thereafter joined the rebel cause, defending others who faced a similar fate.

Pollo, another rebel, shares a comparable tale of despair that hardened his heart and convicted him to resist. "'It was Rinches took my son-in-law. . . . They dragged him on a rope behind a horse all over Hidalgo County—made an example out of him for *questioning* the law, after arresting him for loitering when he dared to meet in public with other tejanos'" (130). The narrator draws attention to the legal mechanisms perpetuating the structural violence that goes hand in hand with physical and psychological violence, commenting, "Laws like that—ban-ning tejanos from gathering in public places—hadn't made it to Morado County yet, but rumors from other counties came over from time to time, reminding us that such things were not so far away" (130).

Joaquín further reflects on the dangers that government officials present, foreshadowing his personal encounter with Morado County sheriff's deputies on the night of his secret rendezvous with Dulceña. "I'd heard tales of what Rangers did out in the chaparral. Out here in the darkness, where lawmen can't tell Mexicans and Tejanos apart, the Rangers were ruth-less, shooting first and asking questions later. It was exactly why I had been worried about our late-night meeting in the first place" (69). Joaquín adds, "I didn't want to come off as paranoid, but I just didn't trust them. Lawmen were just as dangerous as rebels in South Texas these days. Reports from Hidalgo County and Agua Dulce had been running in the rumor mill, of lawmen—Rangers and deputies alike—taking girls away under the pretense of escorting them home and then violating and brutalizing them, oftentimes leaving them for dead in the campo" (70).

The intersection of oppression based on gender and ethnicity becomes even more explicit with repeated commentaries throughout the novel that reiterate the normalcy—or frequency, at least—of sexual assault on Tejanas. As Doña Sarita notes after an attack on her granddaughter Adelita, "'It's not enough that [*Rinches*] hang our young men. . . . Now they're coming after our girls too'" (150). She identifies this tactic of gender-based physical and psychological violence as intentional, commonplace, and effective, explaining, "'They know our men are our strength. . . . But women—well, women are our corazón. They go after our girls to tear us apart, to keep our hearts from growing strong'" (150). The conversation continues, and Joaquín learns that recently at least five other young women had been attacked. "'Two of them are missing, but they were good girls and too young to run off with some boy,'" Doña Sarita declares. "'We all know the Rinches killed them. There's no way of finding out where they dumped their bodies, though. They could be anywhere out there in the monte. God rest their souls wherever they may be'" (151). It is within this broader context that Joaquín witnesses the trauma of Deputy Slater's attack on his beloved Dulceña who, after fighting him off, "was pale with fright" (72) and left with a "bloody lip and bulging left eye" (73).

After unsuccessfully attempting to intervene, Joaquín recognizes the sociolegal power that the attackers wield. Reminding him that they are virtually untouchable, Slater smugly asks, "Joaquín del Toro. . . . What are people going to *think* when we take you in for raping and killing this pretty young thing?'" (73), only further enraging Joaquín. In later conversations involving their superior, Deputy Munro, and the affected families, Munro explains that there will be no repercussions for Deputies Davis and Slater's actions for the benevolent sake of maintaining Dulceña's honor. "'If this got out, it would ruin the girl's reputation,'" he remarks. "'Is that you what you want, son? You want that girl to live with this for the rest of her life? Because that's what'll happen'" (82), further emphasizing the disconnect between the importance of modesty and appropriate etiquette for young women that are included in the interpolated excerpt from *True Politeness: a Hand-Book of Etiquette for Ladies, 1847–1915* (78) and the desires and actions of Dulceña, who refuses to be a victim and would opt for social self-sacrifice in the name of racial or ethnic justice. She calls out the obvious impunity and injustice, questioning, "'Why are we still standing here pretending you're going to do anything about this? . . . Everyone here knows you're going to cover this up. You've said as much. As long as men like you rule this world, women like me, innocent women, will have no justice. Do you think I care about my reputation? I don't care what people think or whisper about me. All I care about is making things better for our people, and if that tarnishes my reputation, then so be it'" (85). Dulceña's rejection of the societal norms regarding expectations of young women's behavior transgresses the patriarchal limitations, thereby shedding light on the misogynistic undertones of sociocultural violence within which the physical and psychological traumas emerge. More explicit, however, is the overarching context of sociocultural violence grounded in anti-Mexican sentiment.

As Deputy Munro insinuates that more harm than good will come to Dulceña should word get out that she was attacked by his colleagues, he underlines that this is particularly the case within the Mexican (American) community. "'People around these parts, they never forget anything. They never let things die. That's the problem with these—these'—'" (82). Although Munro hesitates, his intention is clear, as Joaquín recalls. "The Ranger's words had ignited a fire inside me and I could feel myself getting hotter and hotter, boiling over with rage as I said, '—with these *Mexicans*?'" (83). Munro's bigotry is well known throughout the community and shared by his fellow Rangers, whose "only qualifications were their animosity for Mexican bandits and their willingness to do whatever Munro said without question" (28). Despite the recruitment of Sheriff Nolan, the presumably more objective outsider, to intervene, Deputies Slater and Davis carry on with business as usual, facing no consequences for their brutal attack on Dulceña and Joaquín, and when Joaquín confronts them, the ethnic basis for tensions is clear in the pejorative terms that Davis and other lawmen yell during the action. "'Hit that *bean-eater!*'" (95), one shouts; "'Shut your own mouth, *messy-skin!*'" (97), Slater adds. Inspired by this incident, Joaquín later pens the poem "Rinches"—included in a journal entry dated Monday, August 23, 1915—that emphasizes the vicious ethnically motivated acts of the Rangers:

> Lawmen have
> been given free will
> —orders to shoot
> mejicanos on sight
> in South Texas.
>
> . . .
>
> "Those Rinches," I hear
> campesinos gripe,
> throwing their fists
> in the air.
> "They are bloodthirsty
> salvajes, Godforsaken

fiends—hijos de Satanás!"

. . .

Desert lizards,
trying to discern between
the shades of brown
—distinguish that
which lives and breathes
and separate the brown skin
from the brown earth,
the brown brush,
the brown bark (124–25)

Once again, García McCall takes advantage of the multi-genre approach to develop the voice of Joaquín further and to counteract the traditional narrative regarding the heroics of the Rangers and their efforts to restore order (which, incidentally, is also included as excerpts of nonfiction articles in the novel). The shift in tone and content of the protagonist's journal entries captures how he processes that, despite their historically privileged standing within the community of Monteseco, the del Toro and Villa families find themselves victimized because of their ethnic origin in a chapter of history in which Anglo settlers and Rangers alike were "forcing Tejano rebels to fight for rights that were already theirs" (107). Nevertheless, as Tejanos, they declare their victory of spirit: "'The Texas Rangers think they can dictate how we act and think. But they won't defeat us. . . . Even their brutality will never break our spirits. We are tejanos mejicanos. We are familia. We will always stick together. Our spirits, our hearts, that is something they can never take away from us'" (105). This spirit is elevated, in particular, through the resistance and rebellion on the part of transgressive women like Dulceña and la Estrella, whose true identity is none other than Joaquín's mother, Doña Jovita del Toro.

Known as "the protector of the people" (32), la Estrella is celebrated by Mexicans and Tejanos alike for her willingness to risk
her safety to aid her people. Triumphantly and enthusiastically
reading from an article written by A. V. Negrados and published
in *The Maverick*, la Estrella extols those who "'are still fighting the
evil lawmen of South Texas who would do anything to subjugate
our people as they struggle to protect their families and keep their
ancestral lands from being stolen from under their feet. Our courageous women are our secret weapons, and it is because of them
that we will win this fight'" (104). Once Joaquín comes to understand that his seemingly neutral family has been supporting the
rebels all along under the leadership of his mother, la Estrella, he
reflects, "I'd never seen my mother in this light. She was like a sol-
dadera, a true warrior woman, fighting in the Mexican Revolution"
(132), much like the women featured in the interpolated newspaper
article "Modern Amazons of Mexico Keep Armies Alive," from the
March 14, 1915, edition of *The Sun* (138).

As "the true spirit of the rebellion" (103), la Estrella embodies the epitome of threat to the Rangers. Once her identity is
discovered, Munro shoots and kills her, leaving an entire
community in mourning and making the news in both the
Spanish- and English-language press. "[M]y mother's death had
created a shift in perspective. More and more newspapers written in English were willing to take a chance on covering her
story" (250), Joaquín comments. "La Estrella was no longer a
legend told for and by tejanos. The death of Jovita del Toro, an
American woman of Mexican descent, killed by a deputy sheriff
on American soil, outside a courthouse no less, drew a lot of
attention in our area" (250), speaking to the power of the press
to expose injustice.

While the novel focuses on the coming of age of Joaquín, the
development and evolution of Dulceña, both as a young woman

and as a writer, enhance the complexity of the text and similarly contribute to the notion of the role of writing in the fight for justice. Based on the Mexican American journalist Jovita Idár,[17] the character of Dulceña ultimately reveals that she is, in fact, the mysterious writer behind the pseudonym A. V. Negrados, a thinly veiled reference to Idár's pen name, A. V. Negra. Disrupting gender-based expectations, she explains, "'We all wear masks, Joaquín. No one suspects young girls, especially a waitress, to be smart enough to understand the politics behind the rumor mill around town. Conchita brings me the news she overhears at work and together we listen carefully when we go on our walks'" (183). As a journalist, she feels compelled to remain despite the danger, because "'I have a responsibility to the people of this community. They need me to stay here. I need to be A. V. Negrados—I need to keep writing their stories. If I were to leave, to run away, who would speak for them? Who would voice their fears and document their suffering?'" (185).

Despite suspected arson of her family's print shop, Dulceña resists intimidation tactics—as did Jovita Idár when Texas Rangers attempted to shut down her father's press—and declares, "'The truth must be printed. Evil must be exposed'" (215). In various passages, the text explicitly identifies the power of the word. Not surprisingly, just as the novel opens with a poem from Joaquín's journal, it closes with one as well. There is a remarkable shift, though, from the initial urging on March 23, 1913, to, "Close your ears, / Mind your tongue, / Let the Rangers do their job" (1), to Joaquín's journal entry dated September 18, 1915, in which the poetic voice exhorts, "Stand up. Speak up. / It's the only way to start / an evolution revolution— / thinking with your hearts" (284). Speaking out and harnessing the power of story(telling) to reveal truths and fight injustices is precisely what García McCall aims to do vis-à-vis her novel's counternarrative(s).

In the *Shame the Stars* author's note, García McCall describes the horror she felt when her college-aged son first exposed her to Benjamin Heber Johnson's *Revolution in Texas: How a Forgotten Rebellion and Its Bloody Suppression Turned Mexicans into Americans*, with its description of the political and racial tensions and violence of La Matanza. Appalled, she wondered, "So why didn't I know this part of my culture's history? Well, a long, long time ago I was a small child, and like many a small child in America, I read textbooks that did not include these horrific events in American history. Why don't I know much more now after doing all this research? History books being published and printed for American schools today still make no mention of this part of our history" (294–95). In order to remedy that lack, she set out to create a text that not only acknowledges this chapter of history but offers alternative perspectives and encourages young readers to hone their media literacy as well.

García McCall acknowledges, "No one can ever do justice to the retelling of the extent of the horrific atrocities committed during that time with complete accuracy and authenticity because so much of it was concealed, poorly recorded, or swept under the proverbial rug" (293). Nevertheless, she remarks, "What I can do, I have done. I've included in this book a small ofrenda, a different point of view—a rebellious, contentious voice—along with a small sampling of source materials, both fiction and nonfiction, so that American students might be able to cull through them and better educate themselves" (295). She points to the importance of introducing these difficult topics to students of all ethnic and cultural backgrounds to engage in honest conversation regarding our complicated histories, as well as to distinguish among various types of sources—primary vs. secondary, reliable vs. unreliable, etc.—in their attempt to make sense of the past as well as current events. "We have to dig those old bones up, expose them, share these injustices with the world so that we can be mindful and not let it happen again," she contends. "The struggles on the border are far from over, and we can't afford to repeat old patterns, make the same mistakes; to do so would be indefensible" (Barisich 2016).

In addition to shedding light on obscured histories that are relevant to the issues of today, authors like García McCall and Muñoz Ryan effectively enable the audience to develop an empathetic connection with diverse characters, not only to have a better sense—albeit fictionalized—of their experiences but also to reframe these experiences and descriptions of characters and their attributes as situational rather than essential. As Bracher notes in his studies of literature and cognitive schemas, a robust set of positive and diverse exemplars that resist essentialist depictions of characters will better enable readers to identify the impact of circumstances on a character's identity and/or experience, thereby minimizing the tendency to assume that such circumstances are of the characters' own making or a reflection of their deficiencies.

Beyond this, novels that depict the violence and injustice to which Mexican (and/or Mexican American) families are subject counteract hegemonic discourse around the motives and circumstances of displacement and migration and even counter the narrative of these families as impoverished and uneducated. In *Esperanza Rising*, Muñoz Ryan shares that she has relied upon the story of her grandmother's own experiences with migration and research regarding the marginalization, disenfranchisement, and devastating separation of the Mexican (American) communities in the 1930s to provide an opportunity for upper-elementary readers to connect to the protagonist's story and dismantle any dominant and erroneous assumptions about Mexican migration. Muñoz Ryan highlights the importance of listening to individual voices, explaining, "Seeing isn't knowing. We can't just look at a person—at their countenance or their dress, or the color of their skin, in this diverse world—and understand him or her. We have to first hear the person's *story* for the seeds of understanding to take root. Then we might move on to knowing beyond seeing" (Aldama 2018, 165). Logically, we may then be more apt to move from knowing to empathizing, and perhaps from empathizing to engaging in pro-social and extratextual action in solidarity with the communities that these characters represent.

Although Muñoz Ryan does not incorporate as much narrative innovation or complexity in her novel as does García McCall, she offers a clear and stylistically simple account of the titular character whose juvenile third-person narrative voice perhaps allows for a more palatable approach to broaching polemic topics as she tries to make sense of the world around her. Incorporating Spanish chapter titles that correspond to harvests (e.g., Uvas, Higos, Espárragos), Muñoz Ryan develops specific associated stories within each chapter and signals the cyclical nature of migrant work by beginning and ending with "Uvas." The novel illustrates the evolution of Esperanza from a six-year-old daughter of privilege in Aguascalientes, Mexico, toward maturity, narrating her separation from her father, grandmother, and mother; her developing awareness of social constraints based on gender, class, race / ethnicity; and her inevitable change of worldview because of her own loss of status and exposure to the poor conditions of migrant camps, the mistreatment of workers, and the injustice of being deported for speaking out, regardless of citizenship status. This feminine *Bildungsroman*, then, reveals the diverse traumas that

Esperanza and members of her family and surrounding community endure and, in doing so, functions to dispel stereotypes of Mexican immigrants, contest dominant versions of historical truths, and persuasively argue against unjust treatment of Mexican (American) communities.

Depicting the aftermath of the Mexican Revolution, the novel opens in 1924 and then jumps to six years later, when now twelve-year-old Esperanza looks forward to the harvest and extravagant birthday party that she will enjoy at El Rancho de las Rosas, the "thousands of acres of Papa's land" (Muñoz Ryan 2010, 10). Using free indirect discourse, Muñoz Ryan establishes the continued socioeconomic tensions that remain long after the supposed resolution of the revolution and that ultimately result in the attack on Esperanza's father that turns her life upside down and is the catalyst for the remaining plot elements. Esperanza and Miguel, her close friend and the son of her father's employees, "both knew that even though it was 1930 and the revolution in Mexico had been over for ten years, there was still resentment against the large landowners" (11–12). Although Esperanza identifies her father as a benevolent landowner who sympathizes with his workers (much like Joaquín's father in *Shame the Stars*), Miguel offers a broader perspective, one couched in his experience as a member of the lower class: "'Change has not come fast enough, Esperanza. The wealthy still own most of the land while some of the poor have not even a garden plot. There are cattle grazing on the big ranches yet some peasants are forced to eat cats'" (12).

Consequently, some *bandidos* are taking matters into their own hands to redistribute land and wealth more effectively, and Papa and his *vaqueros* fall victim to a bandit attack. When she receives the news of the former's death, "Esperanza felt her heart drop. A noise came from her mouth and slowly, her first breath of grief grew into a tormented cry. She fell to her knees and sank into a dark hole of despair and disbelief" (22). Esperanza's mother also reels from this and subsequent traumas when she rejects her brother-in-law's proposal of marriage as the sole means to maintain possession of El Rancho de las Rosas, since "'it is not customary to leave land to women'" (30). After Mama sends word that she will not accept, a suspicious fire burns down their home—a clear repercussion of her specific rejection of the proposal as well as the broader sociocultural norms that dictate expectations and limitations for women. Esperanza's uncle continues to intimidate Mama, attempting to manipulate her to marry via guilt about the well-being of her servants and her daughter. Tío Marcos snidely comments, "'Of course, if you prefer, you can live here with the servants, as long as another tragedy does not happen to their homes as well. There is no main house or fields where they can work, so you see that many people's lives and jobs depend upon you. And I am sure you want the best for Esperanza, do you not?'" (44–45). Recognizing the imminent danger of remaining in Aguascalientes, Mama relies on longtime friends and employees to escape to the north while safely avoiding the unique dangers that bandits present for women.

Still processing the shock and heartbreak of her father's death and her incinerated home, Esperanza sustains additional emotional trauma from her forced migration. "Sadness and anger tangled in Esperanza's stomach as she thought of all that she was leaving: her friends and her school, her life as it once was, Abuelita. And Papa. She felt as though she was leaving him, too" (56), the narrative voice describes. As a means to comfort Esperanza, her *abuelita* recounts her own immigration story from Spain and evokes the symbolism of the phoenix in her repeated urging, "'Do not be afraid to start over'" (15, 49).

Abuelita insists, "'We are like the phoenix. Rising again, with a new life ahead of us'" (50). Indeed, Esperanza is poised to embark upon a journey that entails an entirely new life, one that will require her to confront her privilege, or newfound lack thereof, and mature in a variety of ways.

Nearing adolescence, Esperanza has already internalized the dictates of class divisions prior to her migration. She and Miguel used to be inseparable and the best of friends, "But now that she was a young woman, she understood that Miguel was the house-keeper's son and she was the ranch owner's daughter and between them ran a deep river. Esperanza stood on one side and Miguel stood on the other and the river could never be crossed" (18). Yet, the two will ultimately cross a different river—the Río Grande—together to arrive in the southwestern United States, where she will no longer enjoy the status to which she was accustomed.

Not only is Esperanza bewildered that the trunk of clothes for the poor is intended for her and her mother, she consistently compares the nature of her travels to previous, more luxurious train rides. After hiding in the back of a wagon with guavas, she looks forward to boarding the train. "But they did not board the fancy car with the compartments and leather seats or the dining car with the white linens. Instead, Alfonso led them to a car with rows of wooden benches, like church pews facing each other, already crowded with peasants. Trash littered the floor and it reeked of rotting fruit and urine" (66). Not accustomed to being near so many peasants, she stops in the doorway, cautioning her mother, "'We cannot travel in this car. It . . . it is not clean. And the people do not look trustworthy'" (67). Her protest is futile, and her physical movements speak volumes with respect to her sense of superiority

Once settled in the train car, "Esperanza leaned her head against the window. She knew she did not belong here. She was

Esperanza Ortega from El Rancho de las Rosas. She crossed her arms tight and stared out the window" (68). Furthermore, she is horrified at Mama's impropriety in interacting with fellow passengers. "'Mama,' whispered Esperanza, taking on a tone she had heard Mama use many times. 'Do you think it is wise to tell a peasant our personal business?'" (77). In response, her mother pointedly notes, "'It's all right, Esperanza, because now we are peasants, too'" (77). This is but the first of many times that Esperanza will be forced to confront the reality of social / racial / ethnic hierarchies and class differences, as well as her "white" privilege once she is in a context in which she is now a racialized Other.

Prior to arriving at the border, Miguel opens Esperanza's eyes to common notions of the disparity between the rich and the poor, connecting privilege and wealth in Mexican society to Spanish blood and light skin tones. "'There is a Mexican saying,'" he tells her, "'Full bellies and Spanish blood go hand in hand [and] [t]hose with Spanish blood, who have the fairest complexions in the land, are the wealthiest'" (79). Evidently sheltered from such ideas, "Esperanza suddenly felt guilty and did not want to admit that she had never noticed or that it might be true. Besides, they were going to the United States now, and it certainly would not be true there" (80). Not surprisingly, experience after experience would demonstrate that it is indeed true in the United States as well. From the moment she reaches the immigration checkpoint, Esperanza continues to disidentify with those she perceives to be of the lower class or of more marginalized status. Nevertheless, she ultimately comes to recognize the links between socioeconomic status, blood line, skin color, social and legal privilege, and power in her new country.

She recognizes the good fortune of her mother and herself acquiring copies of the documents enabling their border crossing as she sympathizes with the undocumented individuals who do not enjoy such a privilege. "'My heart aches for those people. They came all this way just to be sent back . . . [for] [m]any reasons. They had no papers, false ones, or no proof of work. Or there might have been a problem with just one member of the family so they all chose to go back instead of being separated'" (83–84). Upon arriving at the migrant camp, she is shocked and dismayed at the conditions and promptly alienates herself from the other children even more effectively than her new acquaintance Isabel's explanation of her past could accomplish. Providing her backstory, Isabel explains, "'Esperanza's father owned [the ranch] and thousands of acres of land. She had lots of servants and beautiful dresses and she went to private school, too. Miguel is my cousin and he and his parents worked for them'" (96). Marta, another girl in the camp, poses the cutting question to Esperanza, "'So you're a princess who's come to be a peasant? Where's all your finery?'" (96). After substantial time at the camp, Esperanza still struggles to adapt to new responsibilities that even eight-year-old Isabel has mastered, like cooking or washing diapers. In attempting to explain her ineptitude, "'Well, Hortensia took everything out to the laundry quarters. And the servants, they always . . . '" (115), she trails off as she recognizes how her history of privilege has surfaced once again.

Esperanza's transformation proceeds more gradually than that of her mother, who perhaps due to her age and maturity is better prepared to embrace the changes concomitant with starting over. She exercises agency in her decision to flee her home and in her choice to maintain a positive perspective of these changes. She explains to Esperanza, "'Here, we have two choices. To be together and miserable or to be together and happy. Mija, we have each other and Abuelita will come.

How would she want you to behave? I choose to be happy. So which will you choose?'" (104). Even Mama's physical appearance changes as a manifestation of her broader identity transformation. "She looked different," Esperanza notes. "Was it the long cotton dress and the big flowered apron tied at her waist? No, it was more than that" (108). Mama no longer donned the hairstyle of an aristocratic woman of leisure, "done up in her beautiful plaited bun, or when she was ready for bed, brushed out and flowing. Mama looked shorter and, somehow, not herself. Esperanza didn't like it" (109). An additional unwelcome change that Mama undergoes is her incessant coughing due to contracting Valley Fever and later pneumonia, which necessitate a lengthy hospital stay with minimal visits.

When the doctor shares Mama's diagnosis and prognosis, Esperanza is struck with fear and dismay. "She felt the blood drain from her face. She wanted to tell the doctor that she could not lose Mama, too. That she had already lost Papa and that Abuelita was too far away. Her voice strangled with fear. All she could do was whisper the doctor's uncertain words, 'If she survives'" (157). The narrative voice describes her longing for her mother, and after the first three months of hospitalization and several weeks without visitation, "Esperanza hadn't been acting like herself. She went through the motions of living. She was polite enough, answering everyone's questions with the simplest answers, but she was tormented by Mama's absence. Papa, Abuelita, Mama. Who would be next?" (185). It is as though the separation from her mother has triggered the traumas of loss surrounding the death of her father and the separation and uncertainty about reuniting with her grandmother. It is during this time apart, however, that Esperanza's transformation accelerates, and she adopts a maternal role in caring for her mother, brushing and braiding her hair and assuring her,

"'Don't worry. I will take care of everything. I will be la patrona for the family now'" (178), and again repeating, "'Don't worry, Mama. Remember, I will take care of everything. I am working and I can pay the bills. I love you'" (184).

During this period, Esperanza also becomes more cognizant of social dynamics and the sociocultural trauma that Mexican (Americans) face through microaggressions and outright racial / ethnic discrimination, thanks in large part to Miguel. He explains, for example, "'Esperanza, people here think that all Mexicans are alike. They think that we are all uneducated, dirty, poor, and unskilled. It does not occur to them that many have been trained in professions in Mexico'" (187). Miguel thus offers insights that facilitate Esperanza's process of maturation, and the author once again takes advantage of the innocence of a youthful perspective to launch a barbed insult at the contingent of US society that adheres to this overgeneralization of Mexicans without putting forth any effort to educate themselves about individual and collective experiences and identities associated with Mexican and Mexican American communities.

Miguel continues, "'The fact remains, Esperanza, that you, for instance, have a better education than most people's children in this country. But no one is likely to recognize that or take the time to learn it. Americans see us as one big, brown group who are good for only manual labor'" (187). While taking on the role of primary breadwinner within this manual labor force, Esperanza further matures as she learns about labor relations and the controversy about a potential strike to procure better housing and pay. She also experiences the tensions between those on strike and strikebreakers and becomes aware of the potential for other migrant groups, namely the Okies, to displace the current migrant labor force.

Reminiscent of the association between social prestige and skin tone that Miguel points out early on in the novel, Esperanza also tries to come to terms with the obvious inequities based on ethnic / racial origin when she discovers that the new camp for workers from Oklahoma includes inside plumbing, hot water, and even a swimming pool. Despite performing the same job, the laborers enjoy different amenities, based solely on their origins. Her anger boils over when she picks up on the implicit perception of Mexicans as dirty and inferior, and she questions Miguel's pursuit of the American Dream:

> "Is this the better life that you left Mexico for? Is it? Nothing is right here! Isabel will certainly not be queen no matter how badly she wants it because she is Mexican. You cannot work on engines because you are Mexican. We have gone to work through angry crowds of our own people who threw rocks at us, and I'm afraid they might have been right! They send people back to Mexico even if they don't belong there, just for speaking up. We live in a horse stall. And none of this bothers you? Have you heard that they are building a new camp for Okies, with a swimming pool? The Mexicans can only swim in it on the afternoon before they clean it! Have you heard they will be given inside toilets and hot water? Why is that, Miguel? Is it because they are the fairest in the land? Tell me! Is this life really better than being a servant in Mexico?" (221–22)

Although Miguel recognizes some truth to Esperanza's overall assessment of the inequities, he reminds her of the impossibility of social mobility for someone like him in Mexico, where he "'stood on the other side of the river, remember?'" (222). A change of social station and economic status is at least a possibility that he can hope for in the context of the US. Nevertheless, the road to success is fraught with obstacles and ongoing risks.

One such risk that Esperanza attempts to comprehend is the potential for falling victim to the retaliatory tactic of repatriation of Mexican and Mexican American laborers, particularly after she witnesses an immigration raid targeting the striking workers, regardless of their legal status. Even as Esperanza argues that *la Migra* surely couldn't detain and deport US citizens, Hortensia explains, "'It doesn't matter. They are causing problems for the government. They are talking about forming a farm workers' union and the government and the growers don't like that'" (206). Much like García McCall recuperates the omitted and/or distorted history of La Matanza through its fictionalized depiction in *Shame the Stars*, Muñoz Ryan touches upon the shameful period of "voluntary" Mexican repatriation from 1929 to 1936, offering a brief historical background in her author's note. In rather didactic fashion, the protagonist offers her assessment of the obviously unjust practice, observing, "Something seemed very wrong about sending people away from their own 'free country' because they had spoken their minds" (208). Esperanza later poses a question that is certainly pertinent to contemporary issues of immigration, identity, and legality (and one that García McCall takes up in depth in *All the Stars Denied*), asking, "How was it that the United States could send people to Mexico who had never even lived there?" (211). In stark contrast to her previous leisure, her expectation of receiving exquisite finery, and her minimal regard for anyone else— much less somebody of a lower social stature—Esperanza has evolved into a more conscientious individual who empathizes with others, perhaps modeling the same for the readers.

The narrator reflects on Esperanza's awareness of her growth, noting, "Her other life seemed like a story she had read in a book a long time ago, un cuento de hadas, a fairy tale. She could see the illustrations in her mind: the Sierra Madre, El Rancho de las Rosas, and a carefree young girl running through the vineyard. But now, sitting in this cabin, the story seemed as if it were about some other girl, someone Esperanza didn't know anymore" (157). Similarly, her mother notes her transformation when the former returns from the hospital after five months, remarking, "'Oh, Esperanza, how you've grown. You look so mature'" (230). Despite the months of trials and tribulations, Esperanza emerges confident and hopeful, exemplifying the hope that her name conveys and ready to rise above any additional challenges. Notably, this confidence and hope coincide with the reunification of her family, as Miguel surprises her by arranging to bring Abuelita to California. The restoration of the remaining family unit is evidently enough to offset—or at least to counterbalance—the traumas that Esperanza has sustained as an individual and as a member of a marginalized community.

All the Stars Denied and the Interrogation of Patriarchy and Shameful History

In her sequel to *Shame the Stars*, García McCall once again adopts a multi-genre approach to address the gaps in historical knowledge of systematic policies and practices to target and deport Mexicans and Mexican Americans alike during the 1930s and expose the ensuing interconnected layers of trauma. Like Muñoz Ryan, she develops a compelling fictional story that reveals the human consequences of massive repatriation efforts that largely remain unknown to the general public. In her author's note, she comments, "Raids, roundups, and unconstitutional deportations: None of this is new. What is also not new, but what I find completely unacceptable, is the fact that most Americans still do not know that we've done this many times before" (García McCall 2018, 304). García McCall further remarks, "Students need to inform themselves as to the issues that affect their peers, their neighbors, and their homeland. To remain ignorant of the inequalities of the past is to learn nothing from our mistakes and to perpetuate the cycle of injustices" (307). Indeed, the content of this young adult novel is even more relevant than the author herself likely could have anticipated, with its 2018 publication just a few months after the declaration of the "zero-tolerance" policy of family separation. While many Americans expressed utter shock and disgust at the unconstitutionality and injustice of such policies, most were evidently unaware that similar practices were nothing new.

As a Mexican American author and teacher, García McCall finds it important to recuperate this hidden history of Mexican repatriation following the Great Depression to inform readers that the majority of these deportees were citizens of the United States, many of whom had no knowledge of Spanish or their supposed homeland of Mexico (García McCall 2018, 304–5). This also reflects the contemporary polemic topic of the rights of undocumented youth to remain in the United States, the only home they have known, especially should Deferred Action for Childhood Arrivals (DACA) be suspended. In an effort to inform and to help with collective healing, she implements techniques of both bounded and ambassadorial strategic empathy, creating empathic connections with readers who share heritage and histories and with those who do not. Regardless of the intended audience(s), García McCall comments that "at the heart of it all was my need to tell the truth intertwined with my frustration at the inhumane treatment of mexicanos and the demoralization of an entire group of people—mi gente" (306). Accordingly, she continues the tale of the del Toro and Villa families of Monteseco, Texas, with a renewed focus on the trials and tribulations of the next generation, whose lives of privilege are once again interrupted by the sociocultural and legal tensions of their geopolitical environment.

The novel opens with a note about eco-poetry, the incorporation of which is a technique that enables readers to gain insight as to the protagonist's consciousness as the plot progresses. Much like in the previous text, García McCall inserts fragments of a journal—this time, that of Joaquín and Dulceña's teenage daughter Estrella—throughout, providing alternative perspectives for a more holistic understanding of the characters' experiences and how they process their compounded traumas. Beyond including Estrella's attempts at eco-poetry, the interpolated journal also offers access to Estrella's letters to her deceased grandmother and other fictionalized artifacts like telegrams, an elementary school class roster, newspaper articles, and community meeting agendas. This strategy of incorporating unique framing devices invites readers to take a more active role in experiencing events and emotions and narrows the distance between characters and the audience, thus contributing to the development of narrative empathy. Alongside the more traditional and stylistically unpretentious narrative, these texts within texts round out the straightforward treatment of the community's shifting social dynamic (due to the Great Depression, the arrival of increasing numbers of Anglo immigrants, and the expulsion of Mexicans from the region) and the individual and collective response to these violent and traumatic changes.

Although somewhat aware of, and saddened by, the "desaparecidos . . . mothers, fathers, brothers, sisters, entire families just gone—vanished" (García McCall 2018, 1), Estrella generally occupies her plentiful leisure time writing poetry. Characteristic of an entitled, sullen teenager who is annoyed by nagging to help with housework or babysitting the two-year-old brother that an employee usually attends to, she responds with exasperation, "'What?' I couldn't believe it. More babysitting duties! 'You mean I have to do her job too? Don't I do enough around here? . . . 'Estrella, do this! Estrella, do that!' I never get a break around here. I'm tired of doing other people's work'" (6–7). Beyond this, Estrella harbors resentment that her mother spends a great deal of her time dedicated to her non-maternal duties, running a bookstore and writing investigative newspaper pieces. Dulceña puts her daughter in her place with respect to her privilege, reminding her (and the readers) about the socioeconomic context and its repercussions:

> "I don't think you know what 'depression' means, Mamá said. "You think you have it tough because you don't have time to go outside and write poetry, and that's true. The world as you've always known it is crumbling, Estrella. But there is suffering everywhere. Real suffering. People in every state in this country have lost their homes to this depression, and those that haven't know they're next. Every morning they wake up wondering how they're going to keep a roof over their heads one more month, one more week, one more day. Hardworking fathers and mothers have lost their jobs and are standing in lines hoping the government will give them a few staples to keep their families fed. . . . I hope to God nothing ever happens to make you regret you ever thought this was hard. Because your life isn't hard, Estrella. Your life is very easy. It's very simple. You don't have anything to worry about except homework and chores." (11–13)

This passage also foreshadows the hardships to come for Estrella and her family, as they too will be counted among the "disappeared" when they speak out against the injustices perpetrated by government officials conducting raids and roundups of anybody who could potentially be an undocumented Mexican in Morado County.

The overarching atmosphere of suffering and fear literally intrudes upon her "haven" (25), her mother's bookstore in town, when Cecilia, a classmate Estrella hasn't seen in months, runs in from the commotion outside, terrified and separated from her family. The dialogue that incorporates Dulceña's side of a telephone conversation with her husband establishes the evident regularity of such roundups: "'Joaquín? Sí. Have you heard? They're doing it again. . . . No. . . . No. Not us. The whole plaza is cordoned off. They've got at least twenty people sitting on the ground with their hands on their heads. It's appalling— just appalling!'" (30). The narrator then offers her first-person perspective of the pandemonium, observing, "Through the transparent lace, I could see people running everywhere. Men and women scrambled to get their families out of the streets and into their vehicles. Beat-up ranch trucks sputtered to life and took off" (31–32). As the narrator describes, adding to the ambience of ethnic / racial tensions and violence during the raid, "A group of young Anglo boys were yelling and throwing rocks at the people standing on our side of the street. I flinched and ducked to avoid the rock that broke through the window and came flying across the aisle, rolling on the floor until it stopped halfway down the store" (2).

Despite Cecilia's begging not to go outside for fear of disappearing like her parents, Estrella attempts to lead her outside to a safer refuge. As they run amid other people fleeing, pushing, and screaming, the girls are forcefully stopped by two deputies recruited from out of town. "'Ma'am? . . . Are you Mexican?'" (37), one deputy asks, to which she indignantly responds, "'Am I Mexican? Of course I'm Mexican!' I practically spat the words in his face. 'Look around you. This is Monteseco. Ninety percent of the population is Mexican. And why are you calling me 'ma'am'? I'm fifteen years old!'" (37). When he shows his skepticism, she reflects, "I was livid. 'And I'm an American citizen. I have rights, you know'" (37), demonstrating both ethnic and national pride. In spite of her proclamation of citizenship and the rights pertaining to such, the deputy grabs hold of her arm to take her in. She relates:

> We walked to where the trocas were parked just over the railroad tracks until we stood on the *other* side of town. I looked up at those buildings, trying to scan the perimeter for a place to run, but my spirit was dejected by every sign I encountered. I was more than appalled, I was horrified by the vile words written on business windows and doors. Every poster, every sign screamed hatred. "NO DOGS OR MEXICANS ALLOWED." "GO HOME MEXICAN!" "MEXICANS AND HISPANOS WILL BE SHOT! NO LOITERING!" (37)

Reflecting upon the clear hostility toward, dehumanization of, and discrimination against the Mexican community, Estrella also points to the legal violence and structural injustice inherent in the racial profiling and rounding up of individuals for repatriation hearings at the courthouse. "I looked up at the people already loaded up, huddled together, looking lost as goats on the barricaded farm trucks that would take them away immediately after their 'hearings' with or without consent, whether they were US citizens or not" (38), she describes. Filled with fear and anger, she and Cecilia physically attack the Rangers and manage to escape.

Estrella later pens a letter dated Monday, November 16, 1931, to her deceased *abuela*, Jovita, to process the tumultuous events and to invoke the fearless and rebellious spirit of La Estrella, from whom she inherited her name. She depicts the contemporary terror of "[b]lack-hearted men [who] leap out of shadows, grasp and grapple with our gente and drag them off" (40), capturing the violent and malevolent ambush, and also emphasizing the dehumanizing and unjust repatriation efforts. She continues, "Today, I met them face-to-face, was pulled in tight, wrestled with, and almost hauled away by those who would throw us into cattle cars, drive us to the border, and force us across to Mexico, back to what they say is the land of our ancestors, as if this America was not one land, one heart" (40), recognizing the arbitrariness of borders and also the misconception that the Mexican American community is somehow more Mexican than American. Although Estrella and Cecilia are fortunate to have escaped, twelve community members are not so lucky, including two thirty-something US-born brothers whose birth certificates were lost during their family's move from Massachusetts.

As can be expected, Dulceña and Joaquín, who had committed to fighting injustice in the context of La Matanza during their younger years, are adamant that the local government must be made aware of the moral and ethical problems associated with the unlawful actions of outside agencies and individuals tasked with immigration enforcement and repatriation. They lament the dehumanizing treatment of their *compañeros*: "'Mauled and harangued and loaded up on farm trucks, como bestias,' [Papá] said. 'Disgraceful!'" (44). "'Yes,' [Mamá] said. '¡Como vacas o chivas! That's how they see us, Joaquín. We are nothing more than burdensome beasts, *the neighbor's cattle*, a nuisance to be driven off what they see as *their* land even though *we've* been here far longer'" (44), alluding to the encroachment of Anglo settlers on the region that has been in Tejanos' possession for generations. As if that were not enough, "'And now not even our children are safe?'" (44), Dulceña reiterates, after having expressed her concern that "'they are picking up children without trying to figure out where they came from'" (42). This dialogue bears an uncanny resemblance to the content of conversations that ensued in 2018 and beyond with regard to the incapacity (and perhaps unwillingness) of the federal government to reunite children separated from their caregivers upon crossing the US-Mexico border or to invest sufficient resources and energy to enable these juveniles and their families to present a legal request for asylum. Like the thousands of protesters who participated in the 2018 "Families Belong Together" marches and rallies to demand an end to unjust policies, the del Toro family and fellow community members decide to take action.

Although Estrella would prefer to engage in more explicit civil disobedience like protesting, the adults are wary of endangering the Mexican and Tejano community further, particularly given the escalating tensions. For instance, the last time the Damas de Dios group[18] of "devoted Catholic women, women of wealth and influence from all over Morado County" (45) met in town:

> [T]he Salon de Colores had been raided and more than twenty people had been arrested. They'd been tried quickly in closed chambers and hauled away the very next morning. Even though most of them were US citizens, neither they nor their families were given an opportunity to prove their citizenship in court. Family members were helpless. There was nothing they could do, no time to get papers to them, to hire out-of-town lawyers. Their families were simply picked up, tried, and deported, "repatriated" to Mexico. My parents were sure of one thing: the justice system in Monteseco was askew again. (46)

Dulceña and Joaquín recognize the need to fight back against the inherently violent structural mechanisms but prefer to do so through the power of information, exposing injustices in newspaper articles and disseminating information at arranged meetings in their home for the Mexican community and their allies to come together to formulate an effective plan that will not further endanger their families.

The del Toro family convenes a meeting of the Damas de Dios to discuss the usual business of planning the Posadas, as well as more general concerns about "[s]afety and security" (50). Community members debate a variety of strategies, including demanding an opportunity to present their grievances and propose new ordinances to protect their community at the next meeting of the city council, a body that includes no individuals of Mexican descent. García McCall cleverly includes a typed document directed to the city council that serves as a formal request for consideration of ordinances to be established and those to be eliminated, as proposed by the recently created Council of Mexican American Citizens of Morado County. "This we ask in the name of justice, for the sake of equality for all men, the security of our people, and in respect of and deference to the rights afforded to us as citizens of this country by the Constitution of the United States of America" (64), the document concludes, focusing on constitutional rights of equality and just treatment, neither of which have been protected by a government that legislatively requires separate schools for Mexican versus Anglo children and offers government aid "just for white folks" (52).

Dissatisfied with the more diplomatic and long-term approach of her parents and their associates, Estrella takes it upon herself to engage in direct action, organizing a protest to draw attention to the absurdity of deportation and the emotional devastation of family separation. She and her friends confidently carry signs proclaiming, "DOWN WITH DEPORTATION! and REPATRIATING US CITIZENS MAKES NO SENSE!" (73), or "*Stop the Raids! Stop the Heartbreak!*" (67), referring to the anguish of broken families as well as that of being wrongfully "disappeared" without the ability to prove one's status, especially when out of retaliation. Although other community members have joined their ranks, their confidence, pride, and level of comfort shifts once they enter the Anglo side of the neighborhood to ensure that the commissioner and city councilmen—"the reason the raids were happening" (71)—witness their protest while enjoying their morning coffee at Louie's Hotel & Restaurant.

When Estrella explains that the group's intention is not to create trouble but simply to stand up for their rights, they are met with sociocultural violence manifest in the slinging of anti-Mexican epithets. "'Go home, Mexicans! Go home, mojados!' Phillip Rice, the grocer's youngest son, yelled" (73), as a counter-protest forms. Protected by policemen, the Anglo businessmen yell, "'Arrest them, Chief! Arrest those Mexican dogs!' 'Get those bean eaters!' and 'Run those filthy dogs outta town!'" (73). When Estrella finally responds with "'I am American! I have rights! I can speak my mind! I can speak my heart!'" (74), physical violence breaks out. The policemen attack Estrella and her fellow protestors with clubs and then arrest them. The outrageous happening is later documented and decried in the fictional *El Sureño*.

The discord within Monteseco and the pervasive sociocultural violence directed toward community members of Mexican descent intensify after the incident. The narrator observes, "The division wasn't just evident in the discriminatory signage that had more than doubled since the protest; you could actually feel the discomfort and aggression coming from the glares of the people who lived on this side of town" (78). This undoubtedly contributes to the insidious violence rooted in social and/or economic conditions that Estrella and her community experience. The Council of Mexican American Citizens appears to make headway when the city council grants a special meeting pertaining to their requests regarding ordinances and to discuss the devolving from peaceful protest into violent attacks on and arrests of the young people involved. Nevertheless, they find themselves up against a federal mandate regarding roundups that local authorities ultimately have the power to execute as they wish and a city council body that insists that they should discuss the proposal in a closed meeting, without the input or even presence of the Mexican and Mexican American community members.

As spokesperson for the group, Estrella's father continues to defend the rights of his daughter and her friends as courageous US citizens participating in nonviolent acts of civil disobedience in the face of hatred and to express his concerns about the community. Joaquín remarks, "'As people from different backgrounds, different cultures, we've had our differences, but in the end, we were always a community, a pueblo full of decent people, working toward a better future for our children. But this intolerance, this lack of concern for our laborers, our immigrant friends and family from the other side of the border, and now even our own children have made it impossible for us to remain silent'" (84). Councilman Jones angrily imposes silence, raging against Joaquín's disrespect in referring to the Anglo side of town as a "viper pit" (84), thereby invalidating the concerns brought before him as well as insisting, "'That's quite enough! . . . I refuse to have the whims of a child, let alone a female child, dictate my actions. I suggest you have your daughter sit down before I have her hauled away again. Caceres! Either escort this girl back to her seat or arrest her. We have no more time for shenanigans!'" (85). This one brief portion of dialogue succinctly conveys intersectional oppressions based on ethnicity, age, and gender.

Notably, the narrative and dialogue that García McCall incorporates within these passages of the novel juxtapose the poised and calm demeanor of Estrella's father and the rage of the city councilman, highlighting the obvious injustice(s) of the situation and compelling readers to disassociate from the hateful member of the dominant cultural class and develop a more positive affective relationship to empathize with the marginalized Mexican and Tejano community. In a compelling monologue about the discrimination and inequities that Mexican (American) community members face, Joaquín ultimately invokes the contributions of generations of his people and their constant endurance of interconnected nodes of violence and asks that the city council take action to rectify the situation:

> "We will not be hauled away. We will not be silenced. Not today! You say you feel disrespected? Well, what do you think we feel when we are not allowed to sit next to you in a shop and order something as simple and fundamentally necessary as a glass of water? . . . How do you think we feel when we walk down the streets and see sign after sign proclaiming your contempt? We work just as hard—no, that's not true. Every single one of our campesinos works harder, longer, and for much less pay than the lot of you put together. And for what? To what end? They pick your vegetables, your fruits, your grains. My gente dig the irrigation systems that give you clean food and water from the very soil which was stolen from their ancestors, food and water which you gladly take, and what do they get in return? Hate. Hate and intolerance and now fear. Because that's what the raids have brought us, a foul, fetid fear that taints every breath our workers breathe. Now the question still stands: What are you going to do about it? How are you going to undo these injustices?" (85–86)

In addition to the articulate description of the injustices that his community faces, Joaquín poses pointed questions regarding the unconstitutionality of preserving the law of the land by preemptively deporting anybody who may be "a liability to our country" (87). When he demands respect and fairness with respect to the legal system, the city councilman ejects him with rhetoric that underscores the ethnic tensions: "'Do me a favor, del Toro . . . [t]ake your people and get out of our chambers. We have no use for you and your kind'" (88). Soon thereafter, when a suspicious fire burns down the del Toro home during a raid to arrest Joaquín and take everyone else away, the reader is left to suspect that this physical and psychological act of violence and terror is clearly retaliatory.

As if the trauma of nearly escaping a home purposefully set on fire were not enough, the Morado County Sheriff's Department intentionally separates Joaquín from Dulceña and their children. Estrella realizes, "We were being vanished. We were on our way to becoming more of the many who had simply disappeared from our community" (107). She becomes aware of the fear, anger, uncertainty, and guilt she experiences simultaneously as she blames herself for the family's demise and now separation as she prepares to be a foreigner in her supposed "homeland" of Mexico. Prefiguring the dehumanizing experience of being herded like cattle across the border to Ciudad Juárez and later to a holding facility in Mexico City, García McCall cleverly inserts a poem that describes the steady and calm migration of cows and, in its juxtaposition with the narration of the customs and immigration processing, emphasizes the chaos and frenzy of hundreds or thousands of people trying to make sense of their situation and determine the best path forward. The narrator details the humiliation of "being treated like infectious beasts" (119) as they must walk through trays of disinfectant in the name of protecting the country's livestock. This is but the first of many degrading and frustrating ordeals that Estrella and her mother will face as they attempt to prove their wrongful and unlawful deportation.

García McCall crafts dialogue that makes abundantly clear the legal liminality that the del Toro family members face, especially within the patriarchal structures that necessitate the husband's presence as head of household in order to sort out affairs and verify their identity. Not only does the clerk indicate, "'No husband is a big problem'" (121), prompting Estrella to reflect on the gender inequality inherent in the processes, he entirely dismisses Dulceña's declaration of the illegality of their deportation, correcting her, "'No. You are here by lawful agreement. Between our countries. You are repatriating. Just fill out form for to get [*sic*] Certificate of Residency as well as you can. We try our best, ¿verdad?'" (121).

After agreeing to investigate, the clerk indicates that he found the official orders for repatriation and a certificate of residency, which have clearly been falsified. Dulceña immediately identifies and condemns the elements of legal / structural violence at play, arguing that the del Toros have never been Mexican citizens and thus have no documents to that effect, that they were born in the US, and "'you can't repatriate someone who's never been a patriate of that country'" (133). Moreover, she declares that they are not Communists, nor do they otherwise pose a threat to the United States, and that "'[t]hese are trumped-up charges. They were fabricated in order to deport us'" (134). Despite her insistence on the injustice and illegality of the situation and the need for information about the whereabouts of her husband and her parents, the clerk continues to disregard her, having decided that the documents appear to be official, accusing her of lying, and suggesting that she request a meeting with the American Embassy once she arrives at a repatriation camp in Mexico City. In the meantime, he ushers them out to a corral filled with thousands of desperate people awaiting south-bound trains.

Again focusing on the dehumanization of the deportees, García McCall uses the narrator's juvenile voice to document her consternation and disgust at the horrid conditions of the overcrowded waiting area: "As we exited the customs house, the scent hit us like a tidal wave of decay. . . . [W]e came to a huge corral full of people. I couldn't believe a corral—a fenced-in area meant to keep animals from roaming—was the waiting camp" (139–40). Estrella continues to process the scene, reiterating, "There were no livestock in the corral, only people. I couldn't believe my eyes. Hundreds of Mexican families were standing and sitting around, eyes hollow" (140), in what had been a pasture, as the city is ill-equipped to provide sufficient shelter for so many people. Further reflecting on her displacement, Estrella writes of their treatment in another letter to her grandmother. "Here, in this Mexico," she describes, "we are less than human. Here, we are a threat. Here, we are infected foreigners" (147–48) subject to physical and psychological trauma in "a country where we were homeless, starving, destitute" (149).

Scavenging through trash cans to find scraps as they continue to await the train for days, Estrella recalls the exquisite celebrations at Las Moras and in Monteseco, much like the protagonist of *Esperanza Rising*, and ironically notes, "I ate lamb from beautiful floral porcelain plates, scooped out delicate, frothy strawberry sorbets and airy mousses from tall, sparkling crystal glasses with silver spoons, and sipped Mami's chocolate from dainty teacups, but I never enjoyed the anticipation of eating *any* of that as much as opening a greasy paper bag and finding not one but four red-tortilla taquitos still wrapped in butcher paper" (175). Their dignity and sense of humanity is restored temporarily when, at long last, they board the antiquated train bound for the capital and enjoy the luxury of a clean change of clothes after more than a week of detention and travels. Aside from contending with an overarching trauma of poverty, they simultaneously endure the trauma of class decline.

Already privy to the family's backstory of sustaining one unjust trauma after another and witnessing the characters' adaptability to their unfortunate circumstances, the reader may perhaps develop an even closer emotional connection upon accompanying Estrella, her mother, and her little brother throughout their dramatic chapter of survival in Mexico City as they continue their odyssey to reunite with her father and to rectify their legal situation so that they may return to Texas. Inviting the reader to be an accomplice in solving the mystery regarding Joaquín's whereabouts, García McCall includes a telegram in Spanish from the American Embassy in Mexico City that confirms his presence there as well as his need for medical attention. Also included is a letter that he has addressed to a couple that had kindly paid for his care and indicates his plans to travel to Nuevo Laredo. The narration of the complications that Estrella and her mother withstand all the while—including the need to procure employment and housing, enduring mistreatment and wage theft, and being treated as cultural and linguistic outsiders because of their "corrupted" Americanized Spanish (228)—contribute to a shared sense of indignity at the unfairness of the circumstances, particularly as they individually attempt to make headway at the government offices and face a series of obstacles.

Continuing to employ the epistolary form as another means to facilitate access to the protagonist's inner thoughts, García McCall further documents the emotional trauma that Estrella and her mother continue to face. In a letter to her *abuela* in December 1931, she writes, "I pray that you make the angels listen to the heartbreak in my mother's sobs at night. That you can make them see how vulnerable we are in this strange land" (217). This heartbreak intensifies when the family is subject to yet another separation when little brother Wicho's diagnosis of scarlet fever necessitates his hospitalization and isolation. In a sometimes overwhelmingly didactic fashion, the author establishes crystal-clear connections between each individual trial and the broader context of legal and sociocultural violence that generated it. Because of the terrible conditions while being held in detention, Wicho, who already had a poor constitution, has contracted a dangerous infection. In a rant of frustration and exhaustion, Estrella responds to the clerk who has instructed her to bring her crying brother home because he is disrupting others at the embassy:

> "I would take him home—if we could go home! But our government has thrown us out of our own country. They've left us here in the cold, without food or shelter, without any means by which to live. But you wouldn't know anything about that, would you? You wouldn't know what it's like to starve and freeze and wonder if you'll ever see the rest of your family. You wouldn't know that because you've got a good job here. As long as Mexican Americans are rounded up, forced across the river, and put in corrals to freeze and starve to death, your mortgage will get paid and your children will be fed!" (225)

Although a teenager, Estrella demonstrates a keen awareness of the broader structural factors that have led to the physical and emotional suffering of her family and attacks the role that the Mexican employees play through their indifference and their complicity with the unjust legal system.

Once the hospital releases Wicho, Dulceña decides they will head north to search for her husband. Upon arriving in Nuevo Laredo, they miraculously reunite with Joaquín, who had suffered a memory lapse after the brutal attack following the raid. Together, they plan their border crossing but again face deportation and detention despite having copies of their US birth certificates.

Perhaps due to the compounded trauma, Estrella's response is impassivity, as "there was no comfort in knowing that we were about to be sent back to a country that was not ours. All my energy, all my courage, had dissipated. But I couldn't cry. My eyes were dry of tears, and I was numb inside" (289). The family prepares to spend the night in a jail cell as though they were criminals—a notion the del Toros counteract through dialogue and description of their actions throughout the novel. Indeed, their lawyer reiterates the rights they maintain as citizens of the United States and the illegality of the actions perpetrated against them, pointing instead to the criminality of government officials and policies. They are granted a hearing, during which Estrella makes an impassioned plea to Judge O'Riley, again invoking the argument that the broader legal structures have contributed to the physical suffering of the family, specifically to her brother's severe illness. Estrella pleads against sending the entire family to Mexico, which would present unique dangers for Wicho, and the undue hardship of separation. "'I beg you, let us stay here together. Please—give us back our lives'" (296), she concludes after detailing the impact of the exposure to cold, filth, and disease.

Fortunately for the del Toro family, the judge opts to follow his moral compass rather than the seemingly arbitrary and unjust laws. In a dialogue that critiques the nature of the US legal system and the limitations on prosecutorial and judicial discretion as pertains to immigration policy and enforcement, Judge O'Riley announces the basis for his decision. "'I have been a judge in this great country of ours for more than forty years, and in that time I have had to make some pretty hard decisions—decisions that I wasn't always proud to make, decisions which still keep me awake at night because they were based on laws that weren't always fair and just to the people involved. But as an old man about to retire, one with one foot out the door and the other one in the grave, I can honestly say I've had about as much nonsense as I can stand. And I'm just not willing to add this verdict to my long list of regrets—I refuse to rule in favor of a mandate that, because of its very nature, hurts children by leaving them either homeless or orphaned'" (296). He thus dismisses the charges of improper entry, acknowledges the family's citizenship, and calls for their immediate release from detention. While García McCall conveys the family's elated response to their legal victory, she reminds the reader of "the hundreds of thousands of people who were still destitute and unwanted in a foreign country that didn't trust their American ways" (297), so as not to lose sight of the broader problematic mechanisms that perpetuate trauma after trauma.

As the novel concludes, Estrella turns again to poetry and letter-writing to articulate her emotions in some final reflections on her own evolution in the midst of the trials that her family has faced. Taken together, the two interpolated texts speak to her tendency to, like the prickly pear described in "Too Late," let her heart become hard after exposure to harsh conditions. In her letter penned on the same date—January 6, 1932—she wonders how to remain kind and loving despite being subject to so much violence and trauma. She writes to her grandmother, "It is a miracle that despite all the things that went wrong in your world, you stayed loving and kind not just to your family but to your people. I hope I never grow thorns or become so tough, so hardened by life, that I lose touch with my true self— my identity as a Mexicana, a loving, courageous woman!" (299) This may very well be the culmination of Estrella's journey to adulthood.

The protagonists of all four YA novels examined in this chapter transcend customary cultural expectations of roles and identity based on gender and age, demonstrating the manner in which displacement forces youth (and to a lesser extent migrant women) to redefine and revolutionize family structures and responsibilities. Through experiencing physical and psychological traumas while also being exposed to sociocultural and legal violences, the children and adolescents come of age as knowing subjects, thereby acquiring more personal agency combating patriarchal, ethnocentric, and xenophobic ideas. The reader comes to recognize these texts as individual stories of personal and cultural identity transformation, particularly in the manner in which the protagonists evolve as a result, or in defiance, of the socioeconomic circumstances imposed upon them. As previously mentioned, this evolution parallels that of the male character in a typical *Bildungsroman*, but with significant divergences from the masculine paradigm.

Above all else, the coming-of-age tale of a female protagonist typically offers a degree of critique for the mechanisms of a patriarchal social structure, particularly noticeable within the texts' conclusion. As Coonrod Martínez explains, "La diferencia entre el bildungsroman masculino y el femenino es que mientras el niño madura y se integra a su sociedad como hombre decidido, la niña hecha mujer termina no integrándose a su sociedad, sino alejándose, o teniendo que cometer actos de rebelión. Sólo con esa rebelión puede la mujer inculcarse a su sociedad" (2000, 364). As opposed to the juvenile protagonist of *Across the Great River*, who ultimately integrates back into Mexican patriarchal culture comfortably, the female protagonists of the three other texts embrace their rebellion, not only through taking on new roles and responsibilities in order to survive but also by finding and using their voices to condemn societal injustices. In a similar vein, the authors themselves engage in textual acts of rebellion through their subversion of official historical accounts. Utilizing a variety of empathic narrative techniques to establish bounded and ambassadorial empathy, they depict their cultural heritage's survival in the face of explicit attempts to eradicate and destroy it in the context of La Matanza and Mexican Repatriation via structural / legal and sociocultural institutions that invoke physical and psychological harm. In this way, they unsettle and disrupt the hegemonic versions of "history" and thus exemplify resistance through authorship, shedding light on that which has been erased by writers of official discourse and transmitting experiences of young Mexican (American) migrant women.

Daniuska González González elaborates how such fiction can fill in the gaps within history, describing, "El discurrir de la 'historia en cursivas' (por su ficcionalidad), registra también la recuperación de ciertos vacíos en la memoria oficial. Los senderos que se desvían del camino establecido como verdad, articulan varios puntos de vista, y al no edificarse la historia desde la óptica hegemónica, permite completar los paréntesis de ausencias que han provocado esos anales académicos" (2001, 109). Aside from articulating alternative points of view of historical events, these young adult novels also provide alternative—what Bracher describes as "more adequate"—exemplars of Mexican migrants, Mexicans, and Tejanos that will contribute to the correction (or replacement) of the faulty stereotypical exemplars and prototypes previously embedded in readers' cognitive schemas.

CHAPTER 3
Crying Out for Their Children: Central American Motherhood and Migration

P rojecting a decidedly southward perspective, Graciela Limón focuses primarily on the plight of migrants from Central America and Mexico prior to their arrival at the US-Mexico border. A Chicana author based in Los Angeles, California, who had been part of a 1990 delegation to investigate the assassination of Jesuit priests in El Salvador, Limón textualizes the tenets and ideals of the Sanctuary Movement of the 1980s through her powerful literary condemnations of state-sanctioned violence in Central America and the destructive repercussions of US political and economic intervention in Central America and Mexico more generally in *In Search of Bernabé* and *The River Flows North*. Her use of specific techniques—like alternating perspectives and timelines and incorporation of polyphonic voices—enables readers to develop a greater degree of empathy with a variety of characters and to formulate more comprehensive conceptualizations of the over-whelming layers of trauma and their ripple effects for families. The gripping representations of the interconnected nodes of violence are further amplified by the underlying emphasis on the particular traumas that mothers and children face in an asphyx-iating environment of terror, echoing many of the themes that undergird Helena María Viramontes's short story "The Cariboo Café" published a decade or more before. *In Search of Bernabé* deftly links individual family traumas to surrounding sociocul-tural violence across generations and borders, emphasizing the role of the state in the suffering of individuals, families, commu-nities, and the broader social fabric of El Salvador.

In *The River Flows North*, Limón also addresses the personal consequences of governmental action as well as the startling regularity with which migrants disappear as a result of expo-sure or suspicious circumstances. This later novel, however, focuses not just on the current tragedies or struggles endured by a particular person or family but on the unfortunate series of events that have driven each of the individuals of a group of undocumented migrants to struggle to survive in the Sonoran Desert when, in a twist, their coyote falls victim to an impatient *narco* on the run and can no longer protect them from disori-entation and the dangers of the journey. Limón's more recent text explicitly depicts the suffering and hardships in first- and third-person narrative both prior to and during the 2008 odys-sey *al norte* and simultaneously develops the transformation of the relationships among the seemingly random group of migrants during their ordeal and the powerfully emotional con-sequences of the separation of mothers and their children.

The narrative voice(s) of both texts restore the dignity and humanity of these individuals and both enable readers to vicar-iously experience their suffering and compel them to consider more profoundly the elements—primarily driven by the impact of past US intervention in Mexico and Central America—that contribute to the seemingly inevitable violence and risks inherent in the contemporary migratory journey. Readers who are familiar with Limón's previous works may note a shift from feminist subtlety to rather graphic depiction of torture and murder in *In Search of Bernabé* and *The River Flows North*. Eschewing subtlety enables Limón to effectively capture the horrors for an audience that is distanced from, and unfamiliar with, the depth of the violence and tragedies that serve as the basis for these fictionalized accounts. Consequently, the sense of empathic unsettlement is even further heightened.

In Search of Bernabé: Intergenerational Trauma and the Impossibility of Redemption

A stylistically complex novel, *In Search of Bernabé* implicates the repression and state-sanctioned violence committed during the Salvadoran Civil War (1980–1992) in the exacerbated traumas of an individual family through the use of various narrative techniques that ultimately link multiple storylines that share, at their core, pervasive traumas of loss and shame. The spatial and chronological jumps, shifts in perspective, use of italicized stream of consciousness, and intersecting plot elements contribute to the "fragmentation, displacement, hesitance, repetition and resistance" (Ibarrola-Armendáriz 2014, 138) manifest in collective trauma narrative that effectively conveys the fragmentation of memory and requires more engagement from the reader to follow the various threads that, when intertwined, create a complex tapestry of the experience of violence and longing. Limón also draws on intertextuality, incorporating fragments of nonfiction texts as well as biblical verses to frame and focalize the relevant fictional narration of events within the greater context of heightened violence in the aftermath of Archbishop Óscar Romero's assassination, the military ambush at his funeral, and the ensuing civil war.

Decades before the start of the war, the protagonist's family, which "had been plagued by catastrophes" (Limón 1993, 38), had already initiated a cycle of intergenerational trauma that would leave an indelible mark on mother-son relationships. The novel opens in 1941 with a description of Don Lucio's decision as a teenager to leave Spain for the Americas when "his father's abuse and the stench of rotting fish had become intolerable" (16). This man would later serve as the catalyst for a series of cascading traumas for Luz Delcano when the former, as the thirteen-year-old's grandfather, rapes her, inflicting not only physical and psychological trauma from the incest and internalized shame but also the added layer of psychological and sociocultural trauma after being cast out and forced to give up her son Lucio. Moreover, because of the power and prestige of the Delcano family, Luz has no recourse and eventually experiences structural violence vis-à-vis the personal repercussions of state-sanctioned violence in El Salvador supported by the US.

Immediately following an April 14, 1980, excerpt from *Time* magazine that details the magnitude of the horrors that unfolded at Archbishop Romero's funeral, the fictional narrative jumps into the action, describing the mayhem during the ambush that would result in the disappearance of Luz's second son. Vividly capturing the traumatic event, the narrator describes, "Everyone acted out of instinct, pieces and fragments of tormented beasts driven by a compelling desire to live. All the time, the blasting and the firing of weapons, and grenades continued" (23). Once the attack subsides, Luz and many others search for their lost loved ones. "She called out her son's name, her soft weeping joining that of others. . . . Desperation began to overcome her. In her fears she remembered the loss of her first son Lucio. Now Bernabé, her second born, was also gone" (25), the narrator continues, capturing Luz's anguish as a mother.

Her local search for Bernabé continues in vain in the context of sustained repression, violence, and disappearances until "Luz's intense desire to find her son" (55) compels her to flee toward Mexico City, in hopes that her son had done so as well. In the company of others who are similarly searching for their *desaparecidos*, she notes a "barrage of emotions" (56) and feels the collective grief and fear. Accompanying these emotions are the guilt and shame rooted in her sexual trauma: "For a moment she stared at her image, knowing that if people could see inside of her they would see something worse. The image of Don Lucio Delcano flashed through her mind. Guilt gripped her heart. He was standing in front of her, in the cow shed, and he was taking hold of her hand. She shut her eyes tightly attempting to erase the recurring memory of her youth" (56). Years later, she would still wrestle with this internalized guilt over her encounter with her grandfather and subsequent expulsion from the home at just fourteen, and then her affair with the head of the household for whom she worked until she was thirty-one, confessing to Father Hugh, "'But there's something in me, Padre . . . there's a devil in me that makes me do bad things'" (116). Accompanying Luz's constant shame and guilt, though, is her steadfast maternal instinct to love and protect, which functions subversively through compelling her to continue searching for Bernabé in a repressive environment and beyond borders and to challenge authority figures to protect Arturo Escutia.

When Luz witnesses the terror of this nineteen-year-old during a confrontation with immigration officials and realizes that a revolver is pointed at his head, "she could not restrain herself. In her mind, Arturo could have been Bernabé. Both young men were about the same age and height, and they both had the same look in their eyes. An excruciating heat rose from Luz's belly up to her neck. Something like hot vomit filled her mouth forcing her to open it wide. A terrifying wail escaped from her throat" (58). This is not the first time that Arturo endures a potentially violent altercation. Shooting breaks out at a demonstration he had organized in the name of justice and opportunities, and a few days later, men burst into his home. "Again, they were dressed like campesinos, but those eyes, those cruel eyes told us they were not from the fields. They carried weapons. My father stood, but they didn't give him time to speak. A bullet tore a big hole in his forehead" (63). Immediately after, the men kill Arturo's mother and two brothers, beat Arturo unconscious, and leave him for dead in El Playón. He, too, endures physical and psychological violence perpetrated by the state, in addition to an overwhelming trauma of loss.

In subsequent years, Luz would adopt Arturo as a surrogate son, living and working (and in Luz's case, searching for her lost son) in Mexico City for a year before deciding to migrate farther north to the United States. While in California, Luz and Arturo stay at Casa Andrade, a shelter for refugees and the undocumented, and she laments her liminal status as she continues to search for Bernabé. She "struggled with a nagging sense of floundering, of hanging in suspension, of waiting for something to happen, yet not knowing, when or what it would be. She missed her home city, and as the days drifted by, her heart seemed to sink into numbness" (80), when she is not "grappling with the rage she was still feeling" (83) at the continuing horrors in El Salvador. "Would she be able to survive a life that had left her so shattered and confused?" (83), she wonders.

Years have evidently passed, when five masked men suddenly charge into the apartment that she and Arturo share.

"Seconds seemed an eternity, and Luz's eyes bulged with terror and incomprehension" (84), as the violent scene unfolds:

> The explosions filling the air canceled out everything for Luz. They erased thought, destroyed feeling, killed all hope. It took only seconds, and in that brief interval, Luz understood the speed of smoke and fire. Her eyes relayed to her brain the efficiency with which a gun can kill. She was blinded by the flames jetting out of the assassins' weapons as they pumped death into Arturo's body. For Luz, the shots that spilled from those guns were the split tongues of snakes, lethal and poisonous, and their spewing was devouring Arturo, taking him from her. She witnessed Arturo being butchered as if he were a pig or a rabid dog. (85)

Stunned and traumatized, Luz "let out a lament, a mournful cradle song for a dead son" (85). Mourning the tragic and dramatic death of Arturo, the narrator comments, "One after another, each of her sons had been taken from her, and there was nothing she could have done to prevent her loss" (89). The text frames her powerlessness in the context of structural violence that compounds her loss. The police investigators are not willing to utilize the bloody handprint as evidence and, by default, record the crime as gang-related or linked to drug use, despite the irrelevance of either. (The reader may be inclined to suspect that the same men who murdered Arturo's family in El Salvador may have tracked him down to ensure he face a similar fate.) Moreover, when the police determine that Luz's interrogation is not fruitful, they turn her case over to immigration. Unable to provide proper documents, she is taken to a detention center for imminent deportation.

Back in San Salvador after nearly a decade, Luz finally succeeds in finding Bernabé. A victim of state violence at the hands of his estranged half-brother, he has been tortured, assassinated, and dumped on a garbage heap in El Playón. There, "Luz slowly dropped to her knees, contemplating the remains of the person in front of her. . . . She caressed the mutilated face with her hands, kissing the bloodied cheeks and forehead as she swayed back and forth, moaning softly" (155). Luz reacts to the devastation with "a guttural howling. . . . Luz now wailed, her mouth agape, her face distorted with pain. Her lament expressed all the anguish she had suffered during her years of futile search. It echoed her disbelief and despair at finding her son only to lose him again on the spot. It was more than her body and soul could bear" (155). Limón establishes symbolic connections between Luz and Eve, as the mother of a son who murdered his brother; Rachel of Ramah, as a mother of innocent slaughtered children; and Mary of Bethlehem, whose son made the ultimate sacrifice.[19] Just as Luz's life has been defined by the trauma of the loss of her sons, both Lucio and Bernabé wrestle with the trauma of loss (or absence) of their mother, and this ultimately directs their actions.

Like Luz, Bernabé suffers interconnected layers of violence, as evident from the first scene in which he appears. Amid violence perpetrated by the state, Bernabé experiences physical and psychological terror during the massacre at Archbishop Romero's funeral, followed by the trauma of separation from his mother. Realizing that he has lost Luz, "He screamed out his mother's name, using his able arm to raise himself on whatever shoulder or object he could find, trying to get a glimpse of her. But his mother was nowhere in sight" (24). The narration continues, "His wailing rose above the howling of those around him, and he continued screaming for his mother" (24). Although he is a young man of twenty, he cries in desperation for his mother, and when he later flees, he still yearns for her presence. "Crying for his mother's help, Bernabé plunged head-long toward the river" (35), and he continues to call out to her subconsciously while he is recovering. As months go by, during his time in the resistance movement after unwittingly becoming one of the leaders, "Bernabé spoke to his mother as if she were standing next to him. He worried about her constantly" (31). In his time at the guerrilla camp in the mountains, Bernabé also encounters Arturo Escutia, the young man who, while fleeing the country, would become the next son Luz would lose.

Further enhancing the interlacing of storylines, Limón incorporates repetition of imagery from Luz's story within the passages that focus on Bernabé's crisis of conscience before his participation in the horrific violence of the overarching conflict. Linking Luz's grief for Arturo (and her other sons) and Bernabé's grief over his separation from his mother, the narrative voice describes, "He was haunted by the vision of a mother holding her child's bullet-riddled body in her arms. Her elbows dripped blood, and she moaned and wept. Stunned out of her mind, she had let out a lament, a mournful cradle song for her dead child" (135–36), echoing the same "mournful cradle song" (85) sung for Arturo. The characters' separate stories further merge through spatial and chronological jumps within individual sections. The narrative, for example, utilizes flashback to describe recollections, then a sensorial component (like explosions) returns the narrated action to the present.

At such a juncture, Bernabé and his (unbeknownst to him) half-brother meet. Positioned oppositionally as representing the state and the resistance movement, Colonel Lucio Delcano insists on the arrest of Bernabé, whom he knows to be his half-brother. As the officer approaches the prisoner, Colonel Delcano's "smile veiled the torment raging in his heart" (139). Brought on by his perceived abandonment by their mother, "A lifetime of anger and jealousy surged within the colonel's heart, and his first impulse was to execute his brother on the spot, in spite of witnesses. Nothing could stop him. There was a war going on, and here was a guerrilla leader" (139). Lucio reveals the truth about their relationship, and the story of his own conception, and rages at the audacity of Bernabé in using the Delcano name.

The product of incest, Lucio was taken from his mother and raised as part of the Delcano family, whose lies that his mother had abandoned him for money or because of his unworthiness only contributed to his identity and abandonment issues. "Lucio Delcano had always felt empty when he was a child in spite of the material things he had been given. . . . But he had never experienced the one thing he craved: a mother's love and attention" (39). Like his mother and grandfather, he, too, suffers sexual as well as psychological abuse at the hands of a family member (his aunt/sister). When he finally resists his attacker, she viciously exposes the truth, exclaiming, "'You might look like an angel, but on the inside, you're nothing but a black devil!'" (42). Lucio recalls, "'And then, for the first time, I had the nightmare'" (43), one in which he is a monster of a creature with body parts in the wrong places, a clear indication that he has suffered trauma. At fourteen, Lucio left his home to study, "but even then he had been filled with rancor and hatred" (45). Manipulative, controlling, "talented and cold-blooded" (46), Lucio impressed others with his work ethic and stamina. "No one knew, however, that sleeping was an intolerable agony for Lucio, and that he feared falling asleep because then the nightmare would assault him" (46), suggesting that his unresolved conflicts manifested in his recurring nightmare.

During his time away, Lucio spends all his free time over the span of years searching for his mother, and in the process learns of Bernabé. The narrator explains the emotional impact of the news, describing, "He had found his mother, but now she had another son. He wept as he realized that he had searched for his mother not because he hated her, as he had told himself from the beginning, but because he loved her, and he could not deny that he had secretly hoped that she, too, would love him" (49). Lucio uses his power and resources to track down his mother and half-brother, which only exacerbates his sense of abandonment. "When people described her as affectionate, he felt cheated. . . . A source of even greater torture was the constant supply of photographs he received" (50). Despite knowing her whereabouts, he opts not to contact her, "fearing that she would reject him once again" (50). The brothers' stories intersect, though, when Lucio, a ruthless military strategist, orders the execution of the subversives involved with the Río Sumpul incident.

In his thirst for vengeance, Lucio stuns his inferiors, who expect him to show compassion to his brother and spare the latter's life despite Lucio's reputation for being cold and calculating. Thereafter, instead of the relief, satisfaction, or other positive emotion Lucio anticipates experiencing after Bernabé's execution, "A numbness was invading his body, paralyzing his heart, and he felt afraid and lost, as he often had when he was a child. His obsession had been fulfilled. His brother was dead, yet Delcano felt empty and sick. Like everything else in his life, even the anticipated elation of vengeance had been denied him" (161). Unsuccessfully attempting to overcome the torment he feels due to abandonment, grief, and an internalization of inferiority, Lucio transforms himself from victim to perpetrator of violence in his role with the Salvadoran military. As a result, his brother is subjected to torture and execution, his mother experiences anguish over his loss, and countless others are disappeared or assassinated.

It is through business dealings with the colonel that the storyline of Father Hugh, an American university professor, also becomes more directly intertwined with those of Bernabé and Luz. Describing the search for her son and disclosing what little she knows of her eldest, Luz mentions that he is a 47-year-old powerful military man by the name of Lucio. Wrestling with guilt over the role that he and his childhood friend Augie Sinclaire have played in state violence by knowingly providing arms that would produce such devastating effects on civilians, Hugh immediately recognizes the name, as is evident in his quoted thoughts. Indicating his interior conversation with the now deceased Augie as italicized quotes, Limón provides readers access to the constant barrage of critical accusations that haunt the professor day and night, and that interfere with his ordinary conversations, particularly when triggered. *"Hughie, boy, you're part of the package. How do you think they got those weapons?"* (95), Augie asks from the beyond. Repeatedly implicating Father Hugh in violence, Augie calls out Father Hugh's knowledge that Colonel Delcano was involved in the archbishop's death and in countless others. Denying that he had anything to do with it, Father Hugh continues to hear Augie's voice, "the twanging noise that had robbed him of sleep night after night" (95), arguing, *"Yes you did! We both did! We made the Colonel successful; we saw to it that he got away with what he wanted. We didn't pull the trigger, but we sure as Hell made it possible. I'm sorry for it all, Hugh, why can't you be?"* (146).

Despite his denials of responsibility, Father Hugh appears to be subconsciously tormented by his guilt, which emerges in his recurring nightmares. Among the deceased individuals who appear to him, "Cyprian and Virgil had recently made daily practice of interrupting his sleep. The visits had started to happen right after Father Virgil's death a few months back. The two priests always appeared in Hugh's dreams just before dawn, when the night dipped to its blackest pitch and, when together, they asked the same carping questions, pointing incriminating fingers that made Hugh break out with sweat" (103). When, out of vengeance, Augie had connivingly revealed the details of their unsavory business dealings connected with the university to Father Virgil, Father Hugh's superior, the latter insisted that he resign and cease and desist the business operations. Knowing that to do so would expose his wrongdoing more broadly, Hugh refused, and after a heated argument, Father Vigil suffered a heart attack and died. As opposed to Luz, though, Father Hugh appears to be the maker of his own demise and his burden of guilt is evidently warranted.

Father Virgil and other ghosts like him, Father Hugh suggests, "are really our memories, the ones that we don't, or can't, let go" (126). He elaborates further: "'[I]f we let them, our ghosts come back to pick at us with their sharp edges. They never let us forget anything. They're everywhere, hiding around corners, crouching in little niches where we least expect them. They like to turn their spikes inside of us, trying to make us regret what we've done. And even when we're sorry; even when we're ready to do things in a different way, they still hound and punish us'" (136). When Hugh's path crosses directly with that of Luz Delcano, and she asks him to accompany him to find her son at last, he must face these ghosts head on. Witnessing a mother's anguish at the sight of her tortured and murdered son by the order of the very man to whom he provided weapons, he—like the US government that he symbolically represents—must take responsibility for his part in the destruction, displacement, and despair that have torn so many families apart.

In spite of the litany of violent tragedies to which Luz is subject, she exemplifies resistance and survival, and her personal story of suffering and abuse serves as an allegory for the collective suffering of the people of El Salvador. In narrativizing

the experiences of overlapping nodes of violence in this "modi-
fied testimonial narrative" (McCracken 1999, 61), Limón draws
attention to the interplay between broader sociohistorical contexts of structural violence and specific instances of physical
and psychological violence as experienced by various characters. Following Keen, the text primarily incorporates broadcast
strategic empathy through appealing to universal notions of
motherhood and maternal love, thereby facilitating the establishment of an affective bond between the characters and the
readers, who are likely unaware of the lengthy period of violence and repression during the Salvadoran Civil War, the US
government's role in it, or its implications for patterns of migration. In portraying the immigrant experiences of Luz and Arturo
as refugees who are desperately fleeing in search of safety and,
in Luz's case, her missing son, Limón disrupts the stereotypical
rendering of the figure of the undocumented immigrant.

Converging (Narrative) Streams in *The River Flows North*

Like the tributaries that converge in a flowing river, the voices
of individual characters in Gabriela Limón's *The River Flows
North* come together to represent various migrant communities, underlining the unique nature of the factors that have
forced their displacement. Through heteroglossia,[20] the characters, and the marginalized groups they represent, undermine the conception of a monolithic migrant experience. In a
certain sense, then, one may argue that the unique voices of
the migrants as "the Other(s)" interact dialogically with that of
hegemonic conceptualizations of these individuals as alien and
offer a more comprehensive understanding of the varied historical circumstances that have compelled them to migrate. The
testimonies appear as interpolated vignettes, smoothly transi-
tioning between the narrative of the arduous trek through the

harsh desert and the histories of the characters that led them to this place of desperation and desolation. The accounts may emerge as a character's storytelling, as the product of hallucinations produced by delirium, or even in the seemingly *Pedro Páramo*-esque posthumous rendering of a character's backstory.

Through the unfolding of these histories, regardless of the manner in which they emerge in the novel, we connect more intimately with each of the nine characters and come to identify the trickle-down effect of specific moments in which US intervention serves as the catalyst for their migration. What, after all, could be more personal than divulging one's own story of tragedy and heartbreak unraveling in the wake of social and economic upheaval? By giving voice to these characters' experiences, Limón personalizes the phenomenon of immigration as the migrants battle the physical dangers of the journey while also "confronting their own internal demons" (Limón 2009, 16). Their accounts, narrated in the first person, underscore the impact of broader political, economic, environmental, and cultural forces that have united to strip them of their livelihoods and even the possibility of basic survival in their hometowns, thus driving them to join the ever-expanding migrant stream *al norte*.

Notably, the first of such accounts is that of Imelda (Menda) Fuentes of Chalatenango, El Salvador, who describes her violent victimization at the hands of her government and her husband. Counteracting the stereotypical perception of undocumented migrants as Mexicans seeking wealth or safety from cartels across the border, Limón's text promptly points to the diversity within the immigrant experience and draws attention to the role of US foreign policy in Latin America. As she does throughout the fictional work, Limón incorporates historically accurate details to provide context for Menda's story.

As a teenager, Menda is the only surviving family member of the May 14, 1980, Río Sumpul massacre, the first major "coordinated military operation of the Honduran and Salvadoran armies in which at least 600 people were butchered. Infants were cut to pieces with machetes, and women were tortured and drowned. Pieces of bodies were found in the river for days afterwards" (N. Chomsky 1992, 35). Limón does not directly indict the United States for its provision of military aid to the junta governing El Salvador during the 12-year Salvadoran Civil War in this novel.[21] However, she inscribes this conflict in literary history through Menda's dramatic recollections:

> My life began when I saw my mama, papa and little sister murdered along with hundreds of other people at el Río Sumpul as we tried to escape into Honduras. It was 1980, and I was sixteen years old. It also was the beginning of the war, a time when rebels and government soldiers fought like dogs while they tore at each other's throats. Both sides said they fought for justice, but all they did was destroy our villages and kill those caught in the middle. The war went on year after year. It devastated El Salvador from top to bottom, leaving behind a trail of death, misery and countless broken women left to care for fatherless babies. (Limón 2009, 18)

Menda depicts the mayhem in more detail, recalling, "There were so many dead that the river became clogged with bodies of children, women and men. We didn't know it, but government soldiers were waiting to block us from crossing the river. Killing us was easy for them because they had machine guns and rifles, even helicopters that came at us from above like giant flying scorpions. We had nothing" (18–19).

During her stay in Honduras, Menda develops a sense of normalcy with the help of Doña Altagracia, and her future husband, Jacinto Morales. Despite his apparent calm, restraint, and polite manners, he soon begins to victimize Menda, who is expecting the first of their children. After enduring various miscarriages and years of physical and verbal abuse, and even threats to kill her, Menda leaves Jacinto, returning to her war-torn village, and leaving behind her surviving daughter and son. Wrestling with guilt, she describes, "Burning in my heart were constant thoughts of my children because I knew that I had abandoned them. I didn't forget that I was leaving them without a mother, but they were now old enough to take care of themselves. I knew also that I was the one Jacinto hated" (24–25). She rationalizes, "With me gone, at least my absence would keep them from seeing their mother murdered. Leaving my children was a terrible decision for me, but I had no choice except to live or die, and I chose to live. I hoped this would give me a chance to join them later on in a more human life" (25).

As she had anticipated, Jacinto soon tracks her down, attacks her, and, after she fights back with an iron skillet, ultimately sets fire to the café that has become her livelihood. Certain that remaining in Central America would mean death at the hands of her estranged husband, Menda heeds Padre Ignacio's advice to escape through a US church that offers sanctuary. Although it pains her to put more distance between herself and her children, she realizes this is the only means to increase her chances of survival—despite the unspeakable dangers of the crossing— and to one day fulfill the dream of reuniting with her children north of the border.

Menda's account of the social upheaval that she endures presents the reader with a voice not generally heard in dominant or mainstream discourse, shedding light on the rarely discussed Salvadoran Civil War and drawing attention to the widespread occurrence and cultural acceptance of domestic abuse. Bearing witness to the atrocities of the conflict, Menda must overcome the trauma of the attack and the anguish of losing her family members during her escape to Honduras. One may project that this displacement leads to her not so fortuitous meeting of Jacinto and the more intimate levels of violence that she would subsequently face. What remains clear throughout the text is that US involvement in El Salvador has profoundly impacted individuals like Menda, who becomes one of a community of migrants / refugees paradoxically seeking survival in the very location that initiated the turmoil in their homeland. In similar fashion, neoliberalism and the implementation of the North American Free Trade Agreement (NAFTA) transformed the economy and society of Mexico, prompting the loss of over one million agricultural jobs from 1994 to 2002 (Gibler 2008).

Nicanor and Néstor "Borrego" Osuna, teenaged brothers from Tecolotes, Zacatecas, embody this sector of Mexican farmers whose destinies have been drastically altered by the initiative to foment Mexico's integration in the global economy and the resulting impossibility of economic mobility. Their parents, "humble people with roots deep in the dirt" (Limón 2009, 160), worked somebody else's land for years, always hoping to amass enough money to own their own *rancho.* "This went on for years until one year the worst happened," Borrego explains. "The water that irrigated our *maíz* field plugged up, or changed its direction, or something like that, and, without water, the crop dried up so fast that we didn't even have a chance to harvest at least some of the corn" (160). Upon seeking the *patrón's* assistance, their father was enraged to learn that the water shortage and resulting crop failure came as no surprise to the *patrón,* who would soon sell the land to a tomato harvesting company, perhaps because tomatoes would be more profitable now that there was a post-NAFTA influx of imported corn. "That was the beginning of hard times for our family," Borrego laments. "Our parents were forced to work picking those pinche tomatoes.

Nicanor and I did the same thing, but no matter how many hours we worked, we couldn't put together enough money to get a little house for the six of us so we had to go live with one of amá's sisters" (161). The brothers then found work at a mill that ground corn for tortillas. Alas, "Then that work dried up, too, although it didn't happen suddenly; it happened over months, little by little, until the machines were turned off . . . because of a stinking two-kilo paper sack" (161–62). Borrego continues his rant against the impact of economical and convenient "advances" in agriculture and commerce:

> A new product had come into stores, a dough in powdered form that turned into the real thing when mixed with a little bit of water. . . . Even more important, people saved money because that little two-kilo sack made more dough for less money than what people paid at the mill. . . . What excited everyone, especially women, was that this new thing could be whipped up any time of day. . . . A shitty two-kilo paper sack took away our jobs. Oh, I don't mean that it happened overnight, because it didn't. It took time, but when it happened, it hit everybody. (162)

Desperate to procure the means to feed their starving little sisters, the teenagers followed in the footsteps of the increasing numbers of people heading to the United States.

The brothers made their way north, Borrego recalls, walking and hitching rides in cars and on the roofs of trains and the backs of buses, certain that their dream would begin as soon as they made it to the other side of the border. With their minds and hearts set on farming in order to buy their own land near the ocean and send for their family, they negotiate their crossing with a coyote in exchange for assisting the women and children in the group through treacherous terrain and even sewage pipes. They successfully cross the line and, seeing the shimmering lights and moon reflected in the smooth ocean, celebrate their triumph. "We threw our arms around each other and cried because our dream wasn't a dream. The land by the ocean really existed, and our eyes were looking at it" (166).

Their joy dissipates immediately, though, when la Migra apprehends and deports them to Tijuana, "where we drifted, scared by so many people, and so much noises" (167). Abandoned by the coyote and without the means to attempt another crossing, the brothers resort to working as male prostitutes for months, forever struggling with the shame of the acts that would facilitate their second attempt at crossing, during which they meet Menda and the others. Despite the pain and trauma of the aftermath of their first attempt, they forge onward. "People might wonder what made us try again, even in the face of humiliations, hunger, anger, and stupid decisions," Borrego explains, "but no one stops to think that what we left behind was even worse" (159).

As Limón's novel reveals, the circumstances that migrants leave behind are not confined to poverty or violence wrought by US intervention in their homelands. Rather, women in particular also contest the patriarchy and racial hierarchy in place in Latin America by literally walking away from their homes. In the cases of Celia Vega and Encarnación Padilla, these larger sociocultural factors contribute to an unexpected shift in circumstances and the women's ensuing desperation. A mother in her mid-thirties, Celia Vega has left behind a husband and daughter in Venta Prieta, Hidalgo, Mexico, in order to find work to maintain her family. She begins her history: "Every woman has her story. I have mine, and, in a way, it's a love story, but in another it isn't" (138). She describes her lifelong friendship with Zacarías Tiburcio, with whom she would play and swim in the river, and its evolution into a more intimate relationship alongside the river at the age of eighteen.

In engaging in forbidden behaviors, she continues, "I knew that I had defied what I learned from my beginnings" (139), not only because she was pregnant out of wedlock but, more important, because she had violated the dictates of her class- and race-based society. Although their familial origins were not clear to her, she clarifies, "What I do know is that my family prospered in lands and servants, and that it was people like us who were served by people like the Tiburcios. By the time Zacarías and I were born, our families were locked into those who were above and those who were below" (139). Because the father of her child was "Indio, and poor" (141), Celia's father throws her out of the house and the family spreads gossip about the illicit relationship far and wide to prevent the possibility of her establishing a home and life elsewhere. Just as her life began to deteriorate, Celia reflects, "those people received their own punishment because in time . . . everything in our town began to crumble. The decline took years, but it was steady and it hit everybody. It was a time when jobs were lost; life as people had known it disappeared" (144).

Presumably, Celia's story reflects the consequences of NAFTA and its impact on the state of Hidalgo. She elaborates, "Those were bitter times for all of us, confusing most of us, enraging others, especially since few could explain why such a thing was happening. . . . On the one side, voices said that it was a government thing, and that the greedy politicos were pulling strings to fill up their pockets" (141), reflecting a historical moment during which the Mexican government was embracing foreign investments. "On the other side," Celia continues, "people made bets that it was the gringos who were responsible because everyone knew how greedy they were and how little they respected us. Whatever was the reason, the truth was that we all sank deeper into poverty with each day" (141). When Celia's husband decides to head north without consulting her, they argue and he leaves with no further discussion.

Three weeks later, she learns of his hospitalization in Piedras Negras after his falling from a moving freight train. From then on, their relationship devolves from indifference to coldness due in large part to the lack of intimacy borne of her disgust with his mutilated body and soul. Embittered and angry at the poverty they face, her primary hope is to "shield my daughter from the unhappiness that was polluting our world and even more from the hunger that hounded us every day" (144). She notes the unjust discrepancy in wealth between her home and the home where she works and thus takes advantage of its abundance, regularly stealing food for her hungry child and ultimately being fired for her discreditable behavior. Despite never even venturing beyond her town by herself before, she sets out for *el norte*, agreeing to offer her body once during the crossing as payment to the coyote for her passage, since circumstances and her actions have ruled out any opportunities close to home.

Another young Mexican mother's migration in the wake of the economic downturn of 1994 is the basis for Julio Escalante's journey from Torreón with his ten-year-old grandson, Manuelito. He relates to his companions how their family's thriving shoe-making and leather goods business suddenly began to suffer after generations of expansion. "It happened around 1994, when banks lost money overnight, businesses began to wobble, people lost jobs and the economy went bad. Our life, as we used to know it, seemed to collapse," he declares. "No one could explain what happened except that maybe the gringos and the deals they made with our government had something to do with it" (50). Coinciding with the 1994 Mexican Tequila Crisis, when a 35 percent devaluation of the peso resulted in currency and banking crises (van der Molen 2013), the narrative relates, "In the beginning, it wasn't easy for me to know what people were doing. All I saw was that entire families went away. Whenever I asked, I got vague answers, as if something shameful had happened. It was only after time passed that I realized what was happening: families were uprooting and making their way al norte" (Limón 2009, 51).

Much to his dismay, Julio's sons and son-in-law join the migrant stream. Within a short period of time, his daughter Lucinda, having received a letter and some US dollars from her husband, begins to plot her departure. For months after receiving the letter, she undergoes a transformation, becoming obsessed with the potential to earn money by "leaving us, [and talking] about her new life and about her son learning to speak English" (52). Powerless to stop her, Julio watches as Lucinda and Manuelito board the bus; there is no word from her again. He does, however, later receive notification that the Mexican *Migra* had young Manuelito in custody and that he would have to travel north to Sonoyta to retrieve him.

In the weeks following their return to Torreón, Julio's grieving gives way to an urge to restore spiritual harmony by returning Lucinda's bones to their proper burial place. Julio explains, "Voices murmured of the souls that wandered the earth in search of something left behind, spirits whose bodies had never been buried. No one imagined that each word that I overheard was a knife that pierced my heart. Of course, I knew of las ánimas en pena. Who didn't? But I had never given much thought to a soul wandering the earth in misery until now that it was my Lucinda in search of her body" (54–55). Aware of the "voices [that] were my girl's people, clamoring for her bones" (55) in the local cemetery, he is compelled to retrieve her remains to put Lucinda's soul to rest. To do so, he would need to rely upon his grandson's recollections of watching his mother die after wandering for days when their smuggler abandoned them. Equipped with the faith that they would indeed find Lucinda's remains, Julio and Manuelito unite with the group in La Joyita after already unsuccessfully searching out two or three other common migrant junctures. Despite facing ridicule, they insist that they will pay the full price to go halfway and return on their own upon unearthing the remains of their beloved mother and daughter.

Their quest for closure is akin to that of Doña Encarnación Padilla, whose objective is not to establish a more fruitful life north of the border but to "'stay with the spirits of my ancestors'" (13). The petite ancient Tzetzal woman from the Lacandón Jungle in the highlands of Chiapas, Mexico, clarifies, "'I'm not going to *la Ocho*, nor am I returning. That's why I've come'" (13). She establishes her possession of spiritual gifts, describing her unique role among the Lacandona people as "a dreamer, . . . a gifted messenger, the voice of the ancestors" (90). Even as a child, she would sit with the tribal elders and express what *los tatuches* had communicated in dreams that revealed future suffering and social upheaval, warfare in Chiapas greater than the first encounter with Spanish conquistadores, and past and future displacements and migrations. Rather than focusing on her dreams of past treks southward to the jungles of southern Mexico, the elders were most interested in the "future migrations to the land of our beginnings, a return to the northern deserts from which our ancestors had come" (91). While the reader may initially suspect that hers are the ramblings of a senile woman, this backstory of her relationship with the Mayan spiritual realm ultimately lends more credence to her visions of the dead in the desert and her purpose in heading north.

Claiming to see the guiding spirits of women who have died along their path, Doña Encarnación encourages her companions, explaining that the spirit "walked ahead of us for a long time, waved her arm and told us to follow her. She doesn't want us to die" (40). She continues, "'Look! There she is again. She's asking us to follow her. . . . ' The group strained to see what the old woman was pointing at, but there was nothing except the first signs of light peeping over the high mountain ridges" (59). Acknowledging a previous error in her interpretation of the mystical vision's identity, she later declares that the woman whom she had seen had in fact been Lucinda, Julio's deceased daughter. Despite the group's reluctance to believe Doña Encarnación when she steadily affirms, "'Her bones are here'" (63), they indeed discover the missing woman's body, complete with identifying clothing and personal articles. Having proven her spiritual prowess and the existence of the spirits whom no others can see, Doña Encarnación later offers comfort from beyond her sandy grave as Menda and Borrego desperately cling to life. "She knew Doña Encarnación was out there and that she was looking over them. Menda knew also that the old woman was not alone. Alongside her were the ones she had come to meet" (89). These were Doña Encarnación's ancestors, the founders of the community that ultimately would ostracize her because of her transgression of patriarchal constraints, in part because of her special gifts and role as a dreamer.

Despite these gifts, she asserts, her youth was relatively ordinary and typical of a young woman of her tribe in San Cristóbal de las Casas, marrying as a teenager and becoming a mother soon thereafter. Then came "the day that my destiny shifted its direction, leading me to venture into what was forbidden for any Lacandona woman" (91–92). Captivated by a mysterious Lacandón man's gaze and a sense of longstanding familiarity with him, Doña Encarnación submits to her impulse to surrender to the stranger for the first of multiple encounters. This man, whose "skin smelled of fresh maize"[22] (93) and whose breath was "like the fragrance that lifts from the forest after a rainstorm" (93), she was certain, "was not a man, but a being with the wings of the giant bird that soars above the tallest mahogany trees. I understood this when I felt a cloak of feathers cover me as he mounted and penetrated me. At that moment I surrendered to that birdman" (93).

Upon Doña Encarnación's awaking, as was the case for future encounters, the stranger was gone, convincing her that such encounters must simply have been messages from her ancestors, silent dreams of this particular ritual. Even after the "mysterious birdman" (94) seemingly flees and she discovers her pregnancy, Doña Encarnación believes that her son must be part human and part god. Disregarding the village gossip regarding her infidelity, she is certain that "what had happened to me was reserved only for the blessed" (94) for, she explains, "what I did belonged not to this world, but elsewhere in the land where gods and los tatuches dwell" (94). Not surprisingly, the rest of her village does not share this perspective and she ultimately has to leave the village, forbidden to see her husband and children and forced into the jungle with little hope of survival.

Months later, she gives birth in the midst of a powerful night storm and sees no sign of feathers or other features that would suggest the child was, in fact, the product of a mystical union. Releasing the newborn into the river, she continues to live as an outcast, meandering from one village to the next, accompanied only by "los tatuches who did not turn their faces from me after all. Now they repeated their call," she elaborates, "saying that I was awaited in the desert, but because I didn't know how to fulfill that calling, I allowed years to slip through my fingers" (97). Doña Encarnación's subsequent meanderings leading to her journey to *el norte* open up a narrative space to describe other social changes that she witnesses, allowing for her organic participation in revolutionary processes.

Prior to her wanderings, she had observed the oppression of indigenous tribes and the exploitation of the region's natural resources and "listened to the cry of my people who talked openly of how, over the years, los patrones first squeezed us off our ancestral lands into the dense forest and of how we tolerated that injustice for long years until we grew used to life in the forest" (97–98). Years of this abuse, she explains, resulted in the Zapatista rebellion, an uprising in which she participated in the early 1990s, even as a nearly sixty-year-old woman. Extending a story of personal oppression to that of collective oppression against one's people, Limón effectively weaves historical figures and events within the narrative as Doña Encarnación explains, "It began first with agitation and whispers about uprising and resistance. Then we all heard that the day to overthrow los patrones had come. It happened in our Lacandona villages where new names were whispered: Subcomandante Marcos, Subcomandante Flores and Subcomandante Ramona. We, their followers, became known as Zapatistas, and our army grew larger every day" (98). Despite being a fictitious character within the novel, Doña Encarnación's role as "a living witness to the insurrection that erupted" (99) in a certain sense emphasizes the historically grounded events that explain the migration of the indigenous people of Chiapas whom Doña Encarnación represents.

Moreover, concurrent with her time as a Zapatista, she observes "strangers appear[ed] as if from nowhere, but always they kept on the move as they drifted through our villages" (99). She continues, "At first it was only a trickle of people, many of them who said they came from such distant places as Guatemala and El Salvador. Yet no one settled in our lands.

On the contrary, they were in constant movement, always al norte. In time the trickle became a river that flowed north, most of those people headed for the United States" (99). Upon joining this northward migrant stream, Doña Encarnación bears witness to the hardship and poverty extending throughout Mexico that compelled ever-increasing numbers of migrants to journey to the United States. In solidarity with other displaced souls, she concludes that all her fellow migrants must be "in pursuit of our ancestors' calling. . . . Now we, as children, were returning to the place of our ancestors' beginnings" (101). Accordingly, the flow of "the river of our lives had reversed its course" (101), and the migration north is simply a natural element of a return to one's origins. Thus, the notion of displacement of the migrants is replaced with a restoration of natural harmony, albeit in response to the discord and strife imposed by the intervention of dominant powers.

The journey to harmonious reconciliation, however, is fraught with dangers. Limón effectively depicts the physical perils of the treacherous landscape, but references to the characters' fear of both coyotes and narcos are even more abundant. While the threat narcos pose is not as blatant in *The River Flows North* as in some other "post-Gatekeeper novels" (Caminero-Santangelo 2010) that depict transnational migration, narco-trafficking is, in a certain sense, largely responsible for the outcomes in the text. Running from his associates with just a canvas bag of cash, an edgy Armando Guerrero ultimately forces the group's coyote to abandon them upon becoming incensed that the journey will be delayed by some detours; he not only jeopardizes the group's well-being, but, in a fit of rage, later murders the guide as well.

It is telling that this character is depicted as an outsider of the group, more effectively conveying that most immigrants are nothing like such an individual and thus contesting dominant media discourse that perpetuates notions of the criminal immigrant. "This one stood out from the rest," the narrative voice describes. "His posture and dress spoke of a different class, a different beginning. He was tall and light-skinned. His chestnut-colored hair was wavy and hung down to the collar of his shirt. His hands and fingernails were clean, almost manicured. . . . A ring he wore on the small finger of his left hand accentuated his sleek hands" (Limón 2009, 11). In fact, "Everyone saw that he was unusual. He wore a suit matted with fine dust. . . . His shoes were wingtipped and seemed almost new, and unlike the others, this man did not have a backpack" (12). Even as the members of the group begin to bond with one another, Armando remains apart, more concerned with self-preservation than with establishing any emotional connections with his travel companions, perhaps due to his past.

The last of nine siblings born in Tonalá, Jalisco, Armando is ashamed of, and enraged by, his family's extreme poverty despite the hard work of his parents. Even when he was a young boy, his resourcefulness enhanced his prospects of social and economic mobility. Working at a restaurant at age twelve, he is intrigued by "the mexicanos, the business guys that flashed even bigger rolls than the gringos, and I caught on that beautiful girls always hung around them" (72). By the time he is eighteen or nineteen, he has joined these "narcos and traficantes" (72), acting as chauffeur to the bosses and making deliveries of drugs and money in hopes of obtaining the nice clothes, guns, money, and women that he coveted. By his early twenties, he has abandoned his family and devises a plan to flee with one of the money drops. He explains, "I decided to head for the border, and I would do it with class, just like I was a tourist. I decided not to take anything except a big bag filled with bills and a loaded pistol. One million American dollars was the usual load, and that's how much would be in my bag" (75–76).

When his original plans go awry, he has no choice but to make the crossing with the "bunch of losers that listened to a skinny guy who called himself Leonardo Cerda" (77). Eventually forcing Cerda to abandon the group at gunpoint, he belittles the coyote's concern for the others, shouting, "'Goddammit, Cerda! Drop the bleeding heart routine! I don't give a shit about them and neither do you. Don't even try to make me think it's your first time dumping a bunch of losers. Besides, you should've thought of that when you agreed to my proposition [to get him to Ligurta ahead of the others]'" (104).

Interestingly, Limón positions the figure of the narco and the coyote as opposing forces in her novel, thereby portraying Leonardo in a more positive light, all the while recognizing that he is no angel, having previously engaged in sketchy business dealings. Depicting the manner in which his eyes "looked out from behind high cheekbones with the caginess of a wolf" (6), the narrative voice alludes to the slyness of this "lone wolf" (115, 125) who initially has no interest in learning anything about his group aside from their names. A complex character, he divulges in a *Pedro Páramo*–esque posthumous monologue that he has indeed abandoned other migrants in the desert (after having also abandoned his wife and twin daughters in Mexico to work in the US prior to becoming a coyote). Yet he opts to act benevolently in helping Manuelito find his mother's remains, taking the group on a detour that ultimately results in his murder. Suspecting foul play after being abandoned by Leonardo in the desolate landscape, the group of migrants questions whether "[t]he double-crossing *coyote* had betrayed them" (79). "'[H]e did not show signs of intending to betray us. One can feel treachery'" (82), Doña Encarnación suggests.

As she astutely anticipates, the group suffers inadvertent collateral damage in the broader territorial narco wars that make border crossing even more dangerous. In facing the shared trauma, the group members begin to forge a strong group identity in which the collective comes to supersede the individual. This stands in marked distinction from the start of their journey, during which "[t]hey don't know one another and refuse to reveal their names. They're too shy or too afraid. Instead, they eye one another to calculate age, and guess if that one is Mexican, Guatemalan or Salvadoran" (3). In the initial stages of the trek, "Little by little, eyes take in shoes, or dress, or jacket, hoping to identify material or cut, and they look for anything that might inspire trust. Each one wants to know something about those strangers, but apprehension forces them to withdraw deep into themselves" (3). They "[eye] each other with suspicion. They knew nothing except each other's name, and even that could be fake. How could anybody in the group be trusted? Maybe they were criminals, *narcos* or worse" (16–17). Only later, upon enduring unspeakable physical and psychological trials, will the group become closer and share their stories of hope and heartbreak.

The migrants grasp their insignificance and feebleness before the astonishing power of the vast desert landscape: "Horrified, they watched as the hurtling wind dragged away the deadly wave of sand that had punished everything in its path, and from there they could see it spiraling hundreds of feet upward, creating a ceiling so thick that not even a glimpse of sky was visible" (83). As they survive various sandstorms, their faces appear to be "bloated masks whitened by the blast. Their eyes were sunk into dark sockets, and their hair was spiked around spots that were scraped bald. Blotches of blood showed where the sand had scraped off skin, most of their fingers were bleeding and their clothes were rags barely covering their bodies" (84). Huddling together, the migrants must rely on one another for survival and even the will to survive, particularly in the wake of discovering burial places and the ghastly scene of intertwined and desiccated corpses of men, women, and children who, just like them, had undertaken the same journey.

In celebration of their momentary triumph over fatigue and the natural elements, the group dances around the fire. "As they danced, deep wells locked inside of them opened up and allowed fear, doubt, sadness and confusion to swirl and spike upward, to escape toward the immensity of the star-filled desert sky" (44). At this moment, "they shed tears of relief because the ice that separated them had shattered. No one could explain why, but they knew it had happened" (45). They began to ask one another more about their origins and their destinations.

As the original group of migrants dwindles over the course of a few days, they experience terror, shock, and anxiety together, becoming increasingly devoted to one another, particularly in the case of Menda and Borrego, the last surviving members of the party. As they comfort one another, Menda "wept, and her cries came from a depth that surprised her because she had not realized that she could feel such tenderness for someone she barely knew" (157). Fading in and out of consciousness as she is transported to a clinic, Menda senses her thoughts drifting to her childhood and youth, as well as to memories of her fellow travel companions. Despite their differences, Menda has discovered their common ground: "That journey opened my eyes and taught me that there were many of us doing the same thing. Oh, each one of us had different reasons, but at the bottom of it all, it was to escape intolerable lives. Bus and train stations were clogged with people, all of us with stories that told of bitter reasons for taking such a risk, especially for leaving homes and family" (33).

En route to the US, the migrants' "memories were filled with lovers, and friends, some forgotten and some always remembered. The truth was that each head swarmed with sorrow blurred with hope" (37). They had embarked upon their journey as the only option for a shot at safety and stability. In the juxtaposition of the group's unique stories, the commonalities become evident. Yet, the historically grounded vignettes and testimonies also recuperate the unique experiences and implications of US intervention in Latin America.

Just as the group dynamic shifts so that the migrants establish camaraderie in the face of imminent danger, the reader likewise develops empathy for these characters in a parallel process. Not only does Limón's shifting of narrative perspectives provide a humanized rendering of various migrant figures, the polyphonic novel offers a more holistic conceptualization of the Latinx immigrant community in all its diversity. In a symbolic linkage to one another, various characters' reference to the presence of the river in his or her life further serves as a common thread that acts both thematically and narratively in uniting their individual stories. Notably, none of these rivers is explicitly linked to the Río Grande, the river that typically functions as a trope within border literature. Rather, the motif of the river figures most patently in the stories of Menda and Doña Encarnación, as the site of the Río Sumpul massacre in one instance and the setting of the prohibited acts that lead to Doña Encarnación's ostracism and expulsion from her community.

Forcibly displaced as a result of the actions that occur alongside and within the river, Menda and Doña Encarnación join the stream of migrants flowing north, ultimately assuming the role of guide(s) for their companions, nurturing, encouraging, and directing them along the way. They invoke their maternal instincts as a means to reconcile their previous violations of social tenets regarding motherhood. Menda, having sacrificially abandoned her children in order to protect herself and bring them to the US later, is determined not to abandon hope for her fellow migrants' survival. She declares, "'We're going to live! There has to be a reason for all of this misery. It can't be for nothing'" (153). Similarly, one may presume, some sort of cosmic force may have dictated that this particular group of migrants should come together on this journey. As the narrative threads become more intricately interwoven, the motif of the absent mother rises to the surface.

The Latent Presence of a Mother's Absence

In both of Graciela Limón's novels, the development of the characters' backgrounds highlights the weighty role of the mother— or, more appropriately, the role of the mother's absence in precipitating life events and further exacerbating trauma. Just as the absence of a maternal figure causes anguish for both Bernabé and Lucio and motivates actions with devastating consequences in *In Search of Bernabé*, the loss of a mother has a profound psychological effect on, and serves as a catalyst for the physical journey of, some of the travelers within *The River Flows North*. Witnessing his mother's death during their trek, for example, young Manuelito faces trauma in addition to the grief caused by the continued absence of his mother. In order to help his family come to terms with their loss, he hopes to lead his grandfather to the site of her death to collect her remains. Through the description of Cerda's relationship with his mother, the reader comes to understand his willingness to accommodate the request to find the remains of Manuelito's mother and to lead his group on the detour that ultimately results in his murder.

Born in Texas as the third of five children and raised on both sides of the Río Grande, Cerda "always felt separated" (Limón 2009, 115) from his siblings yet had shared a strong and loving bond with his mother. When tragedy strikes his family when he is sixteen, however, this dynamic drastically transforms. "With just a few months in between, my two brothers died, one in a tractor accident, the other of a mysterious fever, and from that time onward, all the laughter disappeared. Our kitchen got dark and quiet" (117). Struggling to "understand how someone filled with so much laughter could change into the crying, wailing woman that was now [his] mother" (117), Cerda perceives his mother's indifference to him as rejection. "[S]he was buried in sadness," he describes. "She was somewhere else; she hardly even recognized me and, to tell the truth, I couldn't stand it. So on the day everybody headed south, I packed up and set off to drift in and out of cotton fields" (119).

He returns after ten years of a nomadic lifestyle and learns that his mother has passed away, although he and his father acknowledge that her *ánima*, or spirit, had died with her two eldest sons. After a relatively brief stay, he takes to the road again, finding work as a smuggler. Cerda recalls in his posthumous monologue years later, "I remembered her all over again when I faced Doña Encarnación just the other day" (118). The triggering of his mother's memory carves the path that puts an end to his life, for he explains, "After I got to work on the coyote thing, I never stopped until now that a bullet did the job, and all because I decided to lead that bunch of dreamers on a little detour. The kid wanting to find what was left of his amá got to me. Christ! I would have gone into any goddamn desert to dig holes all the way down to Hell for one of my amá's bones" (125). Empathizing with Manuelito, who has lost his mother, Cerda inadvertently sacrifices himself as a result of unresolved issues and love for his mother.

Conversely, Doña Encarnación engages in an "absencing" or disappearing of her maternal role, drowning her son upon discovering that her community may have been justified in ostracizing her. Rather than committing this tragic act out of a sense of sacrifice, she selfishly eliminates this living reminder of her betrayal and abandonment of both her husband and her legitimate children. Given the parallel elements, one cannot help but associate Doña Encarnación's drowning of the product of her illicit affair with the legend of La Llorona (the "Weeping Woman"). Moreover, perhaps this horrific act is produced from a sense of loss, which seems also to be the case for the Salvadoran woman who appears in Helena María Viramontes's "The Cariboo Café" and similarly evokes allusions to La Llorona.

Transnational Migrants Seeking Refuge in "The Cariboo Café"

Through shifting narrative voices, much like in the novels by Limón, Viramontes presents the ramifications of migration on women and children in her polyphonic short story from the collection *The Moths and Other Stories* to expose the alienation, displacement, and oppression of undocumented immigrants in the United States. "The Cariboo Café" does not narrate the migratory journey itself; rather, the story opens with the description of a migrant family's arrival to the unnamed city that is their destination. "They arrived in the secrecy of night, as displaced people often do, stopping over for a week, a month, eventually staying a lifetime. The plan was simple. Mother would work too until they saved enough to move into a finer future where the toilet was one's own and the children needn't be frightened" (Viramontes 1985, 61), the narrative voice explains, establishing the familial motivation for migration as being primarily financial. In contrast to the accounts of children of transnational families who are left behind, Sonya and Macky have accompanied their parents on the trip north. However, socioeconomic circumstances require that they remain unsupervised while their parents work. This situation eventually results in the formation of a transnational "family" by a Salvadoran washer woman, whose own haunting tale of oppression and migration constitutes an integral element of the text.

There remains no doubt that Sonya and Macky have internalized a profound fear of deportation instilled in them by their parents' rules. "Rule one: never talk to strangers. . . . Rule two: the police . . . was La Migra in disguise and thus should always be avoided. Rule three: keep your key with you at all times—the four walls of the apartment were the only protection against the streets until Popi returned home" (61). Only within the refuge of their apartment would the children be safe from the threat posed by the police, the "men in black who get kids and send them to Tijuana, says Popi" (63). He further warns, "Whenever you see them, run, because they hate you" (63), emphasizing the danger of facing officials' animosity toward immigrants like them, in addition to the threat of deportation. Consequently, when Sonya loses the key to their home, she becomes "a living example of the anguish of displacement and the stress of homelessness" (Castillo and Tabuenca Córdoba 2002, 149), seeking refuge at a local seedy diner. Ironically, the children's terror of the police inadvertently results in their kidnapping by a Central American woman, whose own circumstances have forced her across the border to flee guerrilla activity.

Presumably displaced by violence and war in her home country and the disappearance (or murder) of her son, this nameless woman endures the alienation common to the immigrant experience. "Right off I know she's illegal, which explains why she looks like a weirdo" (Viramontes 1985, 66), declares the café owner. Equating her appearance with malevolent intentions, he comments, "Already I know that she's bad news because she looks street to me. Round face, burnt toast color, black hair that hangs like straight ropes. Weirdo . . . " (65–66). In this case, his intuition may be accurate since he later sees "this news bulletin 'bout two missing kids. I recognize the mugs right away. Short Order and his doggie sister" (66); he is identifying Sonya and Macky. Suddenly, the image of the woman's face loses clarity, and he postpones a call to the police to report his sighting. Fragmented like the café owner's memory of the woman's face, the narrative fills in some of the textual gaps, forcing the reader to deduce the woman's rationale for abducting the children. Deranged from the grief of losing her son, Geraldo, she endures the guilt of having prioritized work over family obligations. "When my son wanted to hold my hand, I held soap instead. When he wanted to play, my feet were in pools of water" (70), she laments. Perhaps she believes Macky to be her missing child, or she may be seeking her own sort of refuge in the construction of this makeshift transnational family of individuals who must withstand oppression as undocumented immigrants.

The underlying common alienation experienced by "Others" unites this improvised family, exemplifying the manner in which "borders become bonds among peoples, rather than the articulation of national difference and the basis for exclusion enforced by the collaboration of the United States and Salvadoran regimes" (Harlow 1991, 152), as is also the case among the migrant group in Limón's *The River Flows North*. As Barbara Harlow notes, the onus falls on women like the Salvadoran refugee of "The Cariboo Café" to reformulate personal and political identities beyond gender and race, a task she accomplishes in this case by reconfiguring the traditional structure of family (1991, 152). While the displaced children seek refuge from a world of shadows in the labyrinthine city beyond their apartment doors, the washer woman searches for sanctuary from her physical displacement and psychological torment.

By integrating parallel stories of suffering as a component of migration, "Viramontes commits herself to a transnational solidarity with other working-class people who like all nonindigenous tribes are immigrants to the United States" (Saldívar-Hull 1991, 217), reflecting a combination of feminism and consciousness of race and class. Representing all other female victims of hegemonic agents, this "modern-day *llorona*" (Saldívar-Hull 1991, 219) joins "[t]he women [who] come up from the depths of sorrow to search for their children" (Viramontes 1985, 68), also reflected in allusions to La Llorona in Limón's text. The narrative voice specifically refers to the Mesoamerican archetypal figure of La Llorona, establishing another transnational connection to unite the histories and experiences of the North American borderlands and Central America (Saldívar-Hull 2000, 105). "It is the night of La Llorona," the narrative voice in Viramontes's text asserts. "I hear the wailing of the women and know it to be my own" (1985, 68–69).

Following Saldívar-Hull's suggestion that "The Cariboo Café" exemplifies Chicana political discourse intended to fortify alliances across borders, one may extend this commentary to encompass the cries and laments of all Latina women subjected to suffering. Hence, as in the case with Limón's *The River Flows North*, the author (or reader) comes to identify with the oppression of fellow Latinas and perhaps feels compelled to counteract the injustices in a transnational effort. "The Cariboo Café" drives the reader to empathize with individuals like the washer woman, who, "[a]s refugees in a homeland that does not want them . . . find a welcome hand holding out only suffering, pain, and ignoble death" (Anzaldúa 1999, 34). This call to action heightens the reader's awareness of the structural violence perpetrated against migrants—particularly women and children—regardless of specific geopolitical borders.

Published in the 1980s, in the midst of El Salvador's lengthy civil war, Viramontes's short story operates much like Limón's subsequent biting social critiques of the overarching forces that perpetuate the violence of border crossing through the narration of the domestic and more personal effects of migration. Viramontes exposes the volatile sociopolitical context of 1980s El Salvador through depicting the devastating emotional impact of war on the nameless Salvadoran washerwoman in her text and, consequently, her work educates her readership about issues beyond the national border and documents the experience of but one Central American refugee whose voice is ordinarily silenced or simply ignored. Whether the depiction of this character is flattering or sympathetic is an entirely different matter. One may argue, however, that the trauma she has experienced in her home country and as a result of fleeing from the violence somehow justifies her actions within the short story.[23]

La Llorona as a Maternal Cultural Marker of Trauma

The repeated appearance of La Llorona, a fixture within Mexican and Mexican American (or Chicanx) lore, in these texts is no coincidence.[24] In one of the more common variants of the tale, La Llorona is said to have drowned her children in a fit of rage, grief, and hysteria after being scorned by her unfaithful husband. After she, too, dies in the river, she is denied entry to Heaven and is thus banished to purgatory until she finds her lost children. Out of regret and/or anguish, she continues her search, crying out for her own children and potentially snatching up other children, mistaking them for her own or simply out of sheer desperation. Exemplifying the ultimate "negative mother image" tied to sexuality, death, and the loss of children (Rebolledo 1995, 63), La Llorona incites terror, particularly among children, who are cautioned against bad behavior lest

La Llorona "get" them. Likewise, adults who were raised hearing stories of this Weeping Woman are likely to harbor a deep-seated fear of her and experience a visceral response at the hint of her weeping or presence because of their internalization of the danger that she poses.

Although some literary and artistic representations of La Llorona have subverted this image and instead emphasized her agency and empowerment, others focus on her experience of anguish. Given "the lore's capacity to accommodate contemporary political, social, and economic issues" (Perez 2008, 33), La Llorona has appeared in a variety of contemporary contexts to symbolize a broader experience of grief that extends beyond the confines of the original tale. As Domino Renee Perez remarks, "Though these Lloronas no longer carry the burden of infanticide, they have still lost children for whom they search and mourn" (33), perhaps due to war, gang violence, disease, neglect or assimilation into dominant culture, among other possibilities. The grief of losing a child due to overarching sociocultural and structural violence is present in many of the so-called "flight-plight narrative[s] of the Central American refugee mother" (A. Rodríguez 2001, 400), like *In Search of Bernabé* and "The Cariboo Café," and may be deployed as a strategy to develop the *transfronteriza* alliances grounded in feminism and consciousness of race and class that Saldívar-Hull describes.

These narrative strategies that recognize the potential for solidarity despite differences across the diverse experiences and histories of Latinxs align well with Keen's notion of ambassadorial strategic empathy in their attempt to reach beyond the specific in-group (e.g., Central American refugees) to foster empathy with a specific afflicted group and make an appeal for justice for, or at least recognition of, their experiences. Arguably, though, narratives that invoke La Llorona as a symbol for overarching loss and grief rely upon a focus on these emotions as universals of human experience. That a reader from any ethnic or racial background can relate to them suggests that these texts also incorporate broadcast strategic empathy. Nevertheless, as Perez observes, "Not all Chican@s [or all readers, more broadly], however, are ready to empathize or even sympathize with La Llorona's plight, or to see her as a figure with agency, so while in some cases she inspires others to wage war, in others she is the one against whom war is waged" (Perez 2008, 74).

Indeed, in many narratives of transnational migration written by Latinas—and particularly by Chicanas—La Llorona not only functions as a symbol of the trauma of loss endured by other mothers but also "serves as a powerful means of articulating new threats" (Perez 33). Her mere presence, or the possibility thereof, during migrants' journeys through the desert—nowhere near water, as it were—effectively communicates her capacity for further contributing to the characters' psychological (and physical) trauma, particularly for readers who are familiar with La Llorona. Another example of a tactic of bounded strategic empathy, this reliance on mutual experience or knowledge of that which La Llorona represents only further enhances the significance of the Latina narratives of the violences of transnational migration.

CHAPTER 4
Left Behind and Moving Forward (and Northward)

E ven before media attention turned to undocumented and unaccompanied minors in 2014, US-based authors of fiction had already moved children of Mexican and Central American migration to center stage, as it were, in border narratives capturing the subjectivity and voice of often overlooked individuals who endure profound socioeconomic, physical, and emotional consequences as a result of transnational migration. Like the other writers whose works are highlighted in *Ripped Apart*, the authors of these novels again reveal the interconnected layers of violence associated with immigration, demonstrating the physical vulnerabilities and substantial psychological trauma that derive from overarching sociocultural and legal structures and institutions. In these examples of *Bildungsroman*, however, the focus is on the compounded traumas sustained by children who have been left behind by migrating parents and by kids who themselves embark upon the journey northward.

Rather than portraying juvenile characters as passive victims, *Across a Hundred Mountains* by Reyna Grande and *La Línea* by Ann Jaramillo focus on the evolving identities and roles of the children who suffer the angst of family separation due to piece-meal migration and its various repercussions and, compelled by their circumstances, further develop agency as they head north. Influenced by the shifting dynamics of migration evident in the 2014 surge of unaccompanied minors from the Northern Triangle, Alexandra Diaz in *The Only Road* elucidates the chang-ing motives for migration and narrativizes the transformation that ensues when, this time, youth are the ones who initiate separation from their families in order to flee overwhelming gang violence in their homeland. In revealing their heartbreak-ing and harrowing stories, the authors subvert more traditional conceptualizations of the figure of the migrant—adding to the store of exemplars of contemporary Latinx immigrants within readers' mental schemas—and appeal to the emotions of read-ers who witness the dramatic coming of age of characters who are thrust into adulthood by conditions beyond their control and who unsettle our notions of the distinctions between child-hood and adulthood, legality and illegality, vulnerability and criminality.

Crossing Mountains and Deserts in Search of Answers

Despite the dream that a family member's "crossing over" will provide wealth and stability, Pierrette Hondagneu-Sotelo describes the concerns that women expressed in her sociolog-ical research in *Gendered Transitions: Mexican Experiences of Immigration*. "Women feared that their husbands' migration would signal not a search for a better means of supporting the family but an escape from supporting the family. Their hus-bands' migration promised an uncertain future for themselves and for the children who would remain behind" (1994, 59). Indeed, the female characters of Reyna Grande's *Across a Hundred Mountains* must deal with uncertainty on various levels after the departure and disappearance of the protagonist's father. One of the more obvious of these effects is the physical separation of family, and the implications of such, as a common component of the migratory experience.

"'In a few days I will leave for El Otro Lado'" (Grande 2006, 27), Juana's father explains to the 12-year-old protagonist and narrator of *Across a Hundred Mountains*. "'That's the only way I can ever hope to make enough money to build a house for my family'" (28). Thus begins Apá's search for economic stability, a search that ultimately leads to the detriment of his family on various levels. Aside from the overarching financial insecurity after losing contact with the family's primary breadwinner, Juana and her mother must contend with the emotional turmoil of wondering whether they have been abandoned. Like the women "sitting by the door, embroidering servilletas while waiting outside for the mailman, waiting for the letter from El Otro Lado that rarely, sometimes never, came" (36–37), they have no choice but to wait. And yet, they differentiate themselves from "the forgotten women, the abandoned women" (37), telling themselves that they have been neither forgotten nor abandoned.

The protagonist comments on the deleterious effects of the uncertainty surrounding her father's disappearance, particularly within the context of the Prevention Through Deterrence policies that make border crossing even more dangerous: "For nineteen years I have not known what happened to my father. You have no idea what it's like to live like that—not to know" (3). When she returns home to give her mother her father's remains seventeen years after she had left in search of answers, she believes that knowing the truth will permit her mother to rest in peace, particularly after Amá has endured tremendous suffering due to her socioeconomic circumstances.

Primarily because of her inability to pay the family's creditors after her husband's departure and disappearance, Juana's mother is subjected to the traumas related to the monetization of her forced sexual labor. Don Elías, the funeral-home owner, is well aware that Juana's father has left the *pueblito* and takes advantage of his absence and the family's financial obligations to him, demanding that Juana's mother sexually satisfy him time and time again to physically collect on the outstanding debts. Ashamed, the protagonist's mother tells her, "'Don't touch me, Juana. . . . I'm not clean'" (74). When Don Elías and his barren wife take her baby (although it turns out he is her husband's legitimate son, conceived before Miguel departed in search of work), Juana's mother turns to alcohol to escape her depressing reality. As a result, she becomes the town drunk, "'down at the cemetery, calling out to her children as if she were La Llorona'" (96), and behaving hysterically in public, namely outside the family home of Don Elías.

Her mother's grief and despair at having lost a second child—approximately two years after her daughter accidentally drowned while in Juana's care—along with her excessive alcohol consumption, send her over the edge. Consequently, the traditional mother-daughter relationship inverts, and Juana, at a mere twelve years of age, must adopt a maternal role to care for her mother. Don José, the night watchman, finds Juana to explain, "'Your mother needs your help, child. . . . She's at the foot of your sister's grave, ranting and raving like a loca. I tried to calm her down, but she lashed at me with a broken tequila bottle. You must come and see if you can talk some sense into her'" (96). Illustrating this inversion of roles, Juana attempts to persuade her mother to return home, declaring, "'Amá, we need to go home. You need to get out of the rain. You may catch a chill'" (96).

After Don Elías, in cooperation with his wife, robs Amá of her newborn son, she attacks him and is consequently sent to jail, leaving Juana to fend for herself financially. The legally imposed separation of mother and daughter may be a blessing in disguise, however, as even seventeen years later, Juana's imprisoned mother remains delusional: "'My husband is in El Otro Lado,' she whispered [to herself]. 'Soon he will come back. He told me so. Soon we will be together.' She turned back to the screen and said, 'Verdad, Miguel? You'll be coming back to be with me. Verdad? Soon you will come back to me'" (233). While her mother remains confined to her prison cell, Juana possesses the freedom to migrate in order to procure economic stability and, more important, to go in search of answers regarding her father's disappearance.

Aside from necessarily maturing in order to care for her mother—whose various traumas associated with separation from her husband and her social and economic disempowerment, the consequent monetization of her sexuality for survival, and the devastating loss of her children lead to addiction issues—Juana later ages beyond her years when she further loses her innocence during her attempts to cross the border in search of her father. Still a child, she experiences the physical deprivations and delirium that are part and parcel of the journey northward. "The mountains weren't getting any closer. Or was it just her imagination?" (102), she wonders before La Llorona, a cultural indicator of danger, appears before her in an apparent hallucination. Once Doña Martina, a family friend and *curandera*, finds and revives her, Juana arrives at the sobering conclusion that "Apá was not on the other side of these mountains. And in order to find him, she would have to cross not just these mountains, but perhaps a hundred more" (106). During her journey across those other hundred mountains, she witnesses evidence of the physical danger of migration, presented by elements of nature as well as that which is presented by the coyotes who guide migrants across the border.

To obtain information regarding her father's whereabouts, Juana eventually resorts to working as a prostitute, catering to the wants and demands of these coyotes. She reflects upon the parallels between her situation and that of her mother: "Juana thought about Amá, about the things she had done with Don Elías, the things people used to say about her, the sin that weighed so heavily on her mother's back. Her mother had done what needed to be done. Juana would have to do the same" (179). She would come to feel these sacrifices were justified, as they enable her to resolve the mystery of her father's disappearance and move forward with her life despite her apprehensions. "She, too, was afraid of dying while attempting to cross the border. That was one of the many things she and Adelina had learned from all the coyotes they'd slept with. One never knew if they'd live to see El Otro Lado" (205). Perhaps because of the horror of the multitude of possible dangers that border crossing involves, being caught and deported by the Border Patrol appears to be the least of Juana's worries.

One particular scene in the novel captures the manner in which the officials of la Migra can destroy the hopes and dreams of immigrants just as they finally arrive in the United States. The narrator is elated when at last confronted with "El Otro Lado! Juana breathed a sigh of relief. . . . She was almost there" (216). Nevertheless, "When she finally got to the other side, it was the bright light she had to adjust to. . . . When she opened her eyes, Roberto, Pancho, and the coyote were sitting on the ground, staring at her. Three gringos dressed in green uniforms stood before them" (219).

Although one generally associates the Border Patrol with unfruitful attempts—like this one—to cross the border, Grande establishes the presence of its agents as welcome, and even desirable, assistance in another moment in the text. When the protagonist searches for her father's tomb along the border, the old man with whom she travels tells her she should hide when la Migra comes. However, she views the Border Patrol's presence as positive, perhaps because she has already adopted a new pseudo-legal American identity by using her deceased friend's US birth certificate after Adelina's possessive boyfriend kills her in a violent rage. Juana (now Adelina) "turned around and saw a white vehicle approaching. La migra was here. But they were nineteen years too late to save her father" (4), suggesting that its presence would have been able to save him during his attempt to cross the border decades before. This is a sentiment that Grande echoes in her later novel, *Dancing with Butterflies*.

Having adopted a surrogate identity as Adelina Vásquez, Juana crosses the border relatively easily to begin her life anew—a life that offers social mobility through educational and professional advancement. Although the narrative glosses over Juana/Adelina's experiences north of the border, it is evident that she has undergone a transformation when she returns home to Mexico at the age of thirty-one. Initially surprised to be addressed as Juana by Doña Martina's granddaughter, the protagonist concurs, "'You should call me Juana. That's who I am'" (226). Nevertheless, Sandra disagrees. "I think you're wrong. . . . You aren't Juana anymore. You're now a successful woman who has done what needed to be done. You should keep your new name—Adelina'" (227), because the use of Adelina's citizenship documents permitted Juana "to cross the border, go to college, and get a job" (227), thereby establishing an identity and existence far removed from those that she knew as a girl in her *pueblito*. Further accentuating this change, she no longer wields embroidery needles with the dexterity that she had years before. "Sandra was trying to teach Adelina how to make different stitches with the needle. Adelina pricked her thumb and put it inside her mouth. It had been too many years since she'd embroidered" (235), the narrative voice explains.

Crossing the border to a world of education and professional experiences has shaped Juana/Adelina's identity in such a way that her previous gender roles and identity become obsolete. Much like Mary Pat Brady notes, the concept of borders "implicitly [suggests] that a person can be formed in one temporality but when he or she crosses a border that person transmogrifies, as it were, into someone either more or less advanced, more or less modern, more or less sophisticated" (2002, 50). In this case, the circumstances that compel Juana's migrations result in such a transmogrification and a presumed identification or alliance with her surroundings north of the border. This *Bildungsroman* accordingly narrates the dual journeys—Juana's trip northward and then southward return as Adelina—that demonstrate how she overcomes the suffering that ensues from her father's migration and transcends traditional gender and generational constraints as she independently migrates and successfully establishes a new identity and life across the line.

Confronting Violence in Search of a Unified Family

The protagonists of Ann Jaramillo's YA novel *La Línea* similarly undergo a transformation during the journey across and beyond the US-Mexico border; nevertheless, their experience with migration exemplifies the case of children left behind by both parents. Miguel, one of the protagonists, expresses his awareness and expectations of his personal growth and change, reflecting as an adult, "I thought I'd find the real Miguel, the one I thought I couldn't be in Mexico, once I crossed la línea. I didn't understand that there are thousands of líneas to cross in a life. Sometimes you see the border and you walk right across, eyes wide open. You know you will change. You know everything will be different" (Jaramillo 2003, 124). Indeed, separated from their parents and later escaping their poverty to join them in the United States, Miguel and Elena discover that everything is quite different. In the process of their migration, they leave behind their grandmother and turn to the construction of an alternative transnational family to support them throughout their journey, enabling them to overcome the physical dangers that arise. Although this *Bildungsroman* utilizes an adolescent male's voice in narrating one obstacle after another presenting itself during the trek across the border, Jaramillo places at least as much emphasis on thirteen-year-old Elena's transformation and growth as she transcends prescribed gender norms and comes into her own as a result of the journey.

From the first pages of the novel, the reader understands that Miguel and Elena have grown accustomed to separation from their parents, who have been in the United States for many years. "In almost seven years, we'd seen Mamá just once, a little over three years ago, for three days. She'd slipped home for her sister's, Tía Consuelo's, funeral, using up all the saved money to pay a coyote to get her back across la línea" (5), Miguel explains. When their father writes to Miguel that it is time for him, at fourteen years of age, to join him across *la línea*, his younger sister feels tremendous disappointment that she will not accompany him on his journey and, therefore, have an opportunity to be with her parents once again. After all, as a member of this transnational family, "Elena had to grow up without a mother, so she hoarded what she could of Mamá, her letters. The words were like little drops of water to a person dying of thirst—enough to give hope; not enough to make a difference" (5). Even the children recognize that this familial separation is a sacrifice for the greater good, though. Remaining in their Mexican town with their grandmother, where "[t]hings were tight, really tight" (Jaramillo 2003, 19), Miguel explains, "If Papá and Mamá didn't send a little money every month, we would starve" (6). In fact, he adds, "Even if I wanted to, I couldn't help here anymore" (6), describing the lack of opportunities for economic and social mobility in the *pueblito*. Accordingly, he will head north to contribute to the well-being of his family.

Miguel's departure serves as yet another disruption to the familial configuration, which had already undergone modifications to accommodate his parents' employment in the United States. "[Abuelita had] been my mother. I'd been her son. There was no sense pretending we'd see each other again. She was old. I wouldn't return for many years. I might not return at all" (33), he comments. Socioeconomic circumstances simply dictate that he must abandon his home, grandmother, and sister, following in the footsteps of the many men who had already embarked upon the journey northward. Like many Mexican *pueblos*, "San Jacinto had been emptied of young men. A few left because they wanted to. Most left because they had to. There was no work, nothing worth doing, just odd jobs here and there that paid a few pesos, not enough to feed a family" (12). However, the compulsion to leave is not restricted to the young men of the town. "'Who'd want to stay anymore?'" (12), Elena asks. "'Even the girls are leaving now, if they can. Just last month Jesusita left, with that new boyfriend of hers'" (12). Indignant that her brother would leave her behind in San Jacinto, Elena decides that she, too, will cross the border. "'I know how to get north, and I'm going to do it'" (43), she declares, despite the gender norms that imply a daughter's (or in this case, granddaughter's) responsibility to tend to the home and care for her elders.

When Elena successfully joins Miguel, he reacts with surprise and anger, part of which is due to her transgression of these gender roles. "'How could you make everyone worry? What about Abuelita? How could you leave her alone? You were supposed to stay and take care of her!' [Miguel] said angrily. '¿No tienes vergüenza?'" (51). Nevertheless, he comes to terms with her presence, which ultimately saves his dream of migration from bandits since the resourceful girl had hidden a portion of her money in the lining of her purse (58). Also recognizing the importance of their familial tie, Miguel projects, "Whatever we did, we had to do it as brother and sister. We'd been through too much to separate now" (59). They would need help, though, to reach their destination.

As luck would have it, Miguel and Elena befriend an older Salvadoran gentleman and experienced migrant who becomes a member of their makeshift family while en route to the United States. Javi's wisdom proves to be extremely helpful, particularly in warding off the dangers that Elena, as a young woman, will inevitably face. Despite leafing through the Guía de Seguridad en el Desierto (87), which outlines the hazards of migration and techniques for turning themselves in to the Border Patrol authorities or for returning to civilization if they become lost, the implicitly gendered risks do not seem to cross young Elena's mind. "'You should disguise yourself. The less you look like a girl, the better. There are train gangs. They rob, steal, eat people up. . . . And they rape many women'" (65), Javi explains, informing her of the unique dangers she may encounter during her journey. As an additional precautionary measure, he quietly instructs Miguel, "'Write 'Tengo SIDA' in big letters across her chest. . . . The threat of AIDS might stop some men'" (66). This threat of rape and violence becomes more tangible during their journey once "[a] gang dragged three young girls off the train, screaming and begging to be let go. They disappeared into the bushes on the far side of the water tower" (73).

Visibly shaken by what she has witnessed, "Elena shrank down to the ground, pulled her cap down tight over her head, and hugged her knees" (73). Perhaps those three girls have endured the same suffering as "the Martinez sisters, ten-year-old Juana and twelve-year-old Julietta, sent for by their parents, sent across the desert with a coyote, and never heard from again. No one speculated on the fate of the girls. No one wanted to say how they might have died or, even worse, how they might still live" (28). Traumatic exposure to such gender-based violence and danger for impressionable preadolescents during their migration is the price they pay in the attempt to reunite their transnational family.

Even before beginning their journeys to the United States, the characters hear the stories narrating the horrendous possibilities of what may happen en route to the other side. While some stories are pure exaggeration, the true stories have the same capacity to frighten their listeners, perhaps even more so. "[M]ostly, they told these stories to avoid telling the ones that were one hundred percent true, the ones that we *had* to believe" (28, original emphasis), Miguel reflects before embarking upon his trip. "Maybe I didn't believe everything Señor Gonzalez said, but the basic idea of kidnapping someone and then selling his organs seemed like it could happen" (26). Perhaps their first-hand experience with the death of a mother and child reaffirms their desire to join their parents. Stumbling upon a victim of migration, Miguel notes, "She lay on her side, curled up. Her long black hair fanned out from her head. The skin on her face had blistered and puckered up. I couldn't tell how old she might be. Cradled in her arms was a small child, its face toward her breast" (113). Embracing her child, this woman paid the ultimate sacrifice in hopes of crossing the desert for a better life. Her image would continue to haunt Miguel and Elena, who cannot deny the inherent dangers of their journey and their potential fate.

Attempting to rest, Miguel describes, "But I lay awake, listening to the wind. It was a thousand voices competing to be heard. Hundreds moaned in despair, hundreds in sadness. It was the people lost in this place, calling me to join them. It was the mother and child we left, now arisen and walking with the others" (115). He recalls Doña Maria's warning that, "'In that place of desolation . . . a ghost now walks at night. They say it is La Llorona. . . . She'll attempt to lure you away from your path. Cover your ears so you don't hear her wailing. Don't make the mistake many have made, of following her'" (26). Accordingly, he concludes, "It was La Llorona out to bewitch me, just as Doña Maria had warned. If I listened and followed, I'd be lost forever" (115). Ironically, this threatening archetypal figure normally associated with water is now a threat even to migrants crossing kilometers of desert, nowhere near any river or stream. One may suggest, however, that this image of a dead mother and child may also serve as a reminder to the protagonists that their separation from their parents has not been for naught. Rather than risk the well-being of their children, Miguel and Elena's parents had opted for transnational separation.

A witness to robbery, sexual violence, and death during her migratory journey to reunite with her parents, Elena faces unspeakable traumatic images and experiences that inevitably force her to mature quickly. "'Fairy tales are for little girls,' she screamed above the roar of the train" (69–70), indicating that she has observed and experienced too much to be the girl that she once was. "'I don't believe in el hada madrina anymore. I

173

hate this stupid train!'" (70), she exclaims, expressing her loathing toward "the mata gente," which "was full of boys and girls, just kids . . . looking for our padres and madres" (71). Illustrating that they are but one example of countless children who migrate across the border, Miguel comments, "There must be trainload after trainload of niños, all of them headed north, searching for their families" (71).[25] After such an arduous journey, the luckiest of these children will join their parents in pursuit of the American Dream.

Considering their expectations of a better life of wealth and stability, it comes as no surprise that some of these migrants, like Elena, experience disillusionment after spending time in the United States. After enduring so many physical and emotional trials to arrive across the line, "She says that el Norte never measured up to what she imagined it would be" (122), explains Miguel. In the novel's epilogue, Miguel and Elena share a phone call ten years after their departure from Mexico. Looking at a recent snapshot, Miguel describes, "There's Elena, the one who claimed she wanted to go north more than anyone, right back there on Abuelita's rancho in San Jacinto. Elena returned as soon as Papá let her, right after she finished high school. Even Mamá wasn't enough to keep her in California" (122). Despite her education and experiences north of the border, Elena decides to leave her family, electing instead to return to her life of tradition, living on her grandmother's ranch with her husband and son and growing organic foods to sell to Mexico City restaurants. One presumes from her return to San Jacinto that she does not embrace a new American identity, as Juana/Adelina does in *Across a Hundred Mountains*. However, the reader must project whether (and how) her migratory journeys affect her existence upon her return.

The dangers and disappointment that Elena experiences

largely mirror that which is evident in extant sociological and psychological research regarding the emotional consequences of transnational motherhood and piecemeal migration patterns in which first the father migrates, followed by the mother, and ultimately by some or all of the children. Among the unique challenges for the children of these transnational families is those who do manage to reunite with their parents must adapt to a new language, culture, and social and educational systems while simultaneously coping with feelings of loss surrounding their separation from their "surrogate parent" (Abrego 2014; Arroyo 1997; Artico 2003; Dreby 2010; Glasgow and Gouse-Sheese 1995; Goodman 2018; Suárez-Orozco et al. 2002). Much like Miguel and Elena miss their *abuelita* terribly but dare not speak of this so as to protect their parents' feelings, "Separated children . . . feel unable to openly talk to their parents about their sadness over the loss of the surrogate caretaker and their ambivalence about coming to the U.S." (Artico 2003, 4).

Perhaps more overwhelming, though, is the experience of reconnecting with unfamiliar relatives and possibly meeting a new stepparent or siblings (Artico 2003; Glasgow and Gouse-Sheese 1995). Such is the case in *La Línea*, in which the narrator voices his consternation regarding "the twin sisters we'd never seen, three-year-old Maria and Liliana" (Jaramillo 2006, 11). Before reuniting with his family, Miguel questions, "How was it possible to have sisters I'd never even seen?" (11). Many years later, he explains his ambivalent feelings toward them: "I've grown to love my little sisters, the hermanas I'd never known or held until I came north. . . . But I feel a familiar twinge of envy. Maria and Liliana have advantages they don't appreciate or understand" (122). One such advantage is their mastery of English alongside Spanish, but "What is more, "Papá and Mamá never left my sisters' sides, not even for a day. Maria and Liliana never had to wonder when, or if, they would see their parents again. And the twins are citizens. They can go to Mexico and come back whenever they want. For them, there is no línea" (122).

Envy and resentment similarly surface in Reyna Grande's *Dancing with Butterflies*, which conveys one of the four adult narrators' recollections of her experience of family reunification north of the US-Mexico border. Within the complex novel that weaves the stories of four women connected by their love for Mexican folkloric dance, the story of Soledad, an undocumented immigrant and costume designer for the dance company around which the novel ultimately revolves, emerges. Having successfully migrated north at the age of twenty by borrowing an American's birth certificate, she finds herself again in Mexico when she returns to see her dying grandmother. Her forced stay in her *pueblito* and the experience of crossing the border illegally a second time provoke reflection upon her experiences with her previous migration, reunion with her mother and a stepfather and half-sister she had never met, and the continued pursuit of the American Dream. As in *La Línea*, Soledad's mother migrated north in order to provide for her family once Soledad's grandfather and father, experienced migrants who evidently fell victim to foul play during their latest attempt to cross the border, were found dead in the desert. The narrative voice elaborates, "When they died, Ma had to come to the U.S. to make money because we sometimes didn't have anything to eat. She left me and my brother, Lorenzo, with Abuelita Licha. She met Tomás a year later and she fell in love with him and they had Stephanie. After many years, Ma said to me to come help with Stephanie and the swap meet" (Grande 2009, 48).

Despite the opportunities that her relocation affords her,

Soledad dwells on her difficulty with coping with her separation from her grandmother. "She and I, we were always together. It was so hard to leave her behind when I came here to be with Ma. After so many years of Ma being gone I'd started to see my Abuelita as my mother. Sometimes, I asked myself why I even came" (102–3). She repeats the sentiment, adding, "When I first came to the U.S., it was very hard for me. I missed my grandmother very much. I missed sitting outside our little shack, embroidering napkins with colored threads. Abuelita showed me how to make all kinds of stitches" (102). Soledad maintains her connection with her grandmother, albeit from afar, through her work as a seamstress. After all, her *abuelita* had been a seamstress for El Ballet Folklórico de México when she was young and, once she married and moved to Michoacán, "she tried to make a living by sewing school uniforms, quinceañearas or wedding dresses, but she loved making dance costumes, like me" (102). Her grandmother's legacy lives on through Soledad's work and, in more personal terms, affords her a bit of consolation in their separation, particularly given the difficulty with which she adapts to her new family while grieving the loss of what (and whom) she has left behind.

Just as Miguel and Elena of *La Línea* meet their siblings only upon arriving in the United States, Soledad meets her half-sister Stephanie, for whom she acts as caretaker. As such, Soledad must put her educational and professional dreams on hold. Expressing her resentment at these circumstances, she recalls:

> But I came here and Ma didn't want me to go to school to learn English. Because I was twenty, she said I was too old to learn anything, anyway. She wanted me to work and baby-sit Stephanie. Working at the swap meet didn't make me feel good. I wanted to work with my hands and make beautiful things. I missed the colored threads, the sound the scissors make as they cut the fabric, the feel of cloth against my fingertips. The click-clack of the

sewing machine. (103)

Only once her younger sister is in middle school does Soledad have the opportunity to pursue her own goals, first obtaining a certificate in fashion design and later taking English courses in hopes of qualifying for a Green Card (Permanent Resident Card), obtaining a high school diploma and college degree in fashion design, and ultimately operating a successful US-based business. Although she is now able to concentrate on her own professional pursuits, Soledad's anger and resentment toward Stephanie remain. These emotions mirror the anger and envy that Miguel of *La Línea* expresses regarding his twin sisters' childhood experiences in the United States. Soledad reflects, "Sometimes I feel so angry at the way Ma spoils Stephanie. Angry and jealous. Ma left me when I was thirteen years old, and for seven years I was without a mother. Stephanie's had a mother for all of her seventeen years of life. She doesn't know what it's like to have been left behind by the person you love most" (50). Grande and Jaramillo successfully articulate the sense of abandonment experienced by children of transnational migration that has also been documented within sociopsychological studies.

Relevantly, in *Latino Families Broken by Immigration: The Adolescent's Perceptions*, Ceres I. Artico examines the manner in which Latinx adolescents and young adults communicate their experiences and memories of prolonged separation from transnational parents during childhood with particular attention to how these are integrated within the development of an internal working model of self and others. More specifically, the author posits that the comprehension of their parents' decision to leave the country stems from a primary conflict of interpreting the parental action as abandonment versus sacrifice (Artico 2003, 6). While the majority of Central American mothers who leave their children behind to procure domestic work in the United States consider their departure a sacrificial act (Hondagneu-Sotelo and Avila 2007), many of the individuals in Artico's study indicate that fulfillment of material needs was insufficient compensation for the parents' incapacity to fulfill their emotional needs (2003, 99). Although they may recognize their parents' migration as a sacrifice for the greater good of the family on a theoretical level, the sense of abandonment often remains. As Artico observes, "[E]ven with the most benign set of external circumstances, many of these children could not help but feel unloved and rejected at times. Such a duality of emotions and cognition seemed to be part of a larger, overarching theme of duality that permeated this project" (132–33). Among these dualities, she cites "separation versus reunification; sacrifice versus abandonment; the felt-obligation of loyalty to caretakers versus the expected sense of loyalty towards parents[;] the desire to remain in the country of origin versus the need to join the parents in the US; feeling rejected versus feeling special . . . the list seems to go on forever" (133).[26] I would add that another pertinent duality—albeit one whose distinction is more blurred—is that between childhood and adulthood.

Children of migration, as depicted in these texts, confront physical dangers and wrestle with the psychological fallout of abandonment issues, profound fear associated with family separation and other traumas, and perhaps an awareness of structural and socioeconomic inequities and vulnerabilities, all of which would seemingly strip them of their youthful innocence or experience of childhood.[27] This circumstance brings to mind, then, Chávez Leyva's comments regarding the proper categorization of young migrants historically and how they have often been thrust into adult roles. "When writing about Mexican children, the category of 'child' often remains clouded by familial needs and survival" (Chávez Leyva 2008, 74), she asserts. Historically, "Children frequently lived, worked, and existed in an adult world in which they were in fact, if not by legal definition, adults" (74–75). This was certainly the case for the children of *braceros,* as described by Ana Rosas. In more contemporary terms, Thompson et al. embrace a "non-binary approach [that] recognises [*sic*] the development of agency as a process, embracing children and young people's rights and vulnerabilities, while acknowledging their resiliencies, competencies, goals and strengths" (2019, 235), and thus dismantles the dichotomy of children as either victims or criminals.[28] They argue that we should reject the views of migrant children as either hapless and helpless individuals forced into migration via trafficking or other coercion, on the one hand, and on the other as demonstrating so much agency that they disregard not only social norms about what children should or could do but also legal restrictions by crossing borders without papers (Thompson et al. 2019, 237).[29]

Recognizing that childhood is a social construction dependent on sociocultural norms and values that vary according to socioeconomic and geographic contexts, one might suppose that the typical US-based reader is apt to perceive these young migrants as children who should be protected from the threats involved. Although authors incorporate examples of their young characters' resourcefulness, resilience, and other displays of agency throughout the migratory journey, they tend to couch these within scenarios that emphasize, instead, the situatedness of the characters and their actions as a response to circumstances beyond their control, ones that generally suppress agency through limited socioeconomic opportunities in their countries of origin as well as violence related to their journeys. This is yet another strategic narrative move to develop empathy for these youth and contest their potential characterization as juvenile criminals who intentionally enter the US unlawfully to take advantage of resources unavailable in their home countries.

Seeking Safety and Solace in *The Only Road*

Alexandra Diaz's middle-grade novel *The Only Road* positions its young protagonists as refugees who find it necessary to flee the inescapable violence in their town in Guatemala in hopes of survival rather than as calculating migrants whose intentions are to manipulate the system in the US for their own economic benefit. Diaz aims to dispel misconceptions about current trends in migration and inform young readers (and by extension, parents, teachers, and other adults) about contemporary issues in Central America that have contributed to the recent influx of unaccompanied youth from the Northern Triangle and the layers of trauma that they confront before, during, and after their migration to the US. These children, she explains, are "humans, they're children, they're people who don't have any other choice. What kind of people are we to just turn our backs on this situation and pretend it's not happening?" (Neil 2018).

In an effort to counteract the tendency toward indifference, ignorance, and complacency, Diaz reveals the physical and emotional tribulations of twelve-year-old Jaime and fifteen-year-old Ángela as they leave their family behind and, in the author's note, connects the fictional account to the realities of unaccompanied minors engaged in transnational migration. The book has an accessible style and format that includes twenty-four short chapters with large font, simple and direct language, a glossary with Spanish terms, and third-person narrative that manages to engage with mature themes without being graphic. Moreover, Diaz incorporates familiar literary tropes, like the animal as companion and guide, in an adaptation of Joseph Campbell's hero's journey that depicts the epic quest of two cousins who, like the mythic hero, answer the call to depart on their journey, cross the threshold to the unknown and, with the assistance of helpers, pass through a series of trials to ultimately return, transformed, with their reward.

The cousins' call to adventure occurs within the first few pages of the novel when news arrives of Miguel's death at the hand of the Alphas gang, and the threats and intimidation of Jaime (Miguel's cousin) and Ángela (Miguel's sister) intensify. Diaz thus immediately establishes ongoing and escalating physical and psychological violence as motives for their imminent migration, which is conveyed as "the only choice, the only road. If they stay at home, they will die; if they leave, they might live" (Diaz 2016, 280). The narrative voice describes Jaime's initial reaction of dread when he suspects that the Alphas had made good on a previous threat and further explains the power that they wield beyond the scope of Jaime and Ángela's families: "The gang had a strong presence in their small Guatemalan village and other villages in the area. Kids younger than Jaime were addicted to the cocaine the Alphas supplied. Shopkeepers were 'asked' to pay the Alphas for protection: the protection they offered was from themselves. Protection from being robbed, or killed, if refused" (8).

What is more, the physical and psychological violence at the hands of the Alphas is portrayed as related to overarching structures involving corruption and impunity. "The police in the village had called Miguel's death an unfortunate *accidente*. Of course they would say that. Money meant more than morals and justice to the force; whoever paid most had the power, and the Alphas could pay a lot. It also didn't help that the police chief's drug habit funded many of the gang's operations" (12). Thus, there would be no realistic escape from the gang's influence if the cousins were to stay, for "The Alphas would force both of them to take part in beatings and killings" (18). Carefully using wording to avoid the direct mention of gender-based violence, namely sexual assault, the narrative voice continues, "But with Ángela it would be worse. If the gang members thought she was pretty enough, she'd become one of the gang leaders' girlfriends, whether she wanted to or not" (18). Despite the risks that their northward migration to live with Jaime's brother in the US would entail, the families regard this as the only option, given the inevitable danger of remaining at home, and thus accelerates the characters' process of transformation.

In addition to coping with the grief over Miguel's death, Jaime and Ángela must contend with the trauma of loss inherent in the separation from their other family members and the lives they have known. For Jaime, "hardest of all was the idea of leaving home to live with Tomás" (22), the brother who left Guatemala to work in *El Norte* at seventeen, when Jaime was just four years old. Eight years had passed and the siblings, with thirteen years between them, were practically strangers. Moreover, the move entailed saying goodbye to familiarity. As the cousins set out on the trek, the narrator observes, "The village Jaime had known his whole life, gone. His house, his family, gone. From now on, home would only get farther and farther away" (32).

Compounding this trauma is the fear of potential separation from Ángela while en route to the US. While in the darkness of a box car, panic begins to set in when he is unsure of her whereabouts. He wonders, *"Where was she?* A high-pitched whine escaped his body. It had happened. What he feared more than dying. He was all alone and would never see his cousin again" (137). Shortly thereafter, he finds that she is by his side. As their journey continues, though, his sense of loss heightens:

"He hated this train, hated this land, hated this trip. He wanted to go home, have a bath, eat everything in the house, and let his mama tuck him into the hammock outside. It'd be worth facing the Alphas if it meant being home" (209). This feeling intensifies after exposure to the multitude of dangers the two face.

As in Jaramillo's *La Línea*, Diaz repeatedly describes the psychological traumas connected to the fear rooted in the risks that the protagonists sustain. Even prior to their departure, Jaime reflects: "Everyone knew the stories. Gangs robbed you at every turn. Immigration officers beat you up before sending you back home" (21), and a friend had even been abducted and sold as a slave. Learning about the additional hazards along the way, the narrator notes, "*La migra*, trains, bandits, and more gangs. Everything seemed worse than what they had left behind. Except here there seemed to be a greater variety of ways to die" (40–41). Indeed, they would witness the beating of a Salvadoran woman at the hands of Mexican immigration officials when she beseeches them to let her cross without papers to escape an abusive husband and provide for her children, and experience the heat, hunger, dehydration, and panic of being "locked in a pitch-black train car with no way of getting out, prisoners in their escape for freedom" (138).

Not long after, they prepare for an experience riding atop *la Bestia* (the freight train known as "the Beast"), listening apprehensively to their new acquaintance Xavi's more specific description of the dangers that lie ahead:

> "Gangs run the tracks. *Migra* officers sometimes work with them. It was dark when we were either in Chiapas or just into Oaxaca when twenty gang members got on board. They demanded money and threatened anyone who didn't pay up. One boy about Jaime's age insulted them. They caught him, threw him off the train and shot him in the air like a pigeon. I don't even think they killed him. I imagine him lying helpless by the tracks, bleeding to death." (179)

Seeing no alternative, the cousins prepare themselves for such possibilities as well as that of witnessing and/or enduring potential sexual assault as Xavi continues, "'The gang was horrible to one girl. We kept hearing her screams. If we had tried to help her, they would have done the same to us" (179). This episode has a particularly intense effect on eleven-year-old Joaquín, who "'didn't stop shaking for hours afterward'" (179) and hadn't slept in days. Later, the text reveals the secret that Joaquín is, in fact, a young girl who adopts the physical appearance of a boy (reminiscent of *La Línea*'s Elena's physical transformation in anticipation of her migration) as a means to protect herself.

After being held at gunpoint and later robbed by other young companions, the cousins would dodge an ambush by "Los Fuegos, who made the Alphas back home seem like annoying fleas. When they weren't trafficking drugs into los Estados Unidos, they raided cities and trains, demanded pay, and killed whoever got in their way. It was said they etched marks on their arms to keep a tally of their murders" (209–10). Jaime is especially concerned, though, about the fate of his cousin Ángela since, "He knew why everyone kept saying it wasn't safe for girls to make this journey. He knew why Joaquín pretended to be a boy. He knew what they'd do to his cousin if they caught her" (212–13).[30] Again, Diaz artfully incorporates this very real danger of the journey within the narration, but in a way that is not graphic or inappropriate for a young audience.

She also includes mention of the dangers that the train itself presents. While Jaime prepares for the next segment of their journey on board *la Bestia*, "Scenarios filled his head. The worst, of course: he could trip and get swallowed by the train. He could trip and have the train bite off his arms or legs. He could trip and get left behind. They weren't just horror stories. They were events that happened to real people he'd met" (196), and his fears of these potential fates are compounded by the possibility of suffering a fatal injury and dying alone. "Ever since the news of Miguel, Jaime had thought death was the worst thing that could happen to a person, whether it was being beaten to death by people who had once been friends or suffocating in a soulless train" (187). He recognizes, however, that "At least Jaime had been there, had known his cousin's fate. But this unidentified person chopped to bits by the train, that was worse. He'd died by himself, in a strange country, and his family would never know" (187). He and Ángela fear that they may share a similar destiny, especially once they become separated and are injured and exposed to the harsh elements of the desert.

The action-packed novel presents one dramatic episode after another, through which it becomes evident that aside from facing physical violence and the psychological traumas based on separation, loss, and fear, Jaime is also plagued by a gripping sense of guilt over his family's hefty financial sacrifice (30,000 quetzales, or about $4,000, for the safe passage of the two cousins) and Miguel's death in the first place since the attack occurred while Jaime was home sick and not accompanying his cousin and close friend. That guilt and a sense that he owes it to his family to carry on are largely what keep him moving forward and northward in the face of adversity, which additionally entails what I would categorize as sociocultural violence. The narrator remarks, "In an illegal journey of four thousand kilometers, they were going through places more corrupt than his village, running from gangs more violent than the Alphas, going to a country where no one, except Tomás, wanted them there. Everywhere they'd go on the journey, they'd be unwelcome" (50), signaling the explicit hostility toward migrants they would face in transit in Mexico and in the United States.

Upon arrival in Arriaga and encountering fresh "graffiti painted on the locked partition of one of the storefronts: '¡Váyanse centro americanos [sic]!' followed by rude words" (73), Ángela cautions Jaime, "'We have to be careful. . . . Los mexicanos really don't like us. They think we're all criminals and not as worthy in the eyes of God'" (75). This framework serves to help young readers understand that sentiments they may have heard regarding Mexican immigrants in the US are similarly echoed in the context of Central American migrants in Mexico, again reflecting sociolegal hierarchies and the threat of the "alien Other." Jaime and Ángela recognize their status as unwanted outsiders, both in Mexico and the US, further fomenting their fear of the border crossing ahead. Jaime wonders, "But even with the money [for a coyote], how would they manage it? What he knew of that crossing already terrified him. News reports showed immigration patrol officers shooting anything that moved; detention centers packed with people; politicians over there who said all immigrants were rapists and criminals" (49), a clear reference to the rhetoric of President Trump and policies and practices related to deterrence, apprehension, and detention of undocumented immigrants. Noting the "thousands, maybe even tens of thousands, heading to El Norte everyday" (80), Jaime further internalizes his status as one of a multitude of unwanted foreigners—an implication that their presence is a threat that requires policing—commenting, "'That's why they're building a wall. . . . They say it's to keep their country safe. But really, it's to keep us out'" (81).

How, then, could these two young protagonists possibly overcome the lengthy list of trauma-inducing obstacles to reunite safely with Tomás? As with the standard hero's journey, Jaime and Ángela rely on a lengthy list of guides along the way, from family members and family friends to various strangers who provide them with shelter, temporary employment, food, and transportation. They also benefit from the support, camaraderie, and suggestions of sixteen-year-old Xavi from El Salvador, seventeen-year-old Rafa from Honduras, eleven-year-old "Joaquín" from Honduras, and, of course, Vida, the dog that repeatedly protects them and leads them both to safety and to one another after separation. Notably, Jaime also relies upon the comfort and support that he finds in his prayers to Miguel, his deceased cousin.

That they depend on so many helpers to overcome the trials on their quest does not imply helplessness or victimhood. Jaime and Ángela also demonstrably exercise agency, using their own skills and experiences as a means of financial support and, in the case of Señora Pérez, to reciprocate, when they stumble upon her ranch house in the middle of the desert, after she offers hospitality, water, painkillers, food, and even a drive to Juárez. Pleasantly surprised by their willingness to babysit and do other jobs around the house, she articulates how their actions contest a general perception of migrants in the area, even one that she—presumably a Latina based on her name— has entertained. "'I'm glad you came. You hear all these stories about immigrants robbing and sometimes even killing the residents'" (234), further emphasizing Diaz's portrayal of Jaime and Ángela as migrants who subvert the image of immigrants as criminals. Moreover, when the cousins must come up with additional funds to pay for their safe passage, they never engage in theft, robbery, or other nefarious activities but instead use their sewing and sketching skills.

Jaime's hobby of sketching is a motif that runs throughout the novel and that ultimately takes on a role that goes beyond leisure. In one instance, a sketch seems to help the cousins overcome a sticky situation with an immigration officer; in others, Jaime earns money by drawing caricatures. Beyond this, though, his sketchbook is a coping mechanism that enables him to maintain connections while he suffers the trauma of separation and loss, one that serves as a therapeutic tool to help him process the additional traumas that the journey entails. In the spirit of a *Künstlerroman*, Diaz includes several explicit allusions to drawing and the significance of the sketchbook, noting when and how Jaime captures images of key moments or people, thereby using his art as a tool to remember and also to define himself and his story. Ultimately, that story would include the cousins' arrival in the US. "From leaving their family and everything they'd ever known, to escaping gangsters and drug cartels, extreme heat and dehydration, they'd done it. They were finally here. In the United States of America. The land of the free, where they would make their new home. But they weren't safe yet" (261), the narrator observes.

Once they do reach the safehouse and reunite with Tomás, the heroes have seemingly arrived victorious from their journey into the unknown, equipped with the "prize" of self-awareness, personal growth, the knowledge of the contributions of the helpers, and the sense that their arduous journey to safety had been worth it. Nevertheless, it appears that their journey into the unknown will be ongoing. After Jaime's first experience using a telephone, showering indoors, and eating a strange peanut-butter-and-jelly sandwich, "Now a whole new set of concerns took over. What was it going to be like to live here, where there was no one? Would he ever be able to speak English properly? What if he never stopped missing his family back home? What if, after everything, they still got deported?" (276). Diaz further addresses those questions in *The Crossroads*, the sequel to *The Only Road*.

For Diaz, a Cuban American whose mother left Cuba with her family at the age of seventeen in the wake of the Cuban

Revolution, the experiences of unaccompanied minors fleeing the Northern Triangle resonate with her own family's experiences of displacement and loss. She explains in her author's note, "Both of my parents had to leave everything behind: homes, possessions, friends, but mostly family members they thought they'd never see again" (279). Diaz effectively depicts the psychological traumas that result from displacement and family separation while also capturing the host of physical, sociocultural, and additional fear-based psychological threats to Central American migrants, the unique circumstances that have driven each of the characters from their homes, and even their distinct linguistic variations (like *el voseo*, the use of *vos* as a second-person singular pronoun). The result is a narrative that gives readers access to characters' diverse experiences that contest the hegemonic notion of a monolithic Latinx migrant identity or experience, thereby enhancing the store of related mental exemplars and affording the development of an empathetic connection. Functioning as a reminder of the novel's connection with reality, Diaz's author's note provides additional information and also nudges readers to learn more by consulting the works she recommends in a bibliography, perhaps prompting a progression from empathetic connection to extratextual action.

Directed toward an English-speaking American audience, the texts by Grande, Jaramillo, and Diaz utilize simple language to tell the complex and gripping stories of but a few protagonists who have come to represent the countless other Mexican and Central American youths whose stories have not yet been inscribed within literary or official history. In breaking the silence regarding the profound and traumatic effects of transnational migration on those who have been "left behind," as well as those who find themselves forced to leave others behind, these authors provide unsettling stories. Not only do they subvert or unsettle the dominant images of the Latinx migrant in the US imaginary, they may also stir readers vis-à-vis empathic unsettlement to awaken from the comforts of their lives in the industrialized US to recognize, ironically through fiction, the disturbing truths of the dangers and overlapping traumas that children of transnational migration confront.

Particularly in the case of *La Línea* and *The Only Road*, children who have themselves experienced transnational migration may benefit from seeing their experiences in print and connect with the texts through bounded strategic empathy. The didactic nature of these novels, though, suggests that the primary readership is likely unfamiliar with these experiences. In all three of the texts analyzed in this chapter, the depiction of the interconnected layers of violence using techniques that foster ambassadorial strategic empathy expose readers to the agency that youth must develop to overcome the cascading traumas that current legal structures (directly or indirectly) create or exacerbate. In emphasizing children's vulnerability to these traumas, however, the authors counteract the dominant portrayals of immigrant youth as threats to US economic resources, lawfulness, or the more abstract "fabric of American society," and instead may prompt readers to engage in extratextual, pro-social action by advocating for changes to particular policies or practices related to the policing and detention of unaccompanied minors, or otherwise supporting these newcomers.

CHAPTER 5

The Personal *Is* Political: Narrative Condemnations of Individual Tragedies of Transnational Migration

T he narrative portrayal of more intimate experiences with the phenomenon of immigration and border crossing exemplifies how transnational migration is simultaneously "an inherently political" (Zolberg 2008, 11) and "an inherently personal process" (Dreby 2010, 3), and shatters the illusion of a merely theoretical borderland through depictions of the more tangible and material dimension of the border. Beyond this, the articulation of the personal tragedies and trauma steeped in suffering and injustice serves as an effective point of departure for the expression of political condemnations of the structural mechanisms that sustain the need for migration and simultaneously condone violence, in its various permutations. In offering scathing condemnations of the personal impact of the global phenomenon of immigration, Ana Castillo, Julia Álvarez, and Melinda Palacio utilize their respective novels—*The Guardians, Return to Sender,* and *Ocotillo Dreams*—as instruments to reveal the individual physical and psychological suffering associated with broader legal and sociocultural policies and practices that endanger and separate Latinx migrants and their families, and result in collective trauma that extends beyond Latinx immigrants to include US-born Latinxs.

These texts explicitly critique the inhumanity of US immigration policies and practices that serve as the backdrops to the novels and employ a range of narrative strategies that both enhance empathy and potentially counteract the cognitive inhibitions that prevent readers from taking extraliterary action (Nance 2010, 165). Weaving together themes of migration and the absent mother, these authors abandon subtlety in their attacks on US immigration policy and indifference to the marginalization of migrants in our society and unsettle readers, shaking them from complacency through exposure of the web of violence endured by migrants and their families. Similarly, Josefina López's theatrical piece, *Detained in the Desert,* overtly critiques the hypocrisy of immigration policy and conceptualizations of (il)legality and morality through bringing to the stage various physical, emotional, and legal struggles of migrants and US citizens alike.[31]

Deterrence, Disappearance, and Devastation

Ana Castillo's *The Guardians* is a powerful work that offers a new spin on the migrant narrative, focusing on the psychological repercussions of the migratory journey for family members left behind on either side of the US-Mexico border. In particular, the text revolves largely around the female protagonist, Regina, who lives in the United States, rather than emphasizing the physical and emotional trials of her brother, Rafa, a Mexican migrant who has crossed the border various times and whose most recent apparently unsuccessful attempts at border crossing form the crux of the text despite not being narrated at any point in the novel. In the wake of Rafa's vanishing during his most recent effort to cross the line, Regina adopts a maternal role to care for his son, Gabo, and takes on the investigative challenge of resolving the mystery of his disappearance. Nevertheless, Castillo successfully presents the multitude of dangers that border crossing entails, thereby exposing the perils of migration and condemning the broader global forces that foster Mexican movement northward and the specific Prevention Through Deterrence policies adopted by the US government in the early 1990s.

As in the case of other texts we have seen thus far, the quest for economic stability is the primary factor that motivates Rafa to cross the border. Projecting strong feelings of nationalist loyalty, he had come and gone frequently to maintain a sense of his Mexican *patria*, reflecting the earlier patterns of circular transnational migration evident prior to the implementation of heightened border surveillance and the enforcement of more stringent US immigration policies beginning in the 1990s. "How many times had mi tía Regina begged my father not to return to México, to take his chances and stay, Santo querido?" (Castillo 2007, 85), asks Gabo, Regina's nephew. "But México had a pull on my papá. It was his country. 'No soy un gringo,' he'd say. He came up to el Norte only for the sake of supporting his familia" (85).

Despite their devotion to Mexico, the characters who migrate north cannot resist the temptation of the rumors of wealth and the American Dream. Unfortunately, this dream turns out to be elusive in many cases. In fact, "La búsqueda de un sueño americano puede ser tu peor pesadilla" (115), succinctly states the warning sign on the wall of a humanitarian office that Regina visits in Juárez as she continues the search for her missing brother. The quest for the American Dream may indeed turn out to be a nightmare both for the migrant and for the family members left behind.

Underlining this discrepancy between migrants' dreams and their reality, Regina ponders her nephew's comprehension of the situation. "He is a boy trying to figure things out. Even if you are a hundred, how do you make sense of your parents being killed or disappearing trying to make their way to the Land of Gold? Muchos dólares en Los Estados. That's what people hear in their villages" (97). Gabo and Regina themselves have endured the physical trials of crossing the border in addition to the disappearance of Gabo's mother. Now, they must contend with the anxiety of yet another missing relative. Regina, in particular, is well aware of both the obvious and the less-discussed risks in the wake of Operation Gatekeeper and reflects upon the possible challenges her brother has encountered:

> The Mexican government now even puts out a survival handbook.[32] It advises migrants how to cross, with tips on avoiding apprehension by US authorities. . . . When you try to come over with no papers and vanish, there won't be any dogs or search parties called out. You travel at your own risk. You are at the mercy of everything known to mankind and nature. There is the harsh weather and land, the river and desert. The night is and is not your friend. It provides coolness and darkness to allow you to move. But you can get lost, you can freeze, you can get robbed or kidnapped, you can drown in el río. You can fall into a ravine, get bitten by a snake, a tarantula, a bat or something else. The brutal sun comes with day and anything can happen to you that happens at night but you can also dehydrate, burn, be more easily detected by patrols and thieves. Bandits could kill you as easily as rob you of not just your life's savings but that of your whole familia. Even

> of your village, in cases where communities have decided that get-
> ting one person out will help them all. If you are a pollo smuggled
> with others in an enclosed truck you could die of suffocation. (117)

As in other works discussed in previous chapters, nature *and*
mankind threaten the migrant during his or her journey northward. Even more treacherous than the perils related to climate,
threatening terrain, or wild animals are the actions (or lack
of action) on the part of the cast of human characters in the
borderlands.

The dangers presented by "humanity" are not limited to bandits or official checkpoints on behalf of the Mexican or American
governments. The coyote, whose duty is to ensure that migrants
successfully cross the border, may take advantage of the circumstances and may very well present another danger that
makes other inconveniences seem mundane. "Embarrassment
is nothing when you're at the mercy of not just 'your' coyote but
all coyotes, all traffickers prowling out there for the victims of
poverty and laws against nature" (118), Regina states. Further
identifying this threat, the narrator declares:

> The problem is the coyotes and narcos own the desert now. You
> look out there, you see thorny cactus, tumbleweed, and sand soil
> forever and you think, No, there's nothing out there. But you know
> what? They're out there—los mero-mero cabrones. The drug traf-
> fickers and body traffickers. Which are worse? I can't say. (4)

As the plot of *The Guardians* develops, it is evident that migrants
are at the mercy of the coyotes not only during the act of
crossing the border but also after arriving in the United States.
Furthermore, "Whatever happens to men, in my opinion, is
worse for women" (117), Regina avers, emphasizing the additional risks of gendered violence. This is the case of the "fortunate" woman who has made it across the line. When Rafa
and his wife, Ximena, attempted to cross the border previously,

their coyotes insisted upon their separation. "The coyotes said no, the women had to go in another truck. Three days later the bodies of four women were found out there in that heat by the Border Patrol. All four had been mutilated for their organs. One of them was Ximena" (4). The fact that Gabo's mother had died like this provokes further anxiety for the adolescent in the face of his father's recent disappearance.

This anxiety is but one of the elements of Castillo's portrayal of emotional angst experienced by family left behind as a result of migration. Regina explains the distressing uncertainty: "We've been waiting a week, me and Gabo—for his dad to come back. He's been back and forth across that desert, dodging the Border Patrol so many times, you'd think he wouldn't even need a coyote no more" (4). However, awareness of Rafa's potential fate emotionally impacts his son. "It isn't as if Gabo himself hasn't noticed. I heard him crying into his pillow one night. He probably envisions his father being killed by a coyote and left in the desert like what happened to his mother" (12), the narrator supposes. Facing such trauma necessarily forces Gabo to age prematurely. Recognizing this, Regina explains, "It made me long for the child who said his prayers out loud every night. The last time I had seen him do that was before his papá had gone missing. All his innocence was oozing out of him a little every day and there was nothing I could do to stop it" (50). In fact, Gabo, a spiritual and pious adolescent, consequently "made a pact with the Devil" (81), resorting to a powerful gang's help to acquire knowledge regarding his missing father's whereabouts. As an indirect effect of his relationship with the members of los Palominos, Gabo is murdered before obtaining any pertinent information.

Illustrating the intergenerational trauma (Szeghi 2018, 405) of one family's story of migration affords an opportunity to critique the broader forces that, in conjunction, perpetuate Mexican migration to the United States. More so than the other writers focusing on individual costs of transnational migration, Castillo incorporates polemic commentaries within her work, strongly criticizing national border and immigration policies and identifying drug trafficking as a vice propagated north of the border that has concrete repercussions south of the border. Referring to investigations for his manuscript-in-progress, titled *The Dirty Wars of Latin America: Building Drug Empires*, the character Miguel comments, "Now, the sixty-four-thousand-dollar question, or in this case, billion dollar question, is: How long can the United States contain what its vices and counterproductive prohibitions have wrought?" (Castillo 2007, 151). Miguel's narrative voice offers an alternative to current labor and immigration policies, indirectly casting the blame for economic problems on the outsourcing of jobs rather than on the influx of Mexican immigrants:

> If the country made it easier for professional immigrants to come in, the competition would possibly drive professional salaries *down*. Thereby equalizing the distribution of wealth. Anyway, it's not about people sneaking in but jobs being snuck out. NAFTA, CAFTA, the new treaty with the Pacific rim, all the maquilas along the US-Mexico border and Southeast Asia—companies went there and keep going there to take advantage of the cheap labor to be found abroad. (125)

Further elaborating upon questions of globalization and relations between the two sides of the border, Regina poses a series of rhetorical questions: "What if there had been no war and what if no money could be made on killing undocumented people for their organs? What if this country accepted outright that it needed the cheap labor from the south and opened up the border? And people didn't like drugs so that trying to sell them would be pointless?" (29). The passage acknowledges the complex mechanism that ultimately holds the responsibility for the structural violence against migrants attempting to create a better life for themselves across the border.

Regina's critique encompasses not only immigration policies but also those agencies that require that migrants, in particular, comply with such legislation. In Castillo's novel, el Abuelo Milton describes the unjust treatment of Mexicans on both sides of the border, beginning with the 1924 establishment of the Border Patrol. "'That's when Mexicans got to be fugitives on our own land. Whether you lived on this side or that side, all Mexicans got harassed'" (72), regardless of citizenship status. With its advanced technology and constant vigilance in the name of domestic security, la Migra is but one obstacle to the Mexican migrants attempting to enter the US to support their families. As all of the analyzed texts suggest, however, the Border Patrol may pose the least of threats to migrants' security and well-being in the borderlands. El Abuelo Milton affirms, "'The borderlands have become like the Bermuda Triangle. Sooner or later everyone knows someone who's dropped outta sight'" (132), someone like Rafa, "only one among hundreds every year disappearing or finally turning up dead because of heat and dehydration in the desert or foul play at the hands of coyotes" (148).

The text's first-person narrative and compelling descriptions of physical, psychological, and structural violence may very well contribute to reader empathy. Nevertheless, Nance describes the "cognitive defenses" that may preclude further action in the face of social injustice, referring to Lerner's identification of readers' downplay of suffering, derogation of victims' choices or character, transfer of responsibility, temporizing, invocation of spiritual redress, and a sense that suffering will improve victims' character (2010, 164) as factors. Castillo effectively counteracts such action-inhibiting factors, especially through portrayal of the extensive suffering of one family, which becomes representative of thousands of others within the Latinx migrant community. So as not to minimize the significance and scope of the issue, she explicitly recognizes the overlooked, subaltern individuals of the world in her acknowledgements at the end of *The Guardians*. Castillo writes:

> Finally, the forgotten underclass throughout the world, whose lives, services, and labor are taken far too much for granted, are remembered. May one day the leaders who govern over humanity earnestly seek ways to even the playing field for everyone to live with dignity. (2007, 212)

These comments also illustrate the didactic nature of Castillo's text, which may come across as heavy-handed. Marta Caminero-Santangelo, for example, rightfully identifies the use of "[v]arious characters [who] take turns serving as 'expository' and teacherly narrators not only of the novel's plot but also of its historical context, as though that context is too important for readers not to 'get'" (2016, 69). However, such didacticism and repetition may ultimately contribute to the effectiveness of the novel in communicating its message and prompting prosocial action. Tereza M. Szeghi argues that authors like Castillo "do not just appeal to readers' emotions but also offer readers and would-be activists guidance about what can be done to effect change . . . in order to increase the odds that their novels will prompt readers to take action" (2018, 404). Dawes explains, "When empathy-inspired action cannot quickly find a clear, straightforward, and personalizing solution, it fades" (2016, 429). Thus, it becomes even more prudent for authors to provide an extraliterary path forward to harness the affective power of storytelling. This may also be useful for those readers whom

Nance identifies as overwhelmed by the enormity of suffering in the text and consequently inhibited from action (2010, 165). Yet another barrier to extraliterary action stems from readers' sense of accomplishment or closure upon finishing a text in its entirety. The novel's rupture with genre expectations—namely that a novel will conclude with a sense of poetic justice, or at least the resolution of the primary conflicts driving the plot— may, in fact, compel readers to make productive use of the unsettling sense of this lack of literary closure.

Writing / Righting the Impact of Interior Immigration Enforcement

To better equip students to understand their sociopolitical realities involving migration, Dominican American author Julia Álvarez has turned *to* YA literature.[33] In *Return to Sender*, she incorporates a variety of empathic techniques that encourage young readers to learn about the complex history, and contemporary practices, of immigration enforcement. "I'm not just a writer," she explains. "I've also been an educator for three decades. And a story protects us in a way. In a sense, it's a safe world in which to consider what's going to hit you broadside in the real world. You give kids the things that are bombarding them in their real lives, but it's within a safe context. It gives them a way to navigate through the world" (Álvarez in Cary 2009). In her semi-epistolary novel, then, Álvarez grapples with the complicated issue of undocumented immigration in a manner that is suitable for nine- to twelve-year-olds to help orient not only the largely Mexican[34] migrant student population that had been arriving in her Vermont community in recent years but also their Anglo classmates.

As a Spanish-speaking volunteer in the classroom, Álvarez had observed, "The kids were really traumatized that their classmate had disappeared. . . . This doesn't happen in their United States, that somebody disappears because they're not supposed to be here, and their parents could be rounded up and they would be deported and put in holding. All of this can be very troubling stuff in fourth and fifth grade. And I thought that we need a story to understand what's happening to us" (Álvarez in Cary 2009). Thus, in the context of the Department of Homeland Security's 2006 Operation Return to Sender deportation campaign, the text develops the budding friendship between Tyler, a Vermont farm boy, and Mexican-born Mari, the daughter of one of the migrants who has come to maintain the farm after Tyler's father suffers an accident. Much like the texts geared toward an adult audience, *Return to Sender* alternates narrative planes, weaving perspectives and incorporating diary entries and letters that exemplify more clearly the emotional impact of Mari's displacement, her "otherness," fears of deportation, and concerns about her missing mother. Perhaps more unique to the text, though, Álvarez effectively captures the cultural interplay at hand through offering a voice for both Mari *and* Tyler, who suddenly experiences de-familiarity with his world and ultimately wrestles with issues of morality, legality, friendship, and betrayal as he develops a deeper connection with Mari.

The reader learns early on in the text that Mari and her siblings have already endured a painful separation from their mother. In her first letter, Mari writes, "If you are reading these words, it means you are back in Carolina del Norte! . . . We have missed you terribly the eight months and a day (yes, Mamá, I am keeping count!) that you have been gone" (Álvarez 2009, 17). They would eventually reunite, "[a] whole year, four months, and four days, to be exact" (231) after their initial separation. Through diary entries and letters, Mari's first-person perspective enables readers to develop an understanding of the emotional fatigue of an undocumented immigrant youth's shouldering the burden of caring for her siblings while worrying about her absent mother and adapting to life in Vermont. In fact, through her orchestration, Mari arranges for her mother's transfer from coyotes who are holding her ransom after months of servitude. Summarizing her mother's account in a letter to her father, "[s]o Mamá won't have to repeat this part of the story until she is stronger" (240), Mari writes:

> It turns out that after Mamá left my uncles, she met up with her *coyote* who was taking her through a reservation. But on the way, they got held up by another gang. Mamá now became the property of these new *coyotes*. They brought her to their leader, and— this is where Mamá hesitated and looked unsure what to tell me. "He forced me to be his . . . servant," she said, choosing each word carefully. "I had to cook for him and take care of his clothes and do whatever he told me. He threatened that if I tried to run away, not only would he find me and kill me, but he would track down my family and do the same to them." (239)

Eight months later, Mari's mother has an opportunity to make calls surreptitiously but is violently assaulted when she is caught. Ultimately, though, she is released, but only after payment of a $3,000 ransom. The astute reader understands the implications of the gendered physical and psychological violence that Mari's mother has endured, and in documenting and bearing witness to it, the trauma affects Mari as well.

Álvarez also documents the psychological violence that derives from structural and legal violence throughout the text. Mari reflects on the psychological turmoil of living in the shadows after her father expresses concern that sending letters will raise suspicion and lead to being caught by la Migra: "I think that having to live secretly for years in this country has made him imagine danger where it doesn't even exist" (35). This concern intensifies with the rise of xenophobic attitudes evident at the community town hall, and Mari notes the negative impact of political discourse about border security on her father, explaining to Tyler, "'The president, your Mr. President, was just on TV saying he's sending the National Guard troops down to the border. They're going to build a huge wall'" (259).

The danger to her family, however, is real, and in a climactic scene, Tyler sees "[a] battalion of cars, lights flashing" (263). The narrative voice continues, "Dark figures leap out and surround the small trailer, where three Mexicans are just now watching a game of *lucha libre* and waiting for the three Marías to come home" (263). Later recounted in her diary entry, Mari describes, "Next, they were hauling Papá out, but he was struggling and swinging at the agents. Meanwhile, Mamá was jumping out of the window of our bedroom, but there were agents all around ready to catch her. Two of them grabbed her by the arms and herded her inside one of the cars. She was screaming the whole time" (268). Notably, the text invokes descriptions that criminalize and simultaneously dehumanize Mari's parents. Privileging the voices of the panic-stricken young characters, the text captures the terror of state-sanctioned apprehension and detention, later contextualizing this particular scene within the broader political action of "a national sweep called Operation Return to Sender" (286).

Thanks to Mari's testimony regarding her mother's traumatic experiences and portrayal of her in contrast to the criminal coyotes who had been part of the trafficking ring in North Carolina, Mari's parents are able to attain legal relief. Her practice of writing, then, is a critical element that helps her to overcome the psychological, physical, sociocultural, and legal / structural violence that her family endures. Mari recognizes the therapeutic nature of writing, explaining in a letter to her mother, "As you always used to tell Papá when he found you writing letters, or just writing in a notebook, '*El papel lo aguanta todo.*' Paper can hold anything. Sorrows that might otherwise break your heart. Joys with wings that lift you above the sad things in your life" (22).

In terms of narrative strategies, the use of epistolary elements also facilitates a greater degree of reader engagement, which in turn may lead to additional empathy to spark prosocial action. As Maya Socolovsky suggests, "Because of the way in which epistolary narratives actively involve the reader, the novel's external audience serves as a community of readers that stands in for the letters' recipients and addressees" (2015, 398), particularly since Mari's father insists that the letters go undelivered. "In conjuring up Mari's own internal sympathetic community of readers," Socolovsky continues, "the novel empowers as well a potentially sympathetic community of listeners outside of the text who effect the symbolic, if not the literal, circulation of the undelivered letters" (2015, 389).

As in Castillo's text, the didactic tone is strong throughout *Return to Sender*, overtly calling on readers to remember and honor the true sense of American patriotism—one that welcomes outsiders—and recognizing their contributions. Rejecting Mr. Rosetti's hypocritical anti-immigrant views, Tyler's teacher declares, "'But the bottom line is that this country, and particularly this state, were built by people who gave up everything in search of a better life, not just for themselves, but for their children. Their blood, sweat, and tears formed this great nation'" (Álvarez 2009, 191). Álvarez also critiques the inhumanity of immigration enforcement practices and their agents, often incorporating pithy descriptions like, "They were ICE all right, with cold hearts to do what they'd done to my family!" (280).

Such descriptions may be effective among the anticipated

readership. In a separate passage to clarify the name of Operation Return to Sender, Tyler asks, "'But isn't that what they stamp on a letter, *Return to Sender* . . . When there aren't enough stamps on it?'" (287). "'Precisely,'" Mr. Calhoun responds. "'People as excess baggage.' He looked disgusted" (287). The dialogue attacks the heartlessness of even the official name of the initiative and the sentiment behind it, as it does elsewhere when Mr. Rosetti, who has changed his tune with respect to immigration, decries, "'That's no way to treat decent folks! . . . And what's more, these here girls have rights. They're American citizens!' he added angrily, jabbing the air with his cane" (273). As the proverbial icing on the cake, Álvarez speaks to her readers directly in a letter in lieu of an epilogue or afterword. Further explaining the issue of border crossing and immigration enforcement, she shares, "To keep out these migrants, a wall is being built between Mexico and the United States. National troops have been sent down to patrol the border. We are treating these neighbor countries and migrant helpers as if they were our worst enemies" (321). She describes the adverse effects of raids on the children of both migrant families and those of American farmers.

Like the other writers who depict themes of migration and its impact on families, Álvarez focuses on the human element of the overarching debate. After all, she comments, "At the heart of any political issue there is a person who is not very different from us" (Álvarez 2009, 9). It is imperative that preadolescents come to understand the underlying similarities among us and the issues impacting our communities, especially at the impressionable stage of their formation during which they are inevitably hearing conflicting messages regarding undocumented immigration. Offering students a venue to become familiar with varied perspectives and experiences, as well as the commonalities that extend beyond specific communities, encourages empathy and prevents the perpetuation of fear-based hate through the simultaneous addition of exemplars of Latinx migrants and their families and a shift from the cognitive schema of autonomy to one of solidarity.

Ocotillos, Prickly Politics, and Desert Blood

Melinda Palacio similarly weaves depictions of the hazards of border crossing and overt criticism of state-sanctioned violence affecting all brown-skinned individuals in a suburb of Phoenix, Arizona, in *Ocotillo Dreams*. Isola, the novel's protagonist, condemns the hostility toward Chicanxs (and Latinxs more broadly) when she is caught up in the fictionalized rendition of the 1997 Chandler Roundup—officially known as Operation Restoration—despite being a monolingual English-speaking US citizen. The five days of the sweeps, though, function as a subtext to the broader arc of the novel, which entails Isola's reconciliation with her deceased activist mother and the resulting embracing of her identity as an empowered Chicana vis-à-vis her experiences as a victim of injustice and betrayal, as well as her involvement with victims of the violence and death wrought by transnational migration.

Palacio's text centers the experiences of a privileged young woman who has distanced herself from her Chicana / Mexicana heritage, which she only begins to accept as she engages in new experiences in the Arizonan desert, a geographic and social landscape that is completely foreign to her. Alternating between scenes in Isola's hometown of San Francisco and Chandler, where she must settle her mother's estate, the novel effectively develops the hostile political environment of the late 1990s during which the joint operation between local police and federal agencies took place. Describing this initiative as the latest in

208

a historical pattern of apprehending and repatriating migrants, a secondary character, for example, explains, "Years ago, she had seen la migra round up people. It's all about numbers, she remembered from the last time. The government got scared because they saw too many Mexicanos and then they started with their interrogations, their arrests. She had seen this happen more than once" (Palacio 2011, 140). Tracing the history of such operations further, Isola's attorney provides background for her client, who is baffled at such treatment:

> "It's nothing new. You haven't been around as long as I have. Eisenhower made up something called 'Operation Wetback' to remove 1.3 million illegals in less than a year, as if the word 'operation' made it OK to violate people's constitutional rights with blatant racial profiling. This time the city's been at it for five days and they're starting to feel a backlash from the public because they've made mistakes by detaining citizens like you." (151)

Palacio overtly depicts the manner in which this initiative has exceeded the typical hostility that community members had grown to expect because, "'The city of Chandler thought they needed to do their part to reduce the millions of illegals. They've picked up anyone with brown skin'" (150). Not only are "Mexican women and children at bus stops and Laundromats" (133) new targets of this type of sweep, the descriptions of the 1997 worksite raids underline the unique nature of the operation. Bill Davis, 15-year owner of Thornton Furniture, has obvious experience with paying off the INS officials during the usual raids that threaten his sixty (mostly Mexican) employees. He articulates, however, how these sweeps are an entirely different monster when Bob, the INS officer, refuses the bribe, declaring, "'It's not going down like that. We're working with City Hall, Mesa and Chandler Police. Sheriff [Arpaio]'s in charge of this one'" (130). Indeed, "[Davis] had never been invaded with so much manpower before. It was the first time the police and the city had worked together in immigration affairs. The Feds were unwilling to negotiate. Their hands hovered over their weapons" (131). When all is said and done, forty of Davis's workers have been taken away in three white vans; conspicuously, however, "They hadn't taken Lee and Tran, the Vietnamese brothers, nor the three white guys that stuck together like brothers, Spud, Doc, and Jimbo" (132). Clearly, then, the determining factor in apprehension during these sweeps is not the likelihood of individuals' undocumented status regardless of country of origin but their suspicious Mexican-like appearance.

Hence, Isola's darker skin and indigenous features initially make her of interest to "the men, policemen or Feds, [who] motioned for her to join them" (142). Stunned to discover in that very moment her lover Cruz's ultimate betrayal in robbing her deceased father's identity, "She was too choked up to hear the men yelling at her. They wanted her identification. She was too upset, both at Cruz and at these policemen, to answer" (143). Realizing she had left her wallet and phone at home, "'I don't have ID,' was all she managed. . . . Without further discussion, the officers shoved her in the back of a white van with half a dozen other people who seemed just as bewildered as she was" (143). Isola does not resist and finds herself "squeezed in with the others. Mexican like her. Undocumented or perhaps citizens like herself" (143–44). This critical moment is the first at which Isola describes any type of affiliation with a Mexican identity, yet she quickly thereafter expresses her incredulity at having been mistaken for an undocumented Mexican.

Up until this point, Isola's lack of *mexicanidad* starkly contrasts with that of the Mexicans with whom she interacts in Arizona and even her mother, whose primary allegiance has seemed for Isola to be to family members in Mexico or

marginalized Mexican migrants. Far removed from the experiences of these individuals in Arizona and Mexico, Isola is
unfamiliar with both the Spanish language and the issues
that are integral to Mexican migrants' daily lives. Trying to
communicate with Cruz when she first stumbles upon him
at her mother's house, "She struggled for the Spanish word.
She continued to scream a gibberish of English and Spanish
threats" (6). In a later conversation, she finds herself asking,
"'What's a mica?'" (13), later remembering, "'Oh, right.' Isola
hadn't heard the word mentioned in years, decades. The people her mother had taught often worried about getting a mica
for work" (13).

Isola's distance from her culture and family is evidently taken
as a personal affront to her mother, who despite being extremely
proud of her highly educated daughter questions, "'Since when
do you concern yourself with my affairs? You who study dead
white people'" (23). Perhaps indicative of Isola's awareness of
her practice of disidentification with Chicanx and Mexican cultural experiences, she later pronounces, "'I should've studied
Spanish instead of French Renaissance literature'" (34). Isola's
recognition of her disengagement from the matters of importance to her mother is perhaps the first step in her process of
adopting a Chicana activist identity, a process during which her
sentiments of betrayal and sadness give way to rage.

Infuriated by the circumstances of her detention, Isola lashes
out, questioning, "'What's with this city and the police arresting people for not committing a crime? I wasn't doing anything
but standing in my neighborhood?" (150). As she had previously
articulated, "And the last time she had checked, it wasn't a
crime to walk around your neighborhood without a wallet" (145).
It occurs to Isola, though, that the authorities are fully aware of
the illegality of their actions: "'Wait. I remember hearing the

cops talking about it. Their loud voices from the front of the van were muffled, but I heard them say something about casting a wide net, and that it didn't matter if they made mistakes'" (151). Astounded that the racial profiling of ethnic groups of bygone days has not disappeared, "'It's 1997,' Isola screeched. 'Didn't we learn anything from the Japanese internment camps? They can't do that!'" (150). Although her interest in social justice is motivated first by her romantic relationship with Cruz and later her personal situation as a wronged brown-skinned US citizen, Isola ultimately engages in a metamorphosis that compels her to act on behalf of certain migrants, mirroring the benevolent and passionate actions of her mother.

Isola's attorney brings attention to this transformation, implicitly commending her for wanting to help a fellow detainee, an undocumented woman whose US-born children were left behind when police apprehended her. "'You're just like your mother'" (150), Liz comments, although Isola would deny that such is true, particularly after learning more about the mysterious life of service Marina had insisted remain a secret. Cruz had explained, for example, "'No era coyote. She helped with English classes and jobs and many things.' He wanted to tell her about Marina's work with the Rescate Ángeles, but Marina had once asked him never to mention the group to her daughter. He had to respect her wishes" (8). Later elaborating on his first encounter with Isola's mother and her role within the "group that helps us when the coyotes abandon us in the desert" (34), Cruz explains, "'Doña Marina was working with Rescate Ángeles. She found me in the desert. I needed water and was lost, disoriented. I had tried to cross before, but got caught'" (34). Josefina, a friend and student of Marina's, would concur with the assessment of Marina's instrumental role in the fictional group based on the Border Angels: "'Your mother was la mera ángel de Rescate Ángeles, the leader'" (176). Rather than accepting the doting comments regarding her mother's generosity and commitment to those around her in pride, Isola struggles with her guilt regarding their estranged relationship and the resentment she had always harbored.

Through employment of chronological and spatial jumps, Palacio develops the basis of the tension between mother and daughter. A flashback to a 1993 scene in San Francisco, for instance, depicts the physical altercation that ensues after Isola demands from Marina early access to her father's inheritance. After considering the potential parallel between Isola's benevolence and that of her mother, the narrative voice later reflects upon the broader source of the protagonist's bitterness, for "Isola had always felt betrayed by her mother's commitments to her family in México and her political causes. It never had occurred to her that her mother showed her love by allowing her daughter a wide berth of independence, which often felt like indifference" (177). Afforded a great deal of lonely independence in her formative years,

> Isola remembered never eating grapes and protesting with her parents her entire childhood, but she had become completely disillusioned by her mother's activism in San Francisco and constant protesting and campaigning for Jerry Brown, a man whose political career never ended. The campaigning meant Isola had never gotten to do what she wanted. She was especially unhappy about the fact that her father had always been away, covering the lives of other people, other families, and other children for the *San Francisco Chronicle*. (48)

Compounding these early feelings of abandonment, Isola's project to sort through her mother's belongings results in additional emotional turmoil when more uncertainties surface rather than the clear answers about her mother's life that she hopes would provide a sense of resolution.

Despite the geographic and emotional distance between mother and daughter, Isola had maintained the illusion that she held a relatively accurate notion of her mother's commitments and experiences until her mother passes away from cancer, never having shared the news of the diagnosis with her despite monthly correspondence. Consequently, "She had come to the desert to find answers, closure, to understand her mother's choices. Now nothing made sense" (179). Certain that "her mother had been the one who had shape-shifted into another being" (19), Isola attempts to make sense of "[h]er mother's desert dealings, whether running a school or a safe house, [which] remained a mystery. Isola continued to feel like a stranger as she rummaged through her mother's secrets" (31). As she unravels some of the mysteries regarding her mother's romantic exploits with Cruz, promises of documents for a friend's nephew, political activism, and her illness, Isola undertakes her own process of shapeshifting.

Ironically, her relationship with the man romantically involved with her mother catalyzes Isola's transformation, which entails the development of her politicized Chicana identity. Rather than denying her heritage and opposing any association with anything with which her mother had engaged, "Here she was, literally walking in her mother's shoes, arrested in her mother's Keds" (152). Detained in her mother's community while wearing her mother's clothes and attempting to resolve issues with the common lover she met in her mother's home, Isola quite literally puts herself in her mother's shoes and begins to comprehend her mother's devotion to marginalized individuals in her community. Particularly after being unjustly criminalized for inhabiting a brown body in an environment hostile to all Latinxs (citizenship status and national origin aside), Isola decides, with the assistance of the reunited Rescate *Ángeles*, to help her young niece and nephew cross the border and present them with the opportunities that a life in the US could potentially offer. This willingness to assist stands in stark contrast to a younger Isola's reluctance, and even resentment, of sharing hand-me-downs with these very family members in Mexico.

The bond with her mother and, by extension, the blood relatives south of the border is reestablished and fortified in Isola's process of coming to terms with Marina's desert secrets. Attesting to the strength of even the thinnest of threads, the mother-daughter relationship, initially described as "[a]n invisible string from San Francisco to the desert, however fragile, was all they had needed" (2), ultimately adopts greater significance in Isola's life and choices. Nevertheless, her experience with detention as a consequence of her apparent *mexicanidad* is ultimately the primary factor that compels Isola to concern herself with others of Mexican descent, particularly those who are targets of discrimination and injustice and, in contrast to Cruz, are honest, hard-working individuals with hopes of a better life. Cruz, a self-serving and deceitful ex-lover who happens to be undocumented, and his release, juxtaposed with Isola's detention, exemplify the problematic irony of the immigration system. Even as he expresses regret at having left Isola after showing his own falsified documents, he justifies his actions: "He didn't think the police would be so cold as to arrest the half-gringa-U.S. citizen and let the mojado go free. Qué ironía había en los Estados Unidos" (170). Perhaps an extra layer of irony surfaces in Cruz's insinuated death, with the supposition being that he is the very migrant whom Isola's niece and nephew discovered next to an ocotillo tree with blood-red blooms.

Desert Transformations

Josefina López's theatrical work, *Detained in the Desert*, premiered at CASA 0101 in Boyle Heights, California, in October

2010, under the direction of Hector Rodriguez, less than six months after Arizona SB 1070 was passed. Outraged by the approval of this legislation, studies on hate crimes against Latinxs, and the increase of media hate speech from 2006 to 2010, López offers a hard-hitting yet entertaining condemnation of the criminalization of brown bodies as well as the hateful extremist discourse that perpetuates and justifies this criminalization. Set in Arizona in summer 2010, the play depicts a political ambience of racial profiling and anti-immigrant sentiment uncannily similar to that of Palacio's *Ocotillo Dreams*, implying a continuation of the very practices and philosophies that were decried over a decade before in the wake of the 1997 Chandler Roundup.

The theatrical work incorporates the same ironic hypocrisy of contemporary immigration legislation as well as a comparable metamorphosis in its Chicana protagonist. The underlying message, though, is one of compassion and hope in our capacity to recognize the humanity of all individuals, regardless of country of origin. "I look at this human issue, not the political issue. . . . [I]t's somebody who is living it in their skin and suffering because of laws that are unjust" (2013), López explains. Rather than inspiring anger, then, López hopes "to forge characters to feel our pain so that we can get back to our humanity" (López in Mendoza 2019, 16). Scenes that illustrate the harsh desert conditions incorporate the playwright's viewing of graphic photos of bodies found in the desert as well as her haunting visit to the Holtville, Arizona, cemetery in which over 600 unidentified migrants are buried. She elaborates, "When a human being dies out in the desert, it's the death of all of us. We are connected to that person even if we didn't know them. . . . Those graphic images were imprinted in . . . my mind" (López 2012).

Having lived in the United States without papers for thirteen years, López undoubtedly empathizes with the plight of migrants, noting in particular, "People who are undocumented are the voiceless, powerless. . . . [The media sources . . . vilify Latino immigrants and . . . someone needs to tell the truth" (2012). Hence, she develops an attack on the subjective application of policy as well as the spread of hate through uniting a conservative talk-radio host and a racially profiled Chicana in the Arizona desert, who come to recognize both their own commonalities and those that they share with the tens of thousands of migrants who have suffered and/or died in the borderlands.

The production is rather minimalist in terms of the stage design, which incorporates a symbolic, rather than literal, creation (T. López in Huerta et al. 2011, 175) of a variety of locations including the KRZT 1070 radio station booth, a tent in the desert, a desert road, the front seat of a car, a detention center interrogation room, a water station, and an SUV. The lack of major set pieces or props facilitates swift transitions from one location to the next, an important feature of *cineteatro*, the term coined by López to describe theatrical works like this one that incorporate cinematic elements and structures like framing and the use of jump cuts between scenes. As Jorge Huerta notes, the cinematic nature of this play "calls for fast, efficient transitions, designed to keep the momentum going, to keep the tension building" (2011, 178). Along with the jump cuts, the use of contrasts and fading in the lighting design enhance the convergence and divergence of the primary characters' parallel storylines as they unfold (Jacobs 2016, 284).

The production opens with a dark stage and various audio clips playing, including some from Spanish language radio, to mimic a radio dial that ultimately lands on KRZT 1070. As lights fade in, Lou Becker, host of a conservative talk radio program, sits in the booth and addresses his listeners. "Welcome to Take Back America. My fellow Arizonans I am so proud of us for finally taking the correct measures to keep all the illegals out" (López 2011, 22). The host, Lou Becker, is not so subtly modeled on conservative host Lou Dobbs. Defending his position on SB 1070 and the immigration debate, he explains, "People call us racists, but we just really love this country. I'm a patriot, not a racist" (22). He continues, utilizing racially derogatory terminology and descriptions in his claim that "[t]his is not about racism or racial profiling. We are just sick of paying for all those illegals that come to our country and state to live and breed like cockroaches" (22). The production utilizes voice-over for the radio callers, enhancing the audience's role as "an active imaginative participant in the world of the play . . . because we could draw on our personal archives and differently envision who these callers might be" (T. López in Huerta et al. 2011, 175). Moreover, the audience members unwittingly become listeners of the English-language hate-talk radio.

Exemplifying the fear-mongering and misguided logic of conservative media outlets, the host—himself an immigrant from Scotland who met his Mexican American wife in Canada—is later kidnapped by the siblings of a young Latino who is murdered in a hate-based attack. Casting the blame on Lou, the unnamed "medium figure" asks the simple yet powerful question, "Why do you spread so much hate?" (López 2011, 36). Reiterating this notion, the "tall figure" later argues, "Your hate spreads hate. . . . [Y]ou inspired those teenagers and gave them the words and the justification to kill my brother!" (41). This is the racist rhetoric that López hopes to counteract in instilling a sense of empathy, or at least awareness, in the audience through toying with the concept of whether those who spread hate possess the capacity to empathize.

Less than twenty-four hours before his kidnapping, Lou had argued with Ernesto Martinez, the founder of the fictional Angels of the Border (based on Enrique Morones, founder of Border Angels), about whether the organization's placement of water in the desert encourages migration. Focusing on the migrants' humanity, Ernesto responds, "No human being would cross the border and risk their life just to get my water. Things have to be dire and desperate for someone to decide to cross the border. Everyday [*sic*] one person dies crossing that border" (24). As fellow humans, Ernesto and his group are committed to preventing the death and suffering of those who cross.

Ironically, Ernesto is the one who discovers Lou after the kidnappers release him in the harsh and disorienting desert. Thanks to Ernesto's arrival to restock water stations, Lou will survive. Moreover, his traumatic experiences in the desert result in a transformation of opinions and implicit awareness of his wrongdoing. Such an evolution is manifest even in Lou's self-correction and selection of more neutral descriptive terms: "Ten illegal aliens. . . . Ten migrants were caught at the . . . " (63), he begins, opting to shift gears. Rather than spewing the rhetoric typical of his radio program, Lou shares, "Ah . . . I'm going to deviate today from my normal show. . . . You know I don't think I've ever shared with you the real reasons why I love this country. . . . I am so lucky that this great country is truly the land of opportunity where a poor boy from Scotland with lots of hopes and dreams can end up having his own radio show and living well reaping all the benefits of this great country. . . . I love this country" (63).

Becker plays Woody Guthrie's "This Land is Your Land," evoking the social commentary of this 1940 critical response to Irving Berlin's "God Bless America," and walks out, stunning his colleagues. Quick to recover the station's mission,

Carl Dunlop jumps in as the new host, immediately restoring the hateful oratory: "When are these illegals gonna get it. We don't want you in our state, and we will do whatever it takes to exter—I mean expatriate—or whatever—send you back to your country" (64). Beyond labeling the migrants as "illegals," Carl's accidental slip of "exter—," suggestive of "exterminate," further reveals the degree of anti-immigrant sentiment evident among some conservative Arizonans.

Parallel to Lou's kidnapping is the development of Sandi's experience with racial profiling by Arizona police. Linking the two planes of the play at various points throughout, López's principal attack on the hypocrisy of the policies emerges as the Chicana and her light-skinned Canadian boyfriend are stopped while driving near the US-Mexico border as they return to San Diego from Texas. Like Isola in *Ocotillo Dreams*, Sandi pursues an advanced degree (in this case, an English MA as a scholarship recipient) in a field seemingly distant from her personal or familial roots. Preferring to utilize an Anglicized name, Sandi ultimately undergoes an identity transformation as a result of her experiences in the racially contentious environment in Arizona, much like Isola does in Palacio's novel.

Initially identifying herself as "not a typical Latina like the other girls you might have met in college" (28), Sandi is emotionally depleted from the consistent feeling that she must prove her "Americanness." Arguing with her boyfriend, she expresses, "No, Matt, you will never know what it's like to be me. You don't have dark skin. Nobody ever questions your right to exist or succeed. You have no clue how hard it is to be an American when you look like me!" (43). Indeed, based solely on appearances, the police officer questions Sandi and Matt, and his assumptions about the nature of their relationship and the perceived threat that Sandi poses are clear. López's use of dramatic irony—at this point the audience is aware that the boyfriend is, in fact, an undocumented Canadian—effectively highlights the subjective enforcement of the policy that enables officers to request that individuals produce documentation of legal status.

Despite the fact that Sandi is a citizen, the officer directs his questions to the undocumented Canadian: "So what are you doing here so close the border?" (31), quickly following up with "Let me see her documents" (31) because, "Son, it is a crime to transport an illegal alien in exchange for sexual favors" (32). The stereotyping of Sandi is doubly denigrating in projecting a status of illegality as well as sexual impropriety and is particularly infuriating given the irony of the situation. In justifying his request, the policeman states, "You are six miles away from the border and you look—I mean . . . you have given me reason to suspect your status—" (32). The reason for suspicion is undoubtedly Sandi's Mexican-like appearance and, as in the case of *Ocotillo Dreams*, only the brown bodies in the borderlands evidently warrant apprehension, detention, and expatriation, and are threatening despite citizenship status. What ensues once Sandi refuses to show her California ID or other documents results in a complex process of conflict and cultural disidentification along the lines of what Cuban American scholar José Esteban Muñoz (1999) describes in his work on this topic.

Shouting her justification for not producing documents and pointedly signaling the officer's lack of objectivity, she exclaims, "No! I don't have a 'Greencard' or any documents with me because I am a U.S. citizen, and I don't need to carry any!" (32). Furthermore, she insists, "No! I won't step out of the car. Why don't you ask him for his documents? How do you know he's not an 'illegal Canadian alien'?" (33). Sandi then shifts strategies to describe herself in opposition to the migrants the officer intends to apprehend. She argues, "I'm speaking to you in English. Do you notice I don't have an accent, and I'm not afraid of you? Doesn't that tip you off that I am an over-entitled American who went to college and is exercising her right to civil disobedience?" (33). Upon her arrival at the detention center, Sandi continues to engage in explicit disidentification with Mexican migrants, explaining, "But I'm a U.S. citizen! I don't belong here. I'm not like *these people*" (39, emphasis mine). While Sandi continues to lament the injustice of the law that permits racial profiling, it is telling that she should position herself in opposition to the migrants who presumably should, or deserve to, be detained. Only after what appears to be a hallucinatory reunion, while in the detention center, with Milagros, a woman from her past, does Sandi explore the roots of her conflict and better comprehend her discomfort with her cultural identity.

Hearing Milagros' fears about her US-born children's well-being after being taken from them by authorities, Sandi seeks to console her, and in the conversations that ensue a seemingly coincidental reunion of sorts takes place. The young women reflect on their common experiences of alienation as children in southern California, and Sandi begins to retrieve memories that have continued to haunt her. "White kids would call us names" (51), she recalls, "'Beaners' and 'Wetbacks' . . . It was awful" (51). She elaborates, "At my school in the valley, I was one of a few Latino children. . . . There was only one other Mexican girl in my class. Milagros . . . " (51–52). Identifying the crucial moment of her childhood during which Sandi had opted to associate with the dominant group, she explains further. "But all these White kids . . . well, I was scared. I couldn't stand up to all of them, and I was afraid they would hurt me. . . . So I started calling her a 'Beaner,' too, and joined in the name calling" (52). Still harboring shame about her actions, she articulates the benefit of acting out of self-interest or self-preservation: "After that day, I was no longer seen as one of them. I was accepted, and nobody ever called me a 'Beaner' or a 'Wetback.' I stopped speaking Spanish and stopped calling myself Sandra and started calling myself 'Sandi.' As Sandi, I would fit in better" (52). After her evidently repressed memories surface, Sandi further empathizes with the migrants from whom she had previously disassociated herself when she finds herself stranded in the desert.

Having waited too long to produce documents, she is forced to board a southbound bus packed with migrants, which mysteriously crashes en route to the border. Alone, scared, and dehydrated in the desert, Sandi stumbles across Lou, with whom she is later rescued by Ernesto. Her political consciousness raised, Sandi undertakes an activist role as a Chicana who more fully embraces her culture, evident through her adoption of her given name, Sandra Chávez, as well as her changed opinion about Rancheras. Committed to joining the group to deliver water to migrants as well as to speak out openly about the spread of hate on behalf of all individuals affected, she and Ernesto drive off into the sunset, singing a Ranchera song "at the top of their lungs" (65), as the lights fade out. The audience is left to suppose that this experience in the Arizona desert marks the beginning of a new chapter in Sandi/Sandra's life and to consider the impact of political policy at the level of each individual and the communities to which they belong.

Following the socially engaged tradition of agit-prop theater, *Detained in the Desert* perhaps better fits within what Diana Taylor terms "trauma-driven performance[35] [that] highlights not only what trauma is (etymologically a blow or wound) but also what trauma does, how it affects entire communities and mobilizes demands for social justice" (2006, 1675). López's work enables the audience to bear witness to individual and collective traumas through dramatization of the repercussions of hateful rhetoric and discriminatory policies that violate rights and, by doing so, bears some resemblance to testimonial literature.

In a similar vein, the novels included in this chapter align with Caminero-Santangelo's notion of "post-Gatekeeper fiction" as a continuation of the Latin American *testimonio* turned inward to reflect on US immigration and border policies domestically. Significantly, such texts are "intended to go beyond bearing witness—beyond mere testimony—to have real world impacts" (Caminero-Santangelo 2016, 23). In addition to granting migrants a voice within narrative history, and rehumanizing the image of an often demeaned and demonized figure of the undocumented border crosser, they bear fictionalized witness to sociopolitical realities of physical, psychological, sociocultural, legal, and structural violence. Through the use of narrative strategies to increase the empathic power of storytelling, they exemplify the manner in which the personal is political (and vice versa), particularly for families of transnational migration, and compel readers to pursue ways to effect change in their own spheres of influence.

CHAPTER 6

Making the Invisible Trauma Visible through *Testimonios*, Ethnographies, and Memoirs

L atina writers have also recuperated the voices of Mexican and Central American migrants in recent texts within various life-writing genres that condemn the global systems and power inequities that perpetuate transnational migration, indicting these broader structures as the root cause of the variety of traumatic experiences that migrants and their families face on an individual and more intimate level.[36] Keen has described fiction as a particularly effective forum for evoking empathy among readers because the paratextual label of "fiction" alone potentially "releases the readers to make empathetic connections without fear that they will be required to reciprocate, make commitments, or act in the real world" (2007, 88–89; 2016, 15). However, she more recently notes the potential for certain life-writing genres like testimonials, memoirs, and biographies that "exist right on the borders of their sister genres of fiction" to similarly employ effective strategies for narrative empathy (Keen 2016, 15). With their focus on the "perspectives of human agents," these subgenres "may attract (or form) higher-empathy readers than dryer, more factual and overtly argumentative or analytical forms of nonfiction" (Keen 2016, 16).

Moreover, she argues that authors will strategically employ empathic narrative techniques when their objective is to raise awareness or create change, particularly in texts related to human rights (Keen 2016, 20). In this context, the employment of a combination of ambassadorial strategic empathy, which fosters empathy for a specific marginalized group and related injustices, and broadcast strategic empathy, which invokes a sense of connectedness and solidarity through recognition of universal experiences, may be the most effective for breaking down imagined barriers between groups. I argue, then, that *La Migra me hizo los mandados* by Alicia Alarcón, *Enrique's Journey: The Story of a Boy's Dangerous Odyssey to Reunite with His Mother* by Sonia Nazario, and *In the Country We Love: My Family Divided* by Diane Guerrero and Michelle Burford effectively facilitate a more comprehensive understanding of the experiences of families of Latinx migration largely by appealing to readers' sensibilities about the general dignity and humanity of all people, the right to live in safe and secure conditions, and the preservation of the family unit and adequate parent-child relationships for the sake of children's well-being. Furthermore, by exposing readers to nonfiction accounts that explain the diverse motivations for migration and the compounded physical and psychological traumas that Latinx migrants and their family members sustain as a result, these life-writing texts connect abstract ideas and phenomena with real people whose lives have been profoundly impacted by US intervention in Latin America, US demand for labor, and/or US policies and practices related to immigration and naturalization, detention, and deportation.

As with the fictional texts, these individuals' stories will enhance readers' collections of cognitive exemplars of Latinx individuals affected by transnational migration, perhaps even more effectively because of readers' awareness that the accounts capture authentic circumstances and experiences. They may also contribute to a concomitant shift of cognitive schemas from the assumption of migrants' autonomy and immutability to one that centers their situatedness and malleability by highlighting the ways that broader contexts shape individuals' actions. Furthermore, by underlining commonalities of the human experience, they may spur a parallel shift from atomism to solidarity. These changes may potentially result in more compassion and understanding on a personal level and translate into pro-social actions to change or eliminate detrimental immigration policies and practices.

Ethnographic Exposés of the Violence Inherent in Transnational Separation

Descriptions of various reasons that motivated individuals' migration and the graphic reality of corporeal harm during the trek northward take center stage within journalist Alicia Alarcón's *La Migra me hizo los mandados*. This collection of testimonies presents the presumably autobiographic immigration stories of Alarcón's Radio Única audience in Southern California. Although the vignettes expose the tremendous violence involved during the journey across the border, the radio listeners who contributed their stories have come to and stayed in the United States, suggesting that the horrors they faced while crossing the border without documents may have been worth it for the individual women who headed north in search of a better life without a spouse to meet them on the other side, and for those men and women who found themselves pushed out of their home countries because of the languishing economy or social violence.

One contributor to the collection, Teresa, recognizes that the only possibility for her to pay for higher education and help the family financially is to join her mother in the United States. As she describes in "Unos nachos para llevar":

> El dinero que mandaba mi mamá desde Los [Á]ngeles alcanzaba cada vez menos para sostenerme en la escuela. Menos pensar en entrar a la universidad. La solución era reunirme con ella, estudiar inglés y trabajar. Así le podríamos ayudar a mi abuelo a salir de sus deudas. (A. Alarcón 2002, 33)

Following in the footsteps of her mother, who had left the family behind in order to support them, Teresa heads north.

Seemingly more concerned with the distance from her spouse than with the issue of money, another woman, Fabiola, explains that she opted to accompany her husband across the border, particularly since, "Yo no sería como ellas, una esposa sometida a la espera" (87). Thus begins their honeymoon in the borderlands, an experience that is nothing like what television and the migrants who have returned home to her town have suggested. Perhaps it is wise that Fabiola undertake this journey, if nothing else, to keep tabs on her new husband. For, as another migrant, Iginia, describes, she married and had three children. "Éramos felices hasta que un día se le metió la loquera de viajar a los Estados Unidos. Hice lo imposible para sacarle esa idea de la cabeza. Todo fue inútil. Me dejó sola con mis hijos" (118–19). Aside from the loneliness and heartbreak of separation, "Al principio me mandaba dinero pero de repente no supe más de él" (119). Consequently, she began to work outside the home to provide for her children who, once grown, crossed the border themselves and found their father married to another woman.

She explains further that her children "pidieron que me fuera con ellos a Estados Unidos. Al principio me negué. Pero el amor por ellos fue más grande que mis miedos y mis angustias" (119). With reason, she harbored many fears, for the journey presents a multitude of risks, but she did ultimately opt to embark on the trip north to join her children.

While the Border Patrol certainly functions as one obstacle to migrants, a bigger threat rests in the physical demands of the journey and the very real possibility of violence and, predominantly in the case of women, rape. As opposed to the passing mention of rape in the fictional works, several testimonies within Alarcón's text explicitly depict scenes of sexual violence toward women. Interestingly enough, though, these are largely featured in the stories shared by men, not women. In "Vi cómo la violaban," for example, Henry describes the rape of two sisters with whom he travels:

> La más grande, desnuda, de espaldas sobre la cama, con los ojos abiertos, gemía quedo. La sábana entre las piernas estaba llena de sangre. Sentía que las sienes me iban a explotar. Unos ojos me miraban suplicantes. Pedían auxilio. Era la más chica, la del círculo de luna oscura en el pómulo derecho. Estaba en el suelo como si estuviera gateando, con su ropa totalmente rasgada, estaba la niña de Colombia. Uno de los mexicanos la sujetaba por los cabellos con el pene adentro de su boca mientras que el otro la sujetaba por la cintura violándola por detrás. Al verme, se levantaron furiosos . . . (55)

Henry feels powerless to stop the assault since these same Mexican coyotes hold his future in their hands. Even though Henry does nothing to assist the sisters, the coyotes later treat him more severely, angry that he has interrupted and simply witnessed their sexual predation. Similarly, José Luis describes "el infierno" (133) once he and the other migrants have crossed the border. He incorrectly assumed that dangers were behind them, particularly after one woman from their party was swept to her death while attempting to cross the river. In the room at the Motel 6, three of the coyotes convened and, "Mientras uno me vigilaba, los otros violaban a las muchachas. Eso lo hicieron varias veces. Pensé en la muchacha de Nicaragua. Tal vez fue mejor que se la llevara el río" (133). José Luis notes the effects on the poor girls yet, like Henry, does nothing to stop the violence. "Cuando salimos, las muchachas parecían haber envejecido diez años. Caminaban lento, las piernas apretadas, la cabeza agachada. La mirada no era la misma" (133). Somehow, drowning pales in comparison to suffering the violence and indignity of rape, and these vignettes, in particular, illustrate that both are very real risks that border crossing poses to women. The graphic nature of the scenes forces readers to recognize this, and the narrative voice thereby establishes a certain degree of empathy for the victims without means to rectify or prevent the situation.

In capturing sometimes horrific autobiographical experiences in this collection of testimonies, Alarcón stirs the reader to action or, at the very least, to awareness. As it is written in Spanish, one might presume that the intent is to warn fellow migrants of the potential suffering and danger that await them. Alternatively, the intention may be to honor and inscribe those experiences within History or to provide something with which other readers with similar experiences could identify. Then again, the original publication in Spanish may have been geared toward Spanish-speaking or bilingual (i.e., Chicanx, Latinx, Hispanx) individuals living in the US, in hopes that the blunt descriptions of contemporary migrant realities will ultimately lead to progress toward social change. The subsequent publication of this collection in English certainly allowed for a broader readership to gain exposure to a sampling of circumstances pushing men and women to cross the border and the perils they encounter during the journey. While the *testimonios* largely do not reflect the changing gender or generational dynamics within the family and community as a result of migration, the stylistically austere and jarring articulation of actual trials and tragedies endured compel the reader to consider the personal impact of migration and the forces that led to the individuals' risky journeys to make it to the US.

Sonia Nazario provides a powerful journalistic account that deals with the personal impact of, as well as the underlying forces behind, transnational migration in *Enrique's Journey: The Story of a Boy's Dangerous Odyssey to Reunite with His Mother*. A projects reporter for the *Los Angeles Times*, Nazario extends her Pulitzer-Prize winning newspaper series into this nonfictional text, which narrates the astounding danger and hardship that young Enrique faces as he attempts a journey alone from Tegucigalpa, Honduras, to the United States in 2000, where he hopes to reunite with the mother whom he last saw eleven years earlier, when he was just five years old. One example of the then estimated 48,000 immigrant children annually who seek reunification with parents north of the border (Nazario 2006, 5), Enrique becomes a poster child for transnational migration for Nazario's readers, who necessarily come to identify with his fear, faith, and will while accompanying him on his harrowing journey northward.

Based upon interviews with a number of individuals and agencies and the author's own journey to retrace Enrique's steps, the text effectively returns a level of humanity to migrants like Enrique. Furthermore, the work's prologue illustrates that transnational migration and motherhood hit quite close to home for the author, whose passing conversation with her housekeeper ultimately compels her to explore a mother's

motivation for leaving her children behind—often for years—
and the effects of such a decision on the family as a whole. These
families are not an abstract conceptualization to facilitate the
discussion of more theoretical issues of migration; rather, this
housekeeper, María del Carmen Ferrez, is an authentic human
being with whom the author interacts regularly, a woman who
for years has harbored a secret about the four children she left
behind in Guatemala twelve years before to provide for them as
a single mother.

A year after the conversation, Carmen's son, Minor, decided
to undertake the journey through Guatemala and Mexico and,
miraculously, surprised his mother at her doorstep. After discussing the migratory experience with Minor, Nazario decided
to investigate the phenomenon further. She explains her motivation in narrating the tale of one migrant child: "Perhaps by looking at one immigrant—his strengths, his courage, his flaws—his
humanity might help illuminate what too often has been a black-
and-white discussion" (xiv) regarding illegal immigration. And
so began her search for a typical adolescent Central American
boy who had traveled on the trains, ultimately crossing the
US-Mexico border, in search of his mother.

In following Enrique's journey, the author crossed thirteen
Mexican states and traveled over 1,600 miles, half of which was
traversed atop trains. These trains, Carmen's son had previously explained, present the biggest danger to migrants. "He'd
told me about the gangsters who rule the train tops, the bandits
along the tracks, the Mexican police who patrol the train stations and rape and rob, about the dangers of losing a leg getting
onto and off of moving trains" (xv). Corroborating this obser-
vation, a priest at a migrant shelter in Chiapas whom Nazario
interviews asserts, "Arrayed against them is la migra, along
with crooked police, street gangsters, and bandits. They wage

. . . la guerra sin nombre, the war with no name" (68). Yet, the young migrants are determined to face all these dangers in the blind faith and hope that they will find their mothers.

For, "In their absence, these mothers become larger than life. Although in the United States the women struggle to pay rent and eat, in the imaginations of their children back home they become deliverance itself, the answer to every problem. Finding them becomes the quest for the Holy Grail" (7), Nazario explains. Accordingly, the children put aside whatever feelings of abandonment or resentment they have experienced in their mothers' absence to undertake the perilous journey northward to provide further financial support for their extended family, or simply for the purposes of reunification. In many cases, Nazario observes, a child or adolescent's decision to head north is not approved of by the parents in the United States or the caretakers in the home country.

This is the case for the author's housekeeper, who "left for the United States out of love. She hoped she could provide her children an escape from their grinding poverty, a chance to attend school beyond the sixth grade" (x), and she acknowledges the sacrifices that ensued. Nevertheless, she describes her resistance to bringing her children to the United States above and beyond her inability to save enough money for a smuggler to bring them. "Besides," Nazario writes, "she refuses to subject her children to the dangerous journey. During her own 1985 trek north, Nazario's housekeeper, Carmen, was robbed by her smuggler, who left her without food for three days. Her daughters, she fears, will get raped along the way" (xi). This fear is not without basis, as "A 1997 University of Houston study of U.S. Immigration and Naturalization Service detainees in Texas shows that nearly one in six says she was sexually assaulted" (98).

Similarly, Enrique's mother, Lourdes, "does consider hiring a smuggler to bring the children but fears the danger. The coyotes, as they are called, are often alcoholics or drug addicts. Usually, a chain of smugglers is used to make the trip. Children are passed from one stranger to another. Sometimes the smugglers abandon their charges" (21). Likely capturing the sentiment of most transnational mothers, Lourdes questions, "'Do I want to have them with me so badly . . . that I'm willing to risk their losing their lives?'" (23). Moreover, both Carmen and Lourdes express their concern at bringing children into their "poor, drug- and crime-infested" (xi) neighborhoods. It is clear, then, that these transnational mothers always bear in mind the well-being of their children, even if that means imposing an almost insurmountable distance between them for years and even decades at a time, disappointing hopes for family reunification and ultimately hindering any chances of knowing one another intimately.

Enrique, for example, had fantasized about his mother's return for the holidays year after year. "Christmas arrives, and he waits by the door. She does not come. Every year, she promises. Each year, he is disappointed. Confusion finally grows into anger" (19), and in his case drug addiction and outright rebellion against his caretakers in Honduras. At age 16, he decides to take matters into his own hands, leaving his home with $57, Lourdes's phone number written on a scrap of paper and in the waistband of his pants, a t-shirt, cap, gloves, toothbrush, and toothpaste, to face "la guerra sin nombre" (68). On his eighth attempt, Enrique finds his mother. Does the reunion ultimately fulfill every expectation? Not exactly. As Nazario describes:

> Children like Enrique dream of finding their mothers and living happily ever after. For weeks, perhaps months, these children and their mothers cling to romanticized notions of how they should

> feel toward each other. Then reality intrudes. The children show resentment because they were left behind. They remember broken promises to return. . . . Some are surprised to discover entire new families in the United States. . . . Jealousies grow. . . . The mothers, for their part, demand respect for their sacrifice: leaving their children for the children's sake. . . . They think their children are ungrateful and bristle at the independence they show—the same independence that helped the children survive their journeys north. In time, mothers and children discover they hardly know each other. (191)

Strong feelings of abandonment and bitterness resurface after the treacherous journey for family reunification.

By revealing the experiences and emotional turmoil of actual individuals impacted by transnational migration, Nazario effectively paints a human portrait of this global phenomenon that is often discussed with objectivity, indifference, or little to no compassion for those parents whose desperation drives them to leave their children to seek undocumented entry into the United States, and for those unaccompanied minors who likewise find themselves motivated to embark on the extremely dangerous trek across various borders. In describing the multitude of dangers, Nazario undoubtedly portrays the effects of transnational migration in a negative light. Nonetheless, she is compassionate toward the individuals whose socioeconomic circumstances led them to undertake this journey. One may suggest that the underlying tone of hope and redemption in her text mitigates the negativity of circumstances that provoke migration and sustain the violence inherent in the movement of people across borders and helps her readership to appreciate and acknowledge these migrants' contribution to our society. "The single mothers who are coming to this country, and the children who follow them, are changing the face of immigration to the United States," Nazario declares. Moreover:

Each year, the number of women and children who immigrate to the United States grows. They become our neighbors, children in our schools, workers in our homes. As they become a greater part of the fabric of the United States, their troubles and triumphs will be a part of this country's future. For Americans overall, this book should shed some light on this part of our society. (xxv)

Indeed, *Enrique's Journey* tugs at the readers' heartstrings and encourages them to consider the issue of migration on a more human level. The text also helps to develop an awareness of how US immigration and labor systems are complicit in leading to the separation of transnational families through laws and policies that preclude the legal migration of most migrants and—given the dangers and cost of crossing the border—inevitably turn many anticipated temporary separations into permanent ones. As is evident in *Enrique's Journey*, the psychological impact, especially on the children left behind, is so devastating that their desperation may drive them to gang involvement and addiction issues or may motivate them to face unspeakable dangers on the journey northward in hopes of family reunification. Nevertheless, even if, in the best of circumstances, parent and child manage to reunite, the trauma of separation and loss is extremely difficult to overcome.

Left Behind in the US and Seeking a Sense of Home and Hope

Diane Guerrero and Michelle Burford similarly engage with the profound trauma of separation and loss in *In the Country We Love: My Family Divided*. In her memoir, the actress Guerrero discloses her painful experiences as a US-citizen child left behind when both her parents were deported to Colombia and, without the intervention of ICE or Child Protective Services, she was essentially left to fend for herself. Like *Enrique's Journey*, this text uses the details of one family's heart-wrenching story of being ripped apart to open up a dialogue about the realities and glaring problems of broader systems and institutions that subject Latinx immigrants and their loved ones to harm, regardless of their immigration status.

The memoir opens in dramatic, almost cinematic, fashion, immediately directing attention to what would prove to be a critical juncture in Guerrero's life and around which the entire text is focalized. "One moment—that's all it takes for your entire world to split apart. For me, that moment came when I was fourteen. I returned home from school to discover that my hardworking immigrant parents had been taken away. In one irreversible instant—in the space of a single breath—life as I'd known it was forever altered" (Guerrero and Burford 2017, 1–2), she explains. Guerrero's narrative then recounts and reflects on the family's history that led to that point before returning to a more detailed description of this particular memory of trauma(s) and its torrent of negative repercussions that would change the trajectory of Guerrero's life.

After publishing a 2014 op-ed in which she "outed" herself as the daughter of undocumented immigrants who were deported when she was just fourteen, she somewhat reluctantly embraced the opportunity to reveal more of her story. Aside from the personally therapeutic potential of processing the traumas through writing, Guerrero explains that her primary reasons for sharing a more comprehensive version of her story are twofold. First, she writes "[b]ecause on that afternoon when I came home to an empty house, I felt like the only child who'd ever dealt with something so overwhelming. And in the agonizing years that followed, it would've meant everything for me to know that someone, somewhere had survived what I was going through" (2). In the fashion of bounded strategic empathy, she strives to create and strengthen a connection with readers with a shared experience of family separation due to detention and deportation. "For the thousands of nameless children who feel as forgotten as I did—this memoir is my gift to you. It's as much for your healing as it is for my own" (2), she asserts.

Second, engaging in strategic ambassadorial empathy, Guerrero shares her story with a broader audience unfamiliar with the phenomenon of immigration-related family separation to personalize and humanize it and dispel misconceptions about the experiences of Latinx migrants and their family members. Furthermore, she reveals the harsh and unjust realities of immigration policies and practices and calls upon our shared values and humanity to demand change to protect others from enduring the same hardship. "Behind every one of the headlines, there is a family. A mother and father. An innocent child. A real-life story that's both deeply painful and rarely told" (3), she notes. Hers is one such story. Leveraging her celebrity, she perhaps even more effectively manages to subvert or unsettle the broader readership's preconceived notions with regard to immigrant experiences.

As with the other texts analyzed in *Ripped Apart*, Guerrero's memoir reveals the intertwined layers of physical, psychological, sociocultural, and legal / structural violence[37] with which she and her family members have had to contend throughout their lives, which "revolved around my parents' quest for citizenship" (28). Through inclusion of personal photos to open each chapter and the use of a casual and conversational style, she narrows the narrative distance between author and reader and paints a compelling picture of how her life, which to outsiders would be perceived as typically all-American, was completely upended. In sharing recollections of critical moments and consequent adaptations to ever-changing circumstances through her junior high, high school, and college years and beyond, Guerrero adopts a confessional tone to describe her maelstrom of emotions while dealing with the trauma of loss and separation, attempts at reconciliation with her mother, and struggles with addiction and self-harm. A common thread that runs throughout her reflections is the combination of chronic and deep-seated fear, guilt, shame, and anger that, as a whole, add another layer of insidious trauma.

"*Deported*. Long before I fully understood what that word meant, I'd learned to dread it" (2), Guerrero recalls. "With every ring of my family's doorbell, with every police car passing on the street, a horrifying possibility hung in the air: My parents might one day be sent back to Colombia. That fear permeated every part of my childhood" (2). As a seven-year-old, Guerrero intervenes and threatens to call the police during a heated altercation between her parents about her half-brother. "'Go ahead and call the cops,' [her mother] whispered, her voice raspy from the yelling. She paused. 'Then they can come and send us all back to Colombia'" (23). As Guerrero does not grasp the consequences, her mother clarifies, "'I mean they'll deport us, Diane,' she said. 'They'll take us all away from you'" (23). She had already known that her parents were undocumented, but it was not until this particular moment that Guerrero understood what the implications of their immigration status could be.

Enduring a pervasive fear while living in the shadows, even as a US citizen herself, she feelingly describes her reaction when she calls home and nobody answers:

> One of my parents was always home by this time. Always. And neither of them had mentioned having plans. *Where could they be?* With my hands trembling, I searched my pockets for a second quarter. Empty. . . . *Ring. Ring. Ring. Ring.* Again—no answer. . . . *Let them be home*, I prayed with every step. *God, please—let them*

be there. . . . I slid [the key] into the dead bolt, held my breath, and tried to brace myself for what I'd find beyond that door. I still can't believe what I found. (8–9)

Indeed, her fear was justified in this case, and this was not the first time that she came home to find that a parent had been arrested and detained. Three years earlier, when Guerrero was a sixth grader, her Mami was detained and deported. Describing her immediate reaction, she remembers, "The room became blurry. I felt light-headed. My brother kept talking, but I couldn't comprehend all that he was saying. I was in the Twilight Zone, or more like that Disneyworld ride, the Tower of Terror" (48).

She wrestled with guilt that her actions, in some way, must have brought on this punishment and discloses the deep shame she felt about the situation. "Only my closest friends knew what had happened, and frankly, if I could've kept it from them, I might've. That's how mortified I was" (50), Guerrero describes. She maintains that, when at school, "I just wanted to be home. I felt out of place. Girl in hiding. WTF" (50). A week after her mother returns, a couple of months after her deportation, she was again detained. Not mincing words, Guerrero shares, "Honestly, it felt like the biggest mindfuck ever. Was this really happening to us? What could we have possible done to bring this on ourselves? How could my mother be taken not once, but *twice*?" (56)

Guerrero recalls missing key mother-daughter moments during the two years her Mami was in Colombia after her second deportation but accepts the separation as permanent with resignation and guilt that she didn't somehow prevent her mother's recapture. However, when the latter comes back again, the reunion brings mixed emotions: "I'd yearned to have her close again. But now that I had my wish, I wasn't so sure I wanted it anymore. Papi and I had established our rhythm, and Mami's reentry felt like an interruption. Really, I was just scared. Scared that I would be disappointed again, and I didn't think my heart could take it" (60–61). Then, just as the family began to settle in more comfortably, the proverbial rug was swept from under them, as Guerrero's brother was deported and her father discovered that he had been scammed out of thousands of dollars in his attempt to legalize his status after finally overcoming his fear and mistrust of the system.

Not long thereafter, the fateful event that Guerrero describes at the beginning of the memoir arrives. She enters into more specific details about the day of her parents' arrest, explaining, "For more than a decade, I've relived every detail of what happened during the next twelve hours" (81). She recalls her sense of dread and describes the intense emotions she experienced when a neighbor let her know that immigration officers had taken both of her parents. "I glared at her, all of a sudden feeling dizzy. The foyer began to spin, faster and faster, as if I was stuck in a washing machine. 'No!' I wailed with my palms over my temples. I swayed forward, then back, and caught myself before falling onto the linoleum. 'They're not gone!' I squealed. The woman didn't blink" (85). She continues, "I staggered into the house and slammed the door. *What am I going to do?* My thoughts raced faster than my heartbeat. *I need to call someone*" (85), capturing the emotions of the experience through alternation of past and present tense in a way that enables the reader to imagine experiencing the same. Guerrero elaborates, "Beyond terrified, I scurried back to the front door to be positive it was chained and bolted. I turned off every light, closed all the blinds, went into my room, and locked the door. With the cordless in hand, I got on the floor and scooted all the way under my bed. Our house had never felt more quiet or scary" (86). Alone and abandoned, she calls a friend's mother, who will take her in, and learns that her parents have been taken to separate detention centers and that she should pack suitcases for their imminent deportation.

Aside from the visceral response of panic, Guerrero also articulates the deep shame about her parents' detention that she once again experienced. Having visited them in detention after their arrest, she later describes the surges of anger mixed with disappointment and grief that swell within her. "I studied my mother's face. In the eight weeks since her arrest, she looked like she'd aged twenty years. She seemed tired and frail, like she hadn't slept for days. I'd never seen her so skinny. Her eyes were glossy, her skin pale. Her hair was disheveled, frizzy, and in a messy bun. Her wrists were handcuffed together and resting in her lap" (99). Guerrero observes the obvious emotional and physical toll that detention has had on her mother without recognizing that, in witnessing her mother's transformation, she, too, is enduring another trauma.

Reflecting on her experience as a teenager processing the grief of forced family separation, Guerrero describes, "The summer I lost my parents, it was the strangest kind of heartache. No friends gathered to grieve over the departed. No flowers were sent. No memorial service was planned. And yet the two people I'd cherished most were gone. Not gone from the world itself, but gone from me" (102). She is expected to carry on with her life, and largely does so, even without any protective intervention from the authorities. "Not only had US Immigration and Customs Enforcement been silent," she recalls, "I also hadn't received a call from Massachusetts's Child Protective Services. At fourteen, I'd been left on my own. Literally. When the authorities made the choice to detain my parents, no one bothered to check that a young girl, a minor, a citizen of this country, would be left without a family. Without a home. Without a way to move forward" (90).

242

Yet, she does find a way to move forward, but it is clear that the psychological traumas of the separation and being forced into the role of her own guardian continue to haunt her for years. Even prior to her parents' removal, Guerrero was already aware of her marginalization as a "brown girl from the hood" (15) who, along with her friends, had suffered bullying rooted in sociocultural tensions. She recalls being verbally assaulted because of her Colombian heritage by other Latinxs, noting, "This wasn't the first time we'd been bullied. In our area, which was mostly filled with Puerto Ricans and Dominicans, anybody who wasn't in one of those two groups was usually considered a dirty immigrant. We were spat upon. Cursed at. Looked down upon. And perceived as unattractive because of our indigenous Indian features" (35), reflecting yet another layer of marginalization and internal colonialism. She comments further on her need to overcome the internalization of inferiority as a result of her intersecting identities as a lower-class Latina from a mixed-status family. Nevertheless, it is her experience as the daughter of undocumented parents that have most markedly affected her mental health.

Aside from the sadness and feelings of abandonment and loss over separation, Guerrero has carried shame over her family's situation as well as resentment and anger directed toward her parents and the system for subjecting her to constant displacement, liminality, and instability, despite her being a US citizen, anger that she had lost her parents more generally, and anger that those around her had no awareness of undocumented individuals or their issues. Moreover, she has internalized such a deep-seated fear of authority that even when she was hit by a car, her immediate thought was, *Do not cause any trouble. If the police showed up, they might realize my parents had been deported and throw me in foster care*" (117), or she would otherwise be a burden to the friend's mother who had taken her into her home.

In addition to the guilt she has shouldered for her inability to prevent the rupture of her family, remorse plagues her when she recognizes that she avoided interactions and conversations with her parents for years. "It broke my heart to know that I was breaking theirs. And yet the angst that surged through me whenever I heard their voices was more painful than knowing I was alienating them" (150), she explains. Furthermore, "When we did catch up, the conversations were stilted and awkward. . . . I felt as if my own mother and father were strangers to me, people I'd perhaps known in a former life but whom I did not recognize anymore" (150). When Guerrero would reunite with her mother more than a decade after the latter's final deportation, she realized that "you have to literally relearn the person" (195), and in readapting to one another, work through tensions, much like the ones Nazario identifies in *Enrique's Journey*.

After giving readers access to some of her darkest moments, Guerrero's tone shifts and becomes both more positive and more explicitly didactic in the final chapters. She shares her experience as an invited guest at President Obama's speech on immigration reform at Del Sol High School in Las Vegas, reflecting on how his proposed policies (like DAPA—Deferred Action for Parents of Americans) would have completely altered the experience of her family and prevented much of their heartbreak. In the last chapter, appropriately titled "Call to Action," Guerrero outlines in no uncertain terms how detrimental the US immigration system is to children, sharing statistics and information about the various negative outcomes for families who are ripped apart and invoking terms like "stolen" and "taken" that are imbued with violence and bring to mind *los desaparecidos* and state terror. She corrects misconceptions about processes for legal entry (dismantling the notion of getting in the "back of the line"), refutes proposals to build a wall or implement mass deportation, and condemns structural and legal mechanisms that, for example, relate to the inhumane treatment of detained immigrants, the ridiculously long waiting period for visa processing, and restrictions that require that undocumented parents or spouses wait outside of the country before applying for a Green Card. Ultimately, though, she issues a call to action, beseeching fellow Americans to do better:

> In a nation that values keeping families together and safeguarding children, I was invisible. Either the immigration officials didn't see me or they chose to turn their heads. I'll never know which. But I do know that as Americans, we can do better than that. We can extend greater compassion. And we can push our leaders to protect the most vulnerable among us. It's one way we can help people who desperately need it. (247)

Throughout the memoir, Guerrero establishes her authority as somebody with lived experience as a child whose family was ripped apart by detention and deportation and invites readers in to relive that experience with her (to the extent possible), before issuing a plea that seems directed more toward outsiders than to the "thousands of nameless children who feel as forgotten as I did" (2). She strategically fosters an empathetic relationship between author (and, by extension, others in similar situations) and reader throughout the narrative and then leverages it with an appeal to take action, even including a list of online resources to learn more about immigration reform and to get politically involved.

Guerrero emphasizes her invisibility as a child who was entirely overlooked by the very system that is ultimately responsible for her victimization and who, as an adult, has had to find mechanisms for coping with and processing one unseen trauma after another. Like Alarcón and Nazario, she utilizes her narrative to shed light on the experiences of the otherwise invisible or ignored, fulfilling the role of social activist and cultural mediator as well as author. In turn, in her collection of *testimonios*, Alarcón presents the stories that are often either concealed (by those who have experienced them, particularly out of shame or a desire to avoid triggering further traumatization) or simply not sought out by those who surround them. While *La Migra me hizo los mandados* does include some gratifying accounts of opportunities fulfilled and families reunited or emotional reflections on how and why the storytellers have arrived in Southern California, perhaps the most memorable of the vignettes are those that are the most difficult and uncomfortable to read.

Although the reader is granted access to horrific accounts of sexual assault and violence, the fact that they are offered by men as witnesses enables a certain degree of narrative distancing, while also underlining the psychological trauma of witnessing that these men have experienced. As a secondary witness, the reader may perhaps be able to process the account cognitively *and* emotionally, as opposed to potentially over-empathizing or over-identifying, which could be more likely if the testimonial were written from the perspective of the victim herself. Regardless, while Alarcón's collection may resonate with readers who have similar lived experiences, it appears to be geared more to a broader audience that may never have stopped to acknowledge or notice the presence of these individuals with a precarious immigrant status, much less honor their voices, histories, and experiences.

Sonia Nazario earnestly shares that, despite interacting regularly with her housekeeper for years, a passing conversation led her to realize that she really had no clue as to Carmen's life and story marked by the traumas of transnational motherhood.

Her response to Carmen's revelation was one of shock and, to a point, judgment about the meaning of motherhood and the kind of monster a mother would have to be to leave her kids behind for years, if not decades. This, then, begs the question: How many others among us have suffered similar traumas? In Nazario's characterization, the disintegration of families rooted in family separation due to immigration is essentially a silent epidemic. Compelled by the story of Carmen's son Minor to learn more, she shares Enrique's story as well and suggests a general need for America as a society to understand this issue, because with information and understanding come compassion and empathy. From there, we may harness a critical mass to effect change. Moreover, Nazario's portrayal of Lourdes, Enrique, and their other family members disrupts stereotypical notions, largely internalized through media outlets, of immigrants as embodying the threatening "Other." Like anyone else, Lourdes wants to be able to provide for her children and, out of desperation, makes an agonizing choice and sacrifice that would expose the entire family to violence and trauma on a number of levels.

In trying to provide safety and security for her family, then, Lourdes has inadvertently led to its fracturing and unraveling. Of importance, though, Nazario looks beyond the individual to explore the overarching forces that are ultimately to blame and offers suggestions for resolving some of the underlying political and economic issues by promoting microloans for women-owned businesses in Honduras, creating additional opportunities locally for work, eradicating corruption, etc., that predate the recent rise in violence in the Northern Triangle. While she offers broader political and economic solutions, she focuses on each individual's capacity to demonstrate compassion and understanding. Furthermore, the intent seems less about promoting the need to help the helpless or be the voice for the voiceless and far more about honoring the stories and experiences of families who demonstrate a great deal of resilience and agency in adapting to their circumstances.

Much as Nazario disrupts the stereotypical rendering of the Latinx migrant, Guerrero unsettles readers' notions of identity, immigration, and the American Dream by exposing her truths. She acknowledges that, as a famous figure, she appears to have it all and to represent everything that the country is about . . . from a distance. "My story represents all that should be celebrated about America," she asserts. "Only here could the daughter of immigrants grow up to succeed in the competitive and exciting world of acting. And only here could a girl like me be invited to have a conversation with the president" (Guerrero and Burford 2017, 247). She had been hiding a weighty secret for most of her life, though—one which leads her to continue, "And yet my experience in this country reflects a reality that's still tough for me to face" (247).

When Guerrero exposed her family's story, her article went viral and became the subject of much media programming. She certainly did (and does) not fit within the predominant image of an immigrant as criminal or otherwise intending to take advantage of the system. Perhaps by exposing the unseen and unknown history of her family's migration, separation, and suffering, she is in some way suggesting that she indeed *is* representative of the American experience. There are hundreds of thousands of young people like her who have had similar experiences,[38] if only we would open our eyes and not be blind to them.

As with Alarcón and Nazario, Guerrero makes visible the otherwise seemingly invisible people, drawing attention to their experiences and their invisible traumas, relying on an appeal to compassion and empathy based on shared values for the sake of justice. When we, as readers, are confronted with the horrific realities that families (specifically children) face because of forced separation, we face a moral and ethical challenge to make things right. Whereas Nazario proposes more abstract solutions, Guerrero, having herself found empowerment through sharing her story and becoming an advocate for immigrant rights, indicates that there already *is* more that allies can do and equips readers with not only her powerful story and its broader context but also specific resources to get involved. Whether the reader will answer the call to action is a separate question. However, the role of her memoir and the life-writings by Alarcón and Nazario as instruments for restoring the humanity of Latinx migrant families and effecting social change is clear.

CHAPTER 7
Reaching the Next Generation: Truth, History, and Hope for Change

S everal Latinx authors have penned juvenile literature in recent decades, reflecting authentic experiences of young Latinx readers to inculcate a pride in their heritage and help to preserve their culture(s) in a world characterized by globalization and the tendency toward cultural homogeneity that such implies. These storybooks are also critical in fomenting a respect for the values and perspectives of different cultures among young readers and therefore are appropriate and important for children of all cultures. Not surprisingly, a current trend within children's literature, primarily that written by Latinx authors, includes the emergence of stories that address the personal impacts of transnational migration. This is likely in response to the current social and legal climate regarding immigration, along with a push for more inclusive children's literature and demographic statistics that point to the clear relevance of such issues for children across the nation.

The unauthorized immigrant population in the US more than tripled from 1990 to 2007, from 3.5 million to a record 12.2 million. Although the number declined by 2017, there were still a reported 10.5 million undocumented individuals living in the US (Radford 2019). Perhaps of more significance, though, is that roughly five million US-born children under eighteen were living with at least one undocumented parent in 2016, up from approximately 4.5 million in 2007 (Passel et al. 2018). Previous figures offer additional insights regarding minor children of unauthorized parents more broadly, accounting for children's own immigration status. As a whole, these children accounted for about 3.9 million, or 7.3 percent, of US students enrolled in kindergarten through 12th grade in 2014. US-born children constitute the majority of those students who have at least one unauthorized parent (3.2 million or 5.9 percent), while approximately 725,000 or 1.3 percent of all enrolled students were themselves unauthorized as well (Passel and Cohn 2016).

The numbers alone are enough to draw attention to the need to consider how best to support the educational outcomes and general well-being of children of transnational migration, as well as the importance not only of providing opportunities for these children to see themselves and their families' experiences represented in literature but also for exposing all students to the unique assets, challenges, and diverse realities of their lives. As Sanjuana C. Rodriguez and Eliza Gabrielle Braden explain:

> As former classroom teachers, we have witnessed the agony that children experience when they learn a parent might be deported and the worry they feel for a family member who stayed behind when the children came to the United States alone. We have watched their reactions to news reports of border walls and deportations and to generalizations of a single Latinx experience to the experiences of all. Therefore, we argue that it is imperative that educators and children continue to discuss the issue of

immigration in schools, especially due to the discriminatory rhetoric used by the current president of the United States, Donald
Trump. (2018, 57)

The opportunity to engage in discussions about issues related to
immigration, for both students who are and who are not directly
affected by immigration, is even more critical in regions where
children of undocumented immigrants constitute over 10 percent of total K–12 enrollment—like Nevada (17.6 percent), Texas
(13.4 percent), California (12.3 percent), Arizona (12.2 percent),
Colorado (10.2 percent), and New Mexico (10.1 percent) (Passel
and Cohn 2016). Using Latinx children's books about transnational migration as an inclusive pedagogical tool to broach challenging topics honors the cultural capital that Latinx students
bring into the classroom, facilitates information-sharing and
dialogue, fosters empathy, and recognizes the agency not just
of the juvenile characters (and their real-life counterparts) but
also the capacity of young readers to learn about, understand,
and empathize with the experiences of traumas associated with
migration and family separation.

A Focus on *la Familia* in the Face of Violence and Trauma

As a means to facilitate students' understanding of the construction of identity and the production of knowledge, reading and
discussion of juvenile texts that address transnational migration and incorporate familiar cultural and linguistic elements
may enable students to bridge the divide between their home
and the academic environment. Moreover, they foment respect
for Latinx students whose backgrounds and experiences position them as individuals who can speak with authority about
particular topics. Through facilitating a space in which students may engage in dialogue about politically charged—and,
for some, highly personal—topics, Latinx children's literature

that narrates the personal impact of transnational migration is thus culturally responsive in reflecting the diversity of students' realities.

As with many of the examples of Latinx children's literature more broadly, texts that focus on transnational migration incorporate themes of embracing the contradictions and conflicts of cultural hybridity and the rejection of dichotomies espoused by Anzaldúa in *Borderlands/La Frontera: The New Mestiza*. They instill cultural pride through incorporating various registers of the Spanish language as well as traditions that entail family, food, healing, and spirituality or religion. Further capturing the heterogeneity of Latinx experiences, Latinx authors tell various tales of migration, narrating the unique circumstances and contexts of each. Texts' specific references to experiences of transnational families normalize, to a certain extent, physical displacement or familial separation and its ensuing repercussions. Discussion of these books may afford students the opportunity to articulate sentiments they have felt but were perhaps incapable or ashamed of expressing.

Not only will children with related personal experiences be validated and empowered to contribute to the shared knowledge of the classroom community, children without such experiences will also benefit from exposure to stories that describe various motives and implications of transnational migration and increase the potential for them to better relate to their peers and be informed about broader societal issues. Briana Asmus and Emma Antel concede, "Teachers may not be able to teach empathy itself, but they can increase the imaginative capacity of their students through the use of young adult literature featuring authentic scenarios and voices" (2018, 17). Particularly in relation to contemporary and polemic topics that frequently appear in the media, like immigration, "an informed, empathic pedagogical approach can work to counter deficit narratives and lead students toward experiencing empathy" (17). Although students are inclined to develop more affective relationships with characters they can relate to, it is important to note, "Students often relate to a character's personality, values or morals" (19), not just characters of the same age, gender, ethnicity, culture, national origin, or linguistic background.

Although the juvenile texts offer a wide variety of specific experiences and contexts of immigration, they all tend to evince a connection with the characters through descriptions of their emotions, namely sadness due to family separation and joy at the prospect of reunification. For example, the young protagonist of *Lucita Comes Home to Oaxaca/Lucita regresa a Oaxaca* returns to her birthplace in Oaxaca with her grandmother for a two-month vacation. Despite her initial sadness because of the temporary separation from her parents, who remain in the US to work, Lucita ultimately reconnects with her Zapotec roots during her summer vacation, realizing, "'My home is in the North . . . but it's in Oaxaca, too'" (Cano 1998, 13). Soon thereafter, her parents arrive to visit the extended family and bring Lucita back to the US. The resolution is certainly a happy one, with the reunification of her family as well as the recuperation of Lucita's Mexican and indigenous heritage.

Narrating another young female character's adjustment to displacement and familial separations, and establishing the limited labor opportunities south of the US-Mexico border hinted at in *Lucita Comes Home to Oaxaca*, Amada Irma Pérez contributes *My Diary from Here to There/Mi diario de aquí hasta allá*, based on the author's own experiences of migration from Mexico when she was five years old. Utilizing an epistolary style, the author writes from the first person in brief diary entries that capture a young girl's excitement, anxiety, and confusion upon learning that her family will leave Juárez in search of work in Los Angeles, California. In preparing to leave her home, Amada bids farewell to Michi, her best friend who reminds Amada, "You're lucky your family will be together over there" (A. Pérez 2002, 6). As the narrator explains, "[Michi's] sisters and father work in the U.S." (6), so she daily contends with the long-term separation from her loved ones.

Describing the planned transition, Amada's father explains that he similarly moved at a young age, relocating to Mexico after being born in Arizona; evidently, his citizenship enables the family to acquire the necessary Green Cards to cross the border within a brief period of time. Until then, however, Amada describes her sadness resulting from her father's departure, even once she is surrounded by extended family members at her grandparents' home in Mexicali. Only the arrival of letters from her father brings a relief from her dismay, and the author incorporates these *cartas de Papá*, which detail his work picking grapes and strawberries in Delano, California, and his aware-ness of César Chávez, "who speaks of unions, strikes, and boy-cotts" (19). "These new words hold the hope of better conditions for us farmworkers" (19), Papá writes, thereby enabling the author to integrate historical tidbits that may encourage young readers to learn more about social justice issues around farm-workers' rights, labor unions, and the work of César Chávez and the United Farm Workers.

Pérez includes a similar nod to issues facing undocumented migrants in describing Amada's crossing from Tijuana to San Ysidro, California, and a bus ride to Los Angeles with her five brothers and mother. The narrator recognizes, "One woman and her children got kicked off the bus when the immigra-tion patrol boarded to check everyone's papers" (27), while "Mamá held Mario and our green cards close to her heart" (27), unquestionably grateful to have the legal means to enter the United States. Laura Alamillo (2007) observes that this text addresses the theme of border crossing, as well as those of family relationships, heritage, and tradition. In addition to depicting the circumstances and emotions that are part and parcel of the separation experienced by transnational families, *My Diary from Here to There* reflects the manner in which Amada relies upon her ties to family and cultural customs to overcome her experience of displacement as a result of her migration, which is borne of economic need.

Despite the changing contexts, this economic motivation for crossing the border and the focus on *la familia* are underlying themes that remain relatively consistent throughout over twenty years of Latinx children's literature that broaches transnational migration. For those texts that present examples of border crossing by individuals *sin papeles*, the fear of la Migra, or officials of today's Immigration and Customs Enforcement, is patent and reflects a distrust of, or trepidation toward, US officials and the policies they enforce on the part of migrant children and parents alike. The private sphere that the family inhabits becomes a refuge that offers relative safety, healing, and connections to traditions that extend beyond the geopolitical boundary between the US and Mexico. Such a safe space takes on greater significance for young migrant characters who, beyond the fear of apprehension by authorities and the distress of abandoning their homeland, feel alienated from the dominant Anglo culture in the US as well as US-based Latinxs.

Gloria Anzaldúa depicts a migrant's experience of dual marginalization in *Friends from the Other Side/Amigos del otro lado*, "the story of Prietita, a brave young Mexican American girl, and her new friend Joaquín, a Mexican boy from the other side of the river" (1993, 1), the latter who crossed the border with his mother so that she could find work. Anzaldúa captures the tension between Chicanxs and Mexican migrants as neighborhood children, mostly Mexican American, yell slurs: "'Hey, man, why don't you go back where you belong? We don't want any more *mojados* here'" (8). The young protagonist opts to become Joaquín's friend and ally, defending him from the taunting and also helping him to escape la Migra during its patrols of the street by bringing him and his mother to the wise *curandera*'s house to hide. Further highlighting this cultural tension on a national scale, the narrator describes, "From behind the curtains, Prietita and the herb woman watched the Border Patrol van cruise slowly up the street. It stopped in front of every house. While the white patrolman stayed in the van, the Chicano *migra* got out and asked, 'Does anyone know of any illegals living in this area?'" (25).

The characterization of the immigration official as Chicano is relevant in that it demonstrates the tensions between US-based individuals of Mexican descent and more recently arrived Mexican migrants, explicitly so through the character's derogatory use of the term "illegals." The solidarity between other Chicanx or US-based Mexican characters (in this case, Prietita and the *curandera*) and the migrant child (Joaquín) opens young readers' eyes to the potential for alliances that transcend borders of immigration status or dominant language. Juvenile migrants who are aware that they themselves are undocumented or are US-citizen children of undocumented parents are surely cognizant of the danger of detention and deportation. This text, however, also sheds light on the fact that there are empathetic individuals in their community who do, and would, support them, just as Prietita chooses to do. Alternatively, readers who may not relate to the conflicts that Joaquín endures may also become conscious of their capacity to help others through friendship and apply the lessons communicated in the story to situations in their daily lives.

More so than in the textual examples of the experience of legal migration, children's books that deal with the impacts of undocumented migration effectively enable readers to empathize with the plight of the protagonist, who often exercises limited agency, having been brought to the US by his or her parents without any say in the matter. The personalization of the broader political and economic phenomenon of transnational movement restores the humanity of the migrant while also revealing some of the factors and consequences of migration that are often not overtly discussed in public conversation about immigration. As an example, René Colato Laínez describes eight-year-old Beto's three-year separation from his father, who remained in El Salvador when Beto and his mother were able to obtain a visa through Abuelo's petition after the bombing of the factory where both of Beto's parents worked during the Salvadoran Civil War in *Waiting for Papá/Esperando a Papá*.

Within the context of his classroom, Beto embraces pride in being an immigrant, primarily through his teacher's role in framing the history of immigration. At the encouragement of a Nicaraguan classroom guest, Mr. Mario González from the "Voice of the Immigrant" radio program, Beto and his classmates write a letter explaining why their fathers are special in honor of the coming Father's Day celebrations. "On the back of my letter, I drew my Salvadoran house on fire. I also drew Mamá screaming and Papá holding me in his arms while I cried" (Colato Laínez 2004, 15), the narrative voice describes. Clearly, such a depiction of the traumatic circumstances that have motivated Beto's separation from his father catches the attention of Mr. González, who invites Beto to read his letter to his father on the air. Likewise, it grabs the attention of the readers of this text, particularly through the inclusion of such weighty themes and images within a genre that typically favors celebratory renderings of difference over disclosure of tragic experiences. Despite an unrealistic resolution, Colato Laínez effectively introduces the unique experiences of Salvadoran refugees to the genre of Latinx children's fiction, conveying the emotional aspect of the legally sanctioned separations of families across borders.

Describing the experience and trauma of family separation, this time resulting from the deportation of undocumented parents of US-born citizens, Colato Laínez's *From North to South / Del norte al sur* opens with José's excitement at his upcoming visit to his Mamá in Tijuana at el Centro Madre Assunta, a shelter for migrant woman and children. He later explains, "Two weeks ago, Mamá didn't come home from work. That night, when she called us, we all cried together. She had been working at the factory when some men asked for her immigration papers. But Mamá was born in Mexico and didn't have those papers. The men put Mamá and other workers in a van. In a few hours, Mamá was in Tijuana, Mexico" (Colato Laínez 2010a, 7). Since José's father is a permanent resident, the family hopes the lawyer will successfully arrange his mother's papers, although there is no telling when that might happen.

Despite the ability to visit his mother, José's sadness does not dissipate, as the separation has taken its toll. However, once he meets and plants a garden at the shelter with unaccompanied children who had attempted to cross the border to reunite with their parents, he takes comfort in knowing that other children are going through similar experiences and emotions as a result of transnational migration. In narrating the story of a young boy whose mother has been deported, while also including the detained children left behind with dreams of family reunification, *From North to South/Del norte al sur* allows young readers in a similar situation to identify themselves within the text and, in focusing on the impact of migration on parents and children, restores the humanity of migrants for a broad audience, regardless of cultural or ethnic affiliation.

Similarly, *Mango Moon* by Diane de Anda narrativizes the emotional experiences of Maricela and her brother Manuel after the detention of their father. Maricela, in first-person perspective, describes the pain of separation with an emphasis on the trauma of loss and absence during a period marked by change. "Everything changed the day they came to Papi's work and took him away" (de Anda 2019, 6), Maricela declares, explaining over several pages the series of adjustments the family had to make. Their mother obtains a second job, which alters the siblings' afternoon routine. They now must take the bus home alone and are unable to play outside in order to ensure their safety while their mom is at work. Over the course of various months, Maricela misses having her dad as her soccer coach, laments his absence at her tenth birthday party, and as they prepare to move in with *tíos* and cousins, expresses her sadness about having to change schools and leave her friends behind. Even while her father is relatively nearby in detention, Maricela is unable to visit him. She comments, "They have kept Papi in a place far away from us for a long time. He said it wasn't a good place for children to see, so Mama goes by herself on a bus to visit him" (20).

To maintain a connection with him, she reads and rereads letters that Papi has sent her, as she wrestles with comprehending why he is being held in prison-like conditions and will soon be forced to leave the country. "Mama says Papi never did anything wrong; he just didn't have papers. I don't understand why they would send him so far away because of some papers" (17). Aside from confusion and sadness, Maricela also contends with a great deal of fear. "I got scared and asked if they could take her away too or even me and my brother" (18), the protagonist notes, reassured to discover that she and her brother are US citizens and that their mother has a "special card" that will protect her from being picked up by ICE. As her father's deportation date nears, though, Maricela's fears for his well-being increase when she recalls conversations between adults about the dangers in the country they had left behind.

The author effectively conveys the various psychological repercussions of familial separation and draws attention to the physical manifestation of such. Maricela explains, "My stomach has been hurting a lot lately. The doctor said I wasn't really sick. He said it was because of all the changes and from missing my dad so much" (28). By portraying the experience of family separation due to detention and deportation from a child's perspective, de Anda normalizes it and creates empathy for children like Maricela whose trauma is ongoing. Portrayed as relatively powerless in a broader context of legal structures that have ripped apart her family, Maricela's only consolation is to gaze at the orange full moon, wondering "if Papi is thinking about me too, under the same mango moon" (30).

Juan Felipe Herrera offers a more empowered characterization of the protagonist of *Super Cilantro Girl/La Súperniña del Cilantro* in the context of her mother's detention. The text opens with an author's note that functions like a preface, commenting on his frequent experiences with border crossing as a child living in San Diego, revealing his penchant for superhero movies, and mentioning Mamá Lucha's cilantro-colored Green Card and his childhood contentment at being able to be together as a family. He reflects, "But what about families kept apart by borders? I wondered. Maybe, I dreamed—and still dream—there is a way to bring families back together" (Herrera 2003, 2), declaring that "[i]t will take a heroic effort from someone like *El Santo* or the star of this story, but it can be done" (2). The plot opens at bedtime, when Esmeralda Sinfronteras (translated as "Emerald Without Borders") comes inside with a bunch of cilantro in hand, and her *abuelita* mentions that her *mamá* will be home later than expected because, despite her US citizenship, she has been detained at the border because she did not show a Green Card. "'Green . . . card? Green? Like cilantro?' Esmeralda asks" (5), suggesting her confusion and unfamiliarity with documents for permanent residents. Noting that her grandmother is not terribly concerned, she goes to bed, making a wish to bring her mother home soon while holding the cilantro.

After a bird awakens her the next morning, she notices and attempts to hide her strange transformation during which first her hands, then eyes and teeth, turn green, and her hair becomes green vines of cilantro that eject her from the school nurse's office. The transformation continues, and Esmeralda becomes a giant, dons a superhero-like costume, and, with the help of her bird companion, decides to fly to the border to rescue her mother. Near Tijuana, "She gawks at the great gray walls of wire and steel between the United States and Mexico. She stares at the great gray building that keeps people in who want to move on" (22). Esmeralda, as her alter ego Super Cilantro Girl, triumphantly declares, "'I am taking you back home to your daughter'" (24), nearly revealing her true identity various times as she tucks her mother into her pocket and flies over the border, evading helicopters and Border Patrol vehicles. Super Cilantro Girl uses her powers to make everything green—with cilantro, of course—to conceal the border and camouflage themselves, thereby dodging the officers who enjoy the fragrance and even begin to use Spanish to express their delight. Upon arriving home, she reveals her secret identity and promptly falls asleep, only to be woken up by Abuelita in a passage that suggests that Esmeralda had dreamed the entire escapade . . . or did she? As she welcomes her mother with hugs, she notices green feathers as her bird companion pecks at the window.

Albeit in what appears to be a dream, Herrera positions Esmeralda as a bicultural Latina who exercises agency by taking action to rectify her mother's unjust situation. Symbolically connected with the liberating qualities of a bird that respects no borders, Esmeralda as Super Cilantro Girl transcends borders to retrieve her mother from wrongful detention. As Sonia Alejandra Rodríguez observes, Latina children and adolescents like Esmeralda "use creativity and imagination to challenge and transform the different forms of violence they experience in their lives" (S. Rodríguez 2019, 9). Manifest in her dreams is Esmeralda's (aspirational) perception of her identity as capable and desirous of "disrupting and challenging various systems of oppression" (9), through her daring superhero adventure to rescue her marginalized mother.

Alternatively, Colato Laínez incorporates the implicit illegal immigration of a young character to the US in *My Shoes and I*. The vibrant and detailed images of the text enhance the symbolic value of the new shoes that Mamá has sent to Mario from the US as a Christmas gift. This sturdy footwear will serve Mario well on his journey, for "Papá tells me that it is a very long trip. We need to cross three countries. But no matter how long the trip will be, I will get there. My shoes will take me anywhere" (Colato Laínez 2010b, 2). In a brisk, simple style, the author describes Mario and his father's arduous journey from El Salvador in English, employing onomatopoeia and a sprinkling of Spanish and documenting the parallel transformation of Mario's shoes along the way. Repeatedly comforting his shoes with the common nursery rhyme in Spanish, "'*Sana,*

sana, colita de rana" (5, 9, 14, 18, 21, original emphasis), Mario attempts to "heal" his damaged shoes after each trial he must overcome. Whether covered in dirt, poked by a sharp nail, embedded in mud, simply worn by excessive use, or drenched from rainstorms or crossing the Río Grande, Mario's shoes—and by extension Mario himself—will endure any obstacle in the quest to be reunited with Mamá. Upon their reunion just across the river, in fact, Mario triumphantly reports, "Mamá is waiting for us. We hug. We kiss. We cry with joy. My shoes are with me. They still walk everywhere I walk. We crossed the finish line, together" (27–28).

Although these texts written by Colato Laínez—as well as those by Cano, Pérez, and Anzaldúa—may exemplify the "realistic YA literature about undocumented migration [that] builds understanding because the books individuate undocumented migrants and use their perspectives to humanize a political issue" (Cummins 2013, 58), the same cannot be said of Duncan Tonatiuh's *Pancho Rabbit and the Coyote: A Migrant's Tale*. Rather than developing understanding through making the political personal in the narration of a specific individual character's experiences, Tonatiuh develops an allegory reminiscent of fables like "The Gingerbread Man" with its emphasis on misplaced trust and trickery. He toys with the dual meaning of "coyote" and further describes his impetus for writing and illustrating this work in the author's note. "We seldom see the dangerous journey immigrants go through to reach the US and the longing that their families feel for them back at home. It is my desire that *Pancho Rabbit and the Coyote: A Migrant's Tale* captures some of that sentiment; ironically, the animals convey the human emotions and side of the story" (2013, 29), Tonatiuh clarifies.

Rather than suggesting a dehumanization of immigrants, the use of animal characters perhaps better enables young readers—especially those unfamiliar with the migrant experience—to focus on the story without imposing any preconceived notions of migrants and their experiences derived from exposure to media representation or public discourse. Indeed, the author manages to restore humanity to the figure of the migrant through the characters' anthropomorphism and offers the juvenile readership an understanding of circumstances that force one's migration, and what the odyssey north entails. Moreover, the use of animals and folktale forms puts this text in conversation with the tradition of fables, which are generally short stories with animal characters that communicate a moral, and more specifically, connects this contemporary tale with variations of the Mesoamerican "trickster tale" that pits the rabbit against the coyote. In some early versions of the fable, the rabbit deceives the foolish coyote into helping the rabbit cross a river, not realizing that the coyote intends to eat the rabbit soon thereafter. Thanks to his cunning and community assistance, the rabbit escapes before being attacked. This adaptation similarly positions the animals antagonistically, as the wily coyote intends to deceive and harm the rabbit who, although brave, is ingenuous. Nevertheless, thanks to the intervention of the rabbit's father and other animal friends from the *rancho*, the coyote is scared off and the rabbit is safe (Dillon 2015, 23). In Tonatiuh's adaption of the tale, one notes his use of techniques common to the allegory, a genre that allows for the interpretation of actions or characters as symbolic of larger ideas or sociohistorical circumstances, as the coyotes, snakes, and crows come to represent various nefarious individuals (e.g., smugglers, narco-traffickers, and bandits/robbers) who commonly inflict violence and trauma on the migrant trail.

Accompanied by illustrations that depict Mamá Rabbit and the four young bunnies left behind, the story begins, "One spring

Reprinted from *Pancho Rabbit and the Coyote: A Migrant's Tale*, p. 4.

the rains did not come and the crops could not grow. So Papá Rabbit, Señor Rooster, Señor Ram, and other animals from the rancho set out north to find work in the great carrot and lettuce fields" (Tonatiuh 2013, 2). After an extended period, Papá Rabbit has saved enough money to preclude any future trips across the border, and the community eagerly awaits his return. When his father does not arrive as anticipated, Pancho Rabbit takes it upon himself, as the eldest son, to head north in search of him. Through the narration of Pancho Rabbit's quest to find his father, young readers accompany the protagonist on the treacherous

Reprinted from *Pancho Rabbit and the Coyote: A Migrant's Tale*, p. 13.

journey atop freight trains, through tunnels, and across scorch-
ing deserts, all the while interacting with malevolent characters.

Along the way, Pancho Rabbit encounters the red-eyed coyote with sharp teeth, who consistently offers his services to the
naïve and inexperienced young rabbit, for a price. Reluctant to
hand over his mole, followed by his rice and beans, and later
his aguamiel, the desperate rabbit agrees to the coyote's terms,
repeating to himself, "'As long as it gets me closer to Papá'" (11).
Such is also the case when the coyote suggests passage through
the tunnel that runs below the border wall, "'but the snakes

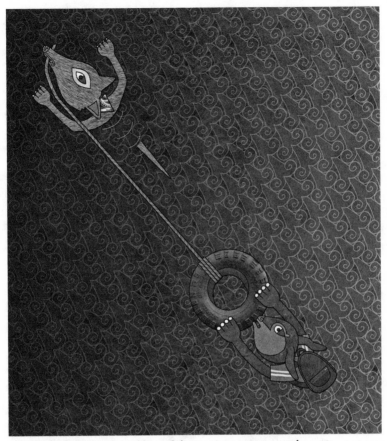

Reprinted from *Pancho Rabbit and the Coyote: A Migrant's Tale*, p. 16.

watch it,'" he explains. However, "'If you give them the tortillas you are carrying, I'm sure they will let us through'" (18). As
might be expected, the snakes, thinly veiled renderings of narco-trafficking cartels, take every last tortilla. Pancho Rabbit's
relief to finally be in *El Norte* dissipates rapidly when, demanding even more of the migrant's already completely depleted
resources, the coyote informs him, "'In that case . . . I will roast
you in the fire and eat you!'" (21). Exhausted from the journey,
"All he could do was huddle in a corner as the coyote slowly
approached" (22).

Reprinted from *Pancho Rabbit and the Coyote: A Migrant's Tale*, p. 22.

This moment of utter vulnerability is interrupted by the fortuitous sudden entrance of Pancho Rabbit's father and friends, whose return has been delayed by an attack by a gang of crows, who stranded them after robbing the migrants of their money and gifts meant for family members back home. Once reunited, Papá prepares his family for the potential future separation despite the inevitable traumas of the trek. In response to his children's begging him not to leave them again, Papá Rabbit pragmatically explains, "'I don't want to leave you . . . but the crows took all our money. If it doesn't rain enough again this

Detail of page 20 from Codex Zouche-Nuttall. Reprinted from the public domain courtesy of Wikimedia Commons.

year, and if there is no food or work here on the rancho, what else am I to do? I will have to leave again'" (26). Emphasizing the limited control that migrants exercise over their circumstances, the story concludes with Mamá's expression of hope that sufficient rain should fall and an illustration of the restored family unit in a circle and holding hands.

That Tonatiuh's illustrations are reminiscent of pre-Columbian codices suggests that this allegory takes on epic historical proportions, capturing a people's collective experience, in this case that of northward migration. Tonatiuh first came across fourteenth- and fifteenth-century Mixtec codices while conducting research for a project about a Mixtec friend and his journey to the US and was inspired to incorporate, and adapt, characteristics of Mixtec art like "strong outlines of external and internal shapes, flat colors within those shapes, faces of humans and animals represented in profile, [and a] stylized perspective" that places flat surfaces vertically, rather than appearing to recede toward a vanishing point on the horizon (Quintero Weaver 2014).

271

While incorporating these characteristics, Tonatiuh also adapts them to reflect modern settings, adds facial expressions that convey emotion, and includes textured surfaces and elements of collage (Quintero Weaver 2014).

Tonatiuh explains that his incorporation of elements of traditional Mixtec art is intended to "celebrate the art from the past and to connect people—especially children of Latino and Mexican descent—with the artistic tradition from hundreds of years ago that produces very beautiful and original images" (Tonatiuh in Turner 2016, 128–29), and to make this tradition both relevant and interesting by connecting it with contemporary issues that are affecting children or those around them.[39]

Describing his good fortune in having dual citizenship and a middle-class upbringing between San Miguel de Allende, Mexico, and the United States, Tonatiuh notes that he has witnessed that his circumstances deviate from the norm; most young people in his Mexican community find themselves migrating north by age eighteen to pursue work opportunities. One of these neighbors, he comments in his author's note, died of dehydration during his attempted border crossing. Cognizant of the complexity of the issue at hand, Tonatiuh incorporates various statistics regarding US dependence on Mexican and Central American migrant labor, as well as recent challenges and triumphs surrounding immigration reform and legislation. Although Tonatiuh shares with other Latinx authors the desire to develop characters with whom young readers will identify, the inclusion of a glossary and additional information regarding migration suggest that this book may, in fact, be more specifically directed toward a broad audience of English-speaking teachers, librarians, and parents as a means to spur dialogue about a difficult topic that even the youngest students are likely to have encountered outside of the classroom.

Teaching Empathy, Cultural Coalitions, and Social Change to the Next Generation

The Latinx authors of the children's books included here introduce factors that stimulate and perpetuate international migration and reveal the experiences of the migratory journey or the
consequences of being left behind in a less graphic, although
still compelling, manner than in recent texts geared toward
adult audiences, reminding readers of all ages that migrants and
their families simply hope and search for a better life north of
the border, risking and sacrificing much to do so. This portrayal
goes counter to popular characterizations of migrants and their
motives for crossing the border, thereby functioning as counter-discourse to hegemonic representations of undocumented
(as well as legal) migrants from Mexico and Central America.
These texts thus serve as vehicles of resistance both through
simply exposing readers to positive and humanized images of
migrant families and, in the case of young Latinx immigrants,
through validating their experiences by reflecting them in print.

As with adult and young adult literature, exposure to distinct perspectives, situations, and experiences tied to immigration within children's literature will increase and enhance the
available cognitive exemplars associated with immigrant families and perhaps counteract dominant stereotypical renderings.
Beyond this, the diversity of experiences manifest in the various
children's books included here deconstructs the notion of Latinx
immigrants and their families as unified, homogeneous, and
essentialist. I would suppose that children who have repeated
textual exposures to various renderings of transnational migration and its impact on Latinx families will, as would adults, be
more apt to recognize the uniqueness of characters' distinct situations and circumstances (and, by extension, the people they

273

represent) and the ways that broader structures or laws create various challenges for Latinx families of migration, especially the children of those families. This may pave the way not only for more positive and empathetic interactions with peers of all backgrounds but also constructive conversations with the adults in their lives and actions to support the undocumented community.

Conclusion

Imagine a scene of a fierce desert sandstorm somewhere near the US-Mexico border, with winds whipping and howling. Through the haze of dust and sand in the air, you can barely make out blurred figures. As the figures approach, their human forms take shape. As they continue to draw near to you, their faces come into focus, and even before hearing their voices you recognize the suffering, desperation, faith, and hope in their expressions as they block the harsh assault of the tiny and relentless grains of sand against their faces. You now realize that the once unidentifiable shapes in the distance are individuals—human beings—fighting against elements of nature, economics, politics, and oppression in their search for a better life north of the border.

In much the same way, the Latina narratives included in *Ripped Apart* personalize the abstract, bringing into focus the unique experiences of men, women, and children affected by transnational migration. These "politically and ethically committed text[s]" (Oliver-Rotger 2006, 200) demonstrate not only the marginality that migrants and their family members face through depiction of the interlocking and overlapping traumas that they sustain but also the US government's complicity with structures that perpetuate immigration, authorized or other-wise. Taken together, these works narrativize the historical policing of the "Other," which is inherently connected to sys-tems and phenomena of our government's own design.

Thus, the distinct plots develop amid backdrops that include, for example, the violence, discrimination, and unconstitutional roundups and forced separations based on notions of difference during La Matanza and the Mexican Repatriation during the 1930s. Others turn their attention to US intervention in Central America and the government's subsequent refusal to recognize its role in the displacement and trauma of fleeing refugees, while still others establish narrative action amid Prevention through Deterrence measures like Operation Gatekeeper that intention-ally made border crossing even more dangerous to keep the "outsider" out. In other cases, contemporary roundups and raids that rely on racial, ethnic, and linguistic profiling serve as the context within which individual characters' trajectories unfold.

Alternatively, narratives that tell the stories of Central American youth embed these in broader conversations about limited economic and educational opportunities, the fallout from transnational motherhood and the disintegration of the family, as well as corruption, the power of cartels (largely driven by US demand for narcotics), the rerouting of narco-trafficking because of both the US and Mexican Wars on Drugs, and gang violence, not to mention the deportation of US-based *maras* who spread their violent networks and tactics in the Northern Triangle decades ago. Finally, a growing number of texts con-textualize their narratives within the uptick of deportations and the broader repercussions for families, particularly after legal mandates like IIRIRA became harsher and harsher, eliminating judicial discretion (and thus consideration of family and com-munity ties), creating more categories of deportable offenses, and retroactively going after individuals for these now-deportable offenses even long after they have served their time.

What, then, is the purpose of writing about this ongoing policing of transnational migrants (as well as those who, by law, have every right to enjoy the protections their citizenship bestows) and its ensuing violence and traumas? In the cases of narratives that incorporate bounded strategic empathy, readers may find a representation of their own experiences and thus validation. By and large, though, the Latina narratives included here utilize techniques related to ambassadorial strategic empathy, bringing to light the distortion and outright omission of certain chapters in American history that exemplify an ongoing use of notions of foreignness and illegality-as-threat as the basis for unjust actions that entail multiple nodes or circles of violence: the physical, the psychological, the sociocultural, and the structural / legal.

These narratives of transnational migration provide various examples of how the overarching structural and legal institutions and practices are to blame by creating situations in which other physical and psychological acts of violence will be perpetrated. Political and structural understandings of whiteness vs. difference and its implications for legality vs. illegality, for example, are also in many ways tied to the sociocultural atmosphere of tensions, discriminatory practices, and/or outright violence. When, historically, have specific groups been targeted to be kept out or separated? When there is a suspicion that they pose a threat economically, socially, or politically, as has been the case with exclusion of Chinese immigrants, American Indian removal and forced separation of families (with children being sent to boarding schools), Japanese (American) internment, roundups, border security, removals, etc. Thus, one can conceive of the interconnected nodes of violence as interlocking

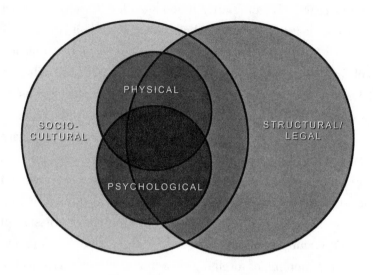

Interconnected Nodes of Violence

and overlapping circles. Within the broader context of over-lapping sociocultural and structural / legal violences, Latinx migrants and their family members are also subject to a multitude of examples of physical and psychological violence, which themselves are often overlapping and difficult to disentangle.

Do these literary texts actually have the capacity to effect change beyond simply "documenting the undocumented" (Caminero-Santangelo 2016), their histories, their experiences, and their voices? In the narrativization of the intersecting nodes of violence, what, if any, power does story or storytelling wield? Arguably, a hostile audience will not have hearts or minds changed by reading these Latina narratives. Perhaps a zone of proximal or effective ambassadorial empathy encapsulates those readers who are relatively open to new concepts, information, or versions of history; for these individuals, these texts could be instrumental in enhancing the conversation about histories of violence and social justice and in taking further pro-social, extratextual action. Juvenile readers, in particular, may demonstrate a greater degree of openness to, or curiosity about, new ideas and experiences and thus might be more apt to be moved to action after setting down the book. This may, in part, explain the proliferation of children's, middle-grade, and young adult texts that address the diverse experiences of immigration and its repercussions.

More important, these narratives provide a wide range of exemplars of Latinx migrants and their family members that contest the threat narrative that foregrounds illegality and unbelonging. We, as readers, empathize with the plight of these individuals through the narrative techniques that writers deploy, recognizing their situatedness and malleability (vs. autonomy and immutability), as well as the common ground of human experience by embracing solidarity (vs. atomism) as a mental schema, thereby rejecting the "us vs. them" mentality. Yet, despite any empathic connection between the reader and the "Other" (in this case, the character with whom the reader presumably does not share specific identities and experiences), the "Other" is recognized as such and, consequently, the reader does not overidentify with the character and appropriate or diminish his or her traumas.

Although the Latina writers utilize a variety of techniques to strengthen the empathic bond between readers and characters, ultimately depictions of the violences associated with transnational migration result in empathic unsettlement and the discomfort that "unsettlement" or "unsettling" implies. Readers are unsettled by the recounting of violence and traumas that affect the characters with whom they have developed an affective relationship and that elicits an emotional response. Simultaneously, they are unsettled in the sense that their awareness of their positionality and privilege—as *not* being the "Other" despite becoming familiar with their trauma via literature—precludes a complete understanding and embodiment of their circumstances. The narratives unsettle not just the readers but also the historical and discursive representations of immigrants and the immigrant experience.

Focusing textually on unique tribulations that entail intersecting violences of transnational migration restores the humanity of individuals affected by immigration and, ironically, results in refocusing on the larger frameworks that subject migrants and their families to violence and trauma. Moreover, in addressing the overarching structural, legal, and sociocultural contexts that engender and exacerbate traumas, these narratives expose the hypocrisy of the "nation of immigrants" that claims to honor their dignity, lives, and stories. The specific details of individual stories are intertwined with examples of an overarching reliance on exploitative labor practices and a history of laws and policies that influence the global economy and limit opportunities for economic and political stability in migrants' countries of origin; determine grounds for lawful entry, belonging, and removal; and police the very presence of the people who are essentially here of our own government's doing. By filling in the gaps left by the omission or distortion of such topics in school curricula, the media, and public discourse, Latina narratives of transnational migration ensure that readers cannot remain blind to the US government's role in the suffering of families that have been ripped apart and the consequent obliteration of the family values the nation proclaims.

Acknowledgments

I would be remiss not to explicitly express my gratitude to the many individuals who have helped this project come to fruition. As trite as it may sound, words are not adequate to capture my appreciation for those who have shaped me and my passions professionally and personally. First, I offer my sincere gratitude to Tey Diana Rebolledo, Francisco A. Lomelí, Kimberlé López, and Enrique Lamadrid for their mentorship and guidance during my undergraduate and graduate studies. I am also grateful for insightful conversations and interactions with past and present students and colleagues at the University of New Mexico and the University of Washington Tacoma, and for the intellectual environment of the UWT School of Interdisciplinary Arts and Sciences, which has further enhanced my commitment to interdisciplinarity and encouraged exploration of new directions for my research. In more tangible terms, this book could not have been completed without research support from the University of Washington Tacoma and the Helen Riaboff Whiteley Center.

I would also like to express my thanks to the team at Texas Tech University Press, namely Joanna Conrad for seeing promise in my project in its earliest phases, Travis Snyder and

Christie Perlmutter for their keen editing insights, Hannah Gaskamp for her fantastic cover design, and John Brock for his work on the publicity front. Thanks, also, to the anonymous reviewers whose comments and suggestions were instrumental in pushing me to delve into exciting new frameworks.

Most important, I must acknowledge the unwavering support of friends and family and their various ways of enabling me to fulfill my professional obligations while simultaneously keeping me grounded and focused on what truly matters. Thank you to my husband, Matthew, for your love, patience, and well-intentioned prodding. To our sons, James and Jonah, I thank you for being such a light in what feels like times of overwhelming societal despair. I hope you are inspired to learn more about our own ancestors' migration, to appreciate our good fortune of never having been subject to forced separations, and to recognize your role in the fight for social justice in the years to come.

Notes

Introduction

1. In using the term "Latina," I adhere to the description posited by Morán González and Lomas of "'Latina/o' American literature" as that created by "writers of Latin American and Caribbean origin who find themselves annexed or incorporated into the United States . . . or who have migrated or descended from exiled or immigrant Hispanic, Latin American, and/or Caribbean peoples residing outside their place of origin" (2018, 1). *Ripped Apart* largely relies on analysis of texts written by female authors of Mexican descent (or Chicanas); however, the use of "Latina" is intended to be inclusive, as some chapters incorporate analysis of works written by women of other Latin American or Caribbean descent. I utilize the gender-neutral term "Latinx" in broader discussion as a means to counteract the linguistic restrictions inherent in selecting specific gender-marked adjective and noun forms (the masculine "Latino" or feminine "Latina") as well as the either-or dichotomy that precludes the inclusion of gender fluidity that the use of "Latina/o," "Latino/a," or "Latin@" may imply. When exclusively discussing works written by Mexican American or Chicana women, I utilize the more

specific term "Chicana."

2. Throughout *Ripped Apart*, "transnational" is intended to describe patterns of movement that extend beyond geopolitical borders and families "who are divided by international borders and who maintain significant emotional and economic ties in two countries" (Dreby, 2010, 5), rather than as a reference to the literary production, where in recent studies "transnational" refers to relevant texts written and published on both sides of the US-Mexico border.

3. The use of "Chicana" here refers to women writers of Mexican descent as opposed to suggesting that the characters of their texts identify as Chicana.

4. Although Jaramillo does not identify as Latina, her text is included within *Ripped Apart* because it aligns closely with the thematics and is largely based on accounts that her middle-school English as a Second Language students (largely of Mexican descent) shared with her.

5. This chapter includes texts written by male and female authors alike to provide a more comprehensive look at the themes and techniques in this emerging genre of children's picture books that address immigration and family separation.

Chapter 1

1. For more on research of narrative impact on emotions and actions, see Dawes 2009, 2016; Green 2004; Green et al. 2012; Hakemulder 2000; Iacoboni 2009; Johnson et al. 2013; Mar et al. 2011; Nance 2006; and Oatley 2002.

2. I find Bracher's use of "sympathy" rather than "empathy"

curious here, as elsewhere he comments on readers' empathy vis-à-vis "involuntary mimicry and perspective taking"
(2013, 201). Developing connections with Iacoboni's study
of the activation of mirror neurons while reading *about*
actions as though one were actually engaged in the actions
(2009, 93–94), Bracher notes, "Involuntary mimicry is elic-
ited by the images of damaged, suffering, and struggling
bodies, both human and animal, which evoke simulations
in readers' brains by activating their mirror neurons" (201).
One would imagine, then, that readers' experience would
be more akin to empathy (vs. sympathy) as described by
Keen, LaCapra, Eagleton, and Sontag.

3. Recent studies that speak to the negative consequences of
family separation, detention, and deportation are Abrego
2014; Artico 2003; Boehm and Terrio 2019; Brabeck et al.
2015; Day Langhout et al. 2018; Dreby 2010, 2012, 2015,
2019; García 2018; Glasgow and Gouse-Sheese 1995;
Rosas 2014; Sampaio 2015; Suárez-Orozco et al. 2002; and
Thronson 2015.

4. Connected to this issue, Molina describes the privileged
role of "medicalized racial profiling" and disease as a basis
for removal in the case of the 1940 Imperial Valley deportations, commenting on how the LPC ("likely to become a public charge") designation undermined the idea of Mexicans
as independent, deserving, "full" citizens and also super-
seded the civil liberties of the union leader whose confiden-
tial medical files were allegedly given to the Border Patrol
(2014, 91, 109–10).

5. Alex Wagner (2017) cites Joe Dunn's research indicating
that 1.8 million men, women, and children were deported.

6. It's worth noting that broader policies pertaining to US intervention in Latin America during the 1950s–1990s also contributed to the instability of social, economic, and political conditions in immigrants' countries of origin, which resulted in massive migration. US involvement in Operation Condor in the Southern Cone in the late 1960s to early 1980s and the provision of funding and military training to support state-sanctioned violence in the context of the Salvadoran (1980–1992) and Guatemalan (1960–1996) civil wars, for example, contributed enormously to the experiences of violence on physical, psychological, sociocultural, and legal / structural levels. Just one example of pertinent legal violence is that under 3 percent of Salvadoran and Guatemalan applicants were approved for asylum by the Reagan administration in 1984 (Gzesh 2006) despite the role it played in the obvious human rights violations in their countries.

7. This is not to say, though, that this is the only reason for migration. A desire for family reunification, educational opportunities, economic stability, etc., are also contributing factors.

8. Notably, these *maras* originated with street gangs in Los Angeles and other US urban areas in the 1980s. With the surge of deportations after the implementation of IIRIRA in 1996, thousands of Central Americans were sent back to the Northern Triangle—among them members of MS-13 and its rival gang, 18th Street (Calle 18, Mara 18).

9. Per the UNOCD Global Study of Homicide, the homicide rates per 100,000 were as follows: for 2010: Honduras 76.1, El Salvador 64.7, Guatemala 40.7, Mexico 22, US 4.8;

for 2011: Honduras 85.1, El Salvador 70.6, Guatemala
38, Mexico 22.9, US 4.7;

for 2012: Honduras 84.3, El Salvador 41.7, Guatemala
33.8, Mexico 21.5, US 4.7;

for 2013: Honduras 74.3, El Salvador 40.2, Guatemala
33.7, Mexico 18.8, US 4.5;

for 2014: Honduras 66.9, El Salvador 62.4, Guatemala
31.4, Mexico 16.1, US 4.5;

for 2015: Honduras 57.5, El Salvador 105.4, Guatemala
29.4, Mexico 16.5, US 5;

for 2016: Honduras 56.5, El Salvador 83.1, Guatemala
27.3, Mexico 19.3, US 5.4;

for 2017: Honduras 41.7, El Salvador 61.8, Guatemala
26.1, Mexico 24.8, US 5.3.

Chapter 2

1. García McCall addresses this idea about uncovering what
    has intentionally been swept under the proverbial rug as
    a motivation for writing: "I never intended to write about
    politics. In fact, I never even considered writing historical
    fiction either. It all just happened organically. The calling to
    write about our historical footprint in these 'United States'
    came from the discovery of hidden histories in America.
    Events like La Matanza (South Texas, 1915), the Repatriation
    Act (US, 1930s), and Project Wetback (US, 1954) have been
    kept out of our history books and thus remain unrevealed
    to the public and consequently our students. The one-sided
    narratives, the askew, curated facts, are much more than
    plot holes in our history books; they are erasures because
    they do not tell our side of the story in the development
    of our country. That's what made me want to write books
    that bring our history of social injustices against Mexicans

and Mexican Americans in this country to light. I believe it is my responsibility as a US citizen to write books that elucidate us. These books and the light they shed on hidden histories can inform conversations about our present political climate so that we can start working toward creating a better future for ourselves, our children, and our children's children" (Huang 2018).

2. Monica Muñoz Martinez elaborates on the vigilantism and extralegal violence during this period (1910–1920) with a particular focus on the normalization of "state racial terror and vigilantism" (2018, 7) that has largely been "forgotten in public memory" (8). Her work captures the strategies of survival and resistance of individuals affected by this violence and serves as a recovery project that preserves the collective memory of this resilience.

3. The patent parallels between the character of Dulceña and Jovita Idár are even more explicit upon consideration of Gabriela González's discussion of the Idár family's commitment to political journalism and civil rights activism in *Redeeming La Raza: Transborder Modernity, Race, Respectability, and Rights.*

4. This group appears to be modeled after the Círculo Social Femenino, México, later changed to Círculo Cultural "Isabel, la Católica," which met twice monthly on Sunday afternoons (G. González 2018, 126). According to Gabriela González, "Ultimately, Círculo Cultural was a vehicle for female benevolence and for restoring the culture of *la patria* (Mexico) in the face of growing Americanization and the dilution of Mexican identity. It promoted a common ethnic identity to unify Mexicans across class lines as

they struggled against racial discrimination and devastating poverty" (2).

Chapter 3

1.	Limón invokes imagery and discourse from Christianity and establishes parallels between Bernabé and Jesus Christ as the sacrificial lamb throughout the novel.

2.	Following Mikhail Bakhtin's theory of heteroglossia, one may understand the presentation of these disparate experiences and worldviews as a result of the dialogical relation of the distinct socio-ideological languages of social groups. According to Bakhtin, "At any given moment of its evolution, language is stratified not only into linguistic dialects in the strict sense of the word . . . but also . . . into languages that are socio-ideological: languages of social groups" (1981, 271–72). These languages or dialects reflect the contradictions of social reality and permit the contribution of various voices, including that of the Other, in the construction of truth and history. After all, Bakhtin proposes, "The truth . . . is born of the dialogical intercourse between people in the collective search for the truth" (1984, 90).

3.	Chicana author Demetria Martínez, on the other hand, does explicitly articulate the detrimental role of the US government in her well-known novel *Mother Tongue* (1994).

4.	Despite highlighting the inherent diversity of the novel's primary characters and the unique backstories driving their migratory journeys, Limón fails to extend such character development to the indigenous characters. Incidentally, one notes a similarly essentialist representation of indigenous characters in Estela Portillo Trambley's *Trini* (1986).

5. Demetria Martínez also situates the plot of *Mother Tongue* within the context of the twelve-year civil war in El Salvador, explicitly drawing attention to the US government's support of the state-sanctioned violence against civilians in the preface to the text. As the protagonist comes to understand the terror experienced by her lover, a refugee from El Salvador, and the broader injustices in El Salvador, she identifies the capacity of writing to serve as testimony. While Martínez's text focuses less on (im)migration than do the novels written by Limón and other Latina authors, it is prudent to recognize her presentation of trans-border issues of social justice through innovative narrative techniques. The power of the characters' documentation of social and political injustice extends to that which is presented by Chicana and Latina authors like Martínez and Viramontes.

6. For nuanced studies of La Llorona and the various artistic representations of this archetypal figure, see the work of Tey Diana Rebolledo and Domino Renee Perez.

Chapter 4

1. In the documentary *Which Way Home*, filmmaker Rebecca Cammisa provides a glimpse of diverse personal stories of immigration of unaccompanied Central American migrant children who brave the illegal journey on freight trains like "la Bestia," presumably the basis for "la mata gente" described in Jaramillo's *La Línea* and Diaz's *The Only Road*.

2. These themes of immigration, abandonment, and the quest for family reunification are also evident in *La misma luna*,

a 2007 feature film directed by Patricia Riggen.

3. Rebecca Cammisa's *Which Way Home* also offers a juxtaposition of children's maturity and independence alongside their fragility and vulnerability, particularly in scenes like that depicting two young friends on swingsets at a playground while awaiting the arrival of yet another freight train to take north.

4. See the work of Heidbrink and Ensor and Goździak for consideration of the simultaneous resiliency and vulnerability of child migrants and the repercussions of such within the US legal system.

5. Dreby similarly addresses the paradox inherent in the roles and responsibilities of children in Mexican migrant families due to unauthorized immigration status, noting both their additional power evident in their relationships with adults and the detrimental consequences of having to shoulder the burden of such (2019, 57).

6. These passages also bring to mind various scenes of similar dangers posed by *maras* in the feature film *Sin Nombre*.

Chapter 5

1. The inclusion of López's theatrical piece in this chapter is based on the parallel thematics and sociopolitical context that it shares with other works in this chapter. It's imperative to note, however, the unique elements of theater and performance art, and the analysis thereof. Consequently, the section that delves into *Detained in the Desert* also incorporates commentary regarding the play's use of sound, lighting design, staging, props, and particular techniques that López considers to be the genre of *cineteatro*,

which applies cinematic elements related to framing and editing, including the use of jump cuts, to dramatic scripts.

2. Indeed, Mexico's Ministry of Foreign Relations began to distribute a 36-page pamphlet in May 2005 that serves as an official guide for those planning to cross the US-Mexico border illegally. While offering advice for a safe arrival in the United States and informing migrants of their rights, the guide largely discourages unauthorized immigration through drawing attention to the inherent risks that such entails. Nevertheless, the publication and distribution of the *Guía del migrante mexicano* has drawn a tremendous deal of criticism from anti-immigration individuals and organizations in the United States. For this and other more recent guides, see Secretaría de Relaciones Exteriores and Secretaría de Gobernación Instituto Nacional de Migración.

3. Again, the specific characteristics and narrative techniques of young adult fiction are distinct from those written for an adult audience (e.g., the use of a teenage voice, a focus less on description or reflection and more on action, and additional experimentation that "challenge[s] traditional linear, chronological, and single-voiced nature of narrative fiction" (Koss 2009, 74). Nevertheless, because *Return to Sender* aligns with the other texts in terms of themes and sociohistorical contexts, its analysis is included alongside that of *The Guardians* and *Ocotillo Dreams*.

4. While this text certainly appeals to all Latinx (and non-Latinx) readers, the author explicitly notes the increase in the Mexican migrant community as a motive for writing *Return to Sender.*

5. Although I am using Taylor's concept in the context of a theatrical stage production, the notion of trauma-based performance is far more inclusive and applicable to, for example, political protests, as described in the article cited here.

Chapter 6

1. Outside of the scope of this book, though certainly laudable, are texts that are similar in theme and approach but written by Latino men, including Luis Alberto Urrea's *The Devil's Highway*, Rubén Martínez's *Crossing Over: A Mexican Family on the Migrant Trail*, and Óscar Martínez's *The Beast: Riding the Rails and Dodging Narcos on the Migrant Trail*.

2. A plethora of interdisciplinary studies, reports, and articles explore the negative consequences of (potential) detention and deportation on youth that largely mirror the experiences Guerrero documents in her memoir. See, for example, American Immigration Council 2019; Boehm and Terrio 2019; Brabeck et al. 2015; Buiano 2018; Day Langhout et al. 2018; Dreby 2012; Dreby 2015; Dreby 2019; Foley 2014; García 2018; Golash-Boza 2012; Golash-Boza 2018; Kanstroom 2007; Kanstroom and Lykes 2015; and Suárez-Orozco et al. 2002.

3. This circumstance may be one of the motives for the publication of the young adult edition of her memoir, *My Family Divided: One Girl's Journey of Loss, Hope, and Home, Loss, and Home*. Nazario has similarly written *Enrique's Journey: The True Story of a Boy Determined to Reunite with His Mother*, an edition adapted for young adults and "reluctant readers."

Chapter 7

1. Tonatiuh similarly incorporates characteristics of artistic production from Mixtec codices in *Undocumented: A Worker's Fight*, which is presented as a two-sided accordion-folded text of twenty-four panels of pictographs accompanied by text. Although the book includes a two-page depiction of border crossing, the primary emphasis is on the need to protect undocumented workers from exploitative conditions in its description of Juan's involvement with organizing at the Workers' Center.

Bibliography

@realDonaldTrump. "Many Gang Members and some very bad people are mixed into the Caravan heading to our Southern Border. Please go back, you will not be admitted into the United States unless you go through the legal process. This is an invasion of our Country and our Military is waiting for you!" Twitter, October 29, 2018, 7:41 a.m. twitter.com/realDonaldTrump/status/1056919064906469376.

Abrego, Leisy J. *Sacrificing Families: Navigating Laws, Love, and Labor across Borders*. Palo Alto, CA: Stanford University Press, 2014.

Adler, Rachel H. *Yucatecans in Dallas, Texas: Breaching the Border, Bridging the Distance*. Boston: Pearson, Allyn, and Bacon, 2004.

Alamillo, Laura. "Selecting Chicano Children's Literature in a Bilingual Classroom: Investigating Issues of Cultural Authenticity and Avoiding Stereotypes." *Journal of the Association of Mexican American Educators* 1, no. 1 (2007): 26–32.

Alarcón, Alicia. *La Migra me hizo los mandados*. Houston: Arte Público, 2002.

Alarcón, Norma. "The Theoretical Subject(s) of This Bridge Called My Back and Anglo-American Feminism." In *Criticism in the Borderlands: Studies in Chicano Literature, Culture, and Ideology,* edited by Héctor Calderón and José David Saldívar, 28–39. Durham, NC: Duke University Press, 1991.

Aldama, Frederick Luis. [Interview with] Duncan Tonatiuh. *Latino/a Children's and Young Adult Writers on the Art of Storytelling,* 241–46. Pittsburgh: University of Pittsburgh Press, 2018.

———. "[Interview with] Pam Muñoz Ryan." *Latino/a Children's and Young Adult Writers on the Art of Storytelling,* 161–66. Pittsburgh: University of Pittsburgh Press, 2018.

———. [Interview with] René Colato Laínez. *Latino/a Children's and Young Adult Writers on the Art of Storytelling,* 56–60. Pittsburgh: University of Pittsburgh Press, 2018.

Alexander, Jeffrey C. "Toward a Theory of Cultural Trauma." In *Cultural Trauma and Collective Identity,* edited by Jeffrey C. Alexander, Ron Eyerman, Bernhard Giesen, Neil J. Smelser, and Piotr Sztompka, 1–30. Berkeley: University of California Press, 2004.

Álvarez, Julia. *Return to Sender.* New York: Yearling, 2009.

American Civil Liberties Union (ACLU). "South Tucson Officials Agree to Important Revision of Police Practices Related to SB1070." American Civil Liberties Union, n.d. Accessed July 30, 2014. www.aclu.org/criminal-law-reform-racial-justice/south-tucson-officials-agree-comprehensive-revision-police

American Immigration Council. "U.S. Citizen Children Impacted by Immigration Enforcement." American Immigration Council, November 22, 2019. Accessed March 28, 2020. www.americanimmigrationcouncil.org/research/us-citizen-children-impacted-immigration-enforcement

Amnesty International. *Human Rights Concerns in the Border Region with Mexico* (Amnesty International Index: AMR 51/03/98). London: Amnesty International, 1998.

Anzaldúa, Gloria. *Borderlands/La Frontera: The New Mestiza.* 2nd ed. San Francisco: Aunt Lute Books, 1999.

———. *Friends from the Other Side/Amigos del otro lado.* San Francisco: Children's Book Press, 1993.

Arroyo, William. "Central American Children." In *Transcultural Child Development*, edited by Gloria Johnson-Powell et al., 80–91. Hoboken, NJ: John Wiley & Sons, 1997.

Artico, Ceres I. *Latino Families Broken by Immigration: The Adolescent's Perceptions.* El Paso, TX: LFB Scholarly Publishing, 2003.

Ashbee, Edward, et al., eds. *The Politics, Economics, and Culture of Mexican–US Migration: Both Sides of the Border.* New York: Palgrave Macmillan, 2007.

Asmus, Briana, and Emma Antel. "Imagination and Empathy: Reframing U.S.-Mexico Border Crossing Narratives." *Language Arts Journal of Michigan* 34, no. 1 (2018): 17–22.

Bakhtin, Mikhail M. *The Dialogic Imagination: Four Essays.* Edited by Michael Holquist; translated by Caryl Emerson and Michael Holquist. Austin: University of Texas Press, 1981.

———. *Problems of Dostoevsky's Poetics.* Edited and translated by Caryl Emerson. Minneapolis: University of Minnesota Press, 1984.

Balderrama, Francisco E., and Raymond Rodríguez. *Decade of Betrayal: Mexican Repatriation in the 1930s.* Albuquerque: University of New Mexico Press, 2006.

Barisich, Justin. "Guadalupe García McCall: Remembering What Has Been Endured, What Has Been Lost." *BookPage* interview, September 15, 2016. Accessed January 2, 2020. bookpage.com/interviews/20423-guadalupe-garcia-mc-call-historical-fiction#.XhIVwkdKiM8

Barrera, Mario. *Race and Class in the Southwest: A Theory of Racial Inequality.* Notre Dame, IN: University of Notre Dame

Press, 1979.

Batalova, Jeanne, et al. "Frequently Requested Statistics on Immigrants and Immigration in the United States." Migration Policy Institute, February 14, 2020. Accessed March 28, 2020. www.migrationpolicy.org/article/frequently-requested-statistics-immigrants-and-immigration-united-states#Unauthorized%20Immigrants

Beltrán Hernández, Irene. *Across the Great River.* Houston: Arte Público, 1989.

Bennett, Jill. *Empathic Vision: Affect, Trauma, and Contemporary Art.* Palo Alto, CA: Stanford University Press, 2005.

Boehm, Deborah A., and Susan J. Terrio, eds. *Illegal Encounters: The Effect of Detention and Deportation on Young People.* New York: New York University Press, 2019.

Brabeck, Kalina M., et al. "Immigrants Facing Detention and Deportation: Psychosocial and Mental Health Issues, Assessment, and Intervention for Individuals and Families." In *The New Deportations Delirium: Interdisciplinary Responses*, edited by Daniel Kanstroom and M. Brinton Lykes, 167–91. New York: New York University Press, 2015.

Bracher, Mark. *Literature and Social Justice: Protest Novels, Cognitive Politics, and Schema Criticism.* Austin: University of Texas Press, 2013.

Brady, Mary Pat. *Extinct Lands, Temporal Geographies: Chicana Literature and the Urgency of Space.* Durham, NC: Duke University Press, 2002.

Buiano, Madeline. "ICE Data: Tens of Thousands of Deported Parents Have U.S. Citizen Kids." The Center for Public Integrity, October 12, 2018. Accessed March 28, 2020. publicintegrity.org/inequality-poverty-opportunity/immigration/ice-data-tens-of-thousands-of-deported-parents-have-u-s-citizen-kids

Caminero-Santangelo, Marta. *Documenting the Undocumented: Latino/a Narratives and Social Justice in the Era of Operation Gatekeeper*. Gainesville: University Press of Florida, 2016.

———. "The Lost Ones: Post-Gatekeeper Border Fictions and the Construction of Cultural Trauma." *Latino Studies* 8, no. 3 (September 2010): 304–27.

Cammisa, Rebecca, dir. *Which Way Home*. HBO Documentary, 2009.

Campbell, Joseph. *The Hero with a Thousand Faces*. Princeton, NJ: Princeton University Press, 1972.

Cano, Robin B. *Lucita Comes Home to Oaxaca/Lucita regresa a Oaxaca*. Translated by Rafael E. Ricárdez. Englewood, NJ: Laredo, 1998.

Carlson, Elizabeth, and Anna Marie Gallagher. "Humanitarian Protection for Children Fleeing Gang-Based Violence in the Americas." *Journal on Migration and Human Security* 3, no. 2 (2015): 129–58.

Caruth, Cathy. *Unclaimed Experience: Trauma, Narrative and History*. Baltimore: Johns Hopkins University Press, 1996.

Cary, Alice, interviewer. "Julia Álvarez: Understanding Children Caught between Cultures." *BookPage*, January 2009. Accessed April 11, 2015. bookpage.com/interviews/8104-julia-alvarez

Castillo, Ana. *The Guardians: A Novel*. New York: Random House, 2007.

———. *The Mixquiahuala Letters*. Tempe, AZ: Bilingual Review Press, 1986.

Castillo, Debra A., and María-Socorro Tabuenca Córdoba. *Border Women: Writing from La Frontera*. Minneapolis: University of Minnesota Press, 2002.

Chabram-Dernersesian, Angie. "And, Yes . . . The Earth Did Part on the Splitting of Chicana/o Subjectivity." *Building with Our Hands: New Directions in Chicana Studies*, edited by

Adela de la Torre and Beatríz M. Pesquera, 34–56. Berkeley: University of California Press, 1993.

Chávez, Leo R. *Covering Immigration: Popular Images and the Politics of the Nation.* Berkeley: University of California Press, 2001.

———. *The Latino Threat: Constructing Immigrants, Citizens, and the Nation.* Palo Alto, CA: Stanford University Press, 2008.

Chávez Leyva, Yolanda. "*Cruzando la Línea*: Engendering the History of Border Mexican Children during the Early Twentieth Century." In *Memories and Migrations: Mapping Boricua and Chicana Histories*, edited by Vicki L. Ruiz and John. R. Chávez, 71–92. Champaign: University of Illinois Press, 2008.

Chishti, Muzaffar, and Faye Hipsman. "The Child and Family Migration Surge of Summer 2014: A Short-Lived Crisis with a Lasting Impact." *Journal of International Affairs* 68, no. 2 (2015): 95–114.

Chomsky, Aviva. *Undocumented: How Immigration Became Illegal.* Boston: Beacon Press, 2014.

Chomsky, Noam. *What Uncle Sam Really Wants.* Berkeley: Odonian Press, 1992.

Clemens, Michael A. "Violence, Development, and Migration Waves: Evidence from Central American Child Migrant Apprehensions—Working Paper 459." Center for Global Development, July 27, 2017. Accessed March 30, 2020. www.cgdev.org/publication/violence-development-and-migration-waves-evidence-central-american-child-migrant

CNN. "Alabama Governor Signs Tough New Immigration Law." CNN US, June 9, 2011. Accessed June 29, 2011. articles.cnn.com/2011-06-09/us/alabama.immigration_1_illegal-immigration-immigration-law-immigration-status?_s=PM:US

Colato Laínez, René. *From North to South/Del norte al sur.* San

Francisco: Children's Book Press, 2010a.

———. *My Shoes and I*. Honesdale, PA: Boyds Mills, 2010b.

———. *Waiting for Papá/Esperando a Papá*. Houston: Piñata Books, 2004.

Congressional Research Service. *Unaccompanied Alien Children: An Overview* (R43599), Prepared by William A. Kandel, October 9, 2019. Accessed March 21, 2020. fas.org/sgp/crs/homesec/R43599.pdf

Coonrod Martínez, Elizabeth. "Crossing Gender Borders: Sexual Relations and Chicana Artistic Identity." *MELUS* 27, no. 1 (2002): 131–48.

———. "La historia antes del viaje al otro lado: La novela *Trini* de Estela Portillo Trambley." In *Pensamiento y crítica: Los discursos de la cultura hoy*, edited by Javier Durán et al., 360–73. Mexico City, n.p., 2000.

Cornelius, Wayne. "Death at the Border: Efficacy and Unintended Consequences of US Immigration Control Policy." *Population and Development Review* 27 (2001): 661–85.

———. "Evaluating Enhanced US Border Enforcement." Migration Information Source, May 1, 2004. Accessed January 11, 2020. https://www.migrationpolicy.org/article/evaluating-enhanced-us-border-enforcement

Craps, Stef, and Gert Buelens. "Introduction: Postcolonial Trauma Novels." *Studies in the Novel* 40, nos. 1–2 (2008): 1–12.

Cummins, Amy. "Border Crossings: Undocumented Migration Between Mexico and the United States in Contemporary Young Adult Literature." *Children's Literature in Education* 44 (2013): 57–73.

Dawes, James. "Human Rights in Literary Studies." *Human Rights Quarterly* 31, no. 2 (2009): 394–409.

———. "Human Rights, Literature, and Empathy." In *The Routledge Companion to Literature and Human Rights*, edited by Sophia A. McClennen and Alexandra Schultheis Moore, 427–32. New York: Routledge, 2016.

Day Langhout, Regina, et al. "Statement on the Effects of Deportation and Forced Separation on Immigrants, Their Families, and Communities." *American Journal of Community Psychology* 62, no. 3 (July 2018): 3–12.

de Anda, Diane. *Mango Moon*. Park Ridge, IL: Albert Whitman & Co., 2019.

De León, Jason. "Risky Border Crossings." *Illegal Encounters: The Effect of Detention and Deportation on Young People*, edited by Deborah A. Boehm and Susan J. Terrio, 19–31. New York: New York University Press, 2019.

Department of Homeland Security Office of Inspector General. *Removals Involving Illegal Alien Parents of United States Citizen Children* (OIG-19-15), January 12, 2009. Accessed March 30, 2020. Prepared by Deborah Outten-Mills et al., www.oig. dhs.gov/assets/Mgmt/OIG_09-15_Jan09.pdf

Diaz, Alexandra. *The Crossroads*. New York: Simon & Schuster, 2018.

———. *The Only Road*. New York: Simon & Schuster, 2016.

Diaz Gonzalez, Christina. *The Red Umbrella*. New York: Yearling, 2011.

Dillon, Katrina. "An Educator's Guide to *Pancho Rabbit and the Coyote: A Migrant's Tale*. Consortium for Latin American Studies Programs Américas Award Curriculum Teaching Resources, 2015. Accessed March 16, 2020. laii.unm.edu/ info/k-12-educators/assets/documents/literature-guides/pancho-rabbit-educators-guide.pdf

Dreby, Joanna. "The Burden of Deportation on Children in Mexican Immigrant Families." *Journal of Marriage and Family* 74, no. 4 (July 2012): 829–45.

———. *Divided by Borders: Mexican Migrants and Their Children.*

Berkeley: University of California Press, 2010.

———. "Illegality and Children's Power in Families." In *Illegal Encounters: The Effect of Detention and Deportation on Young People*, edited by Deborah A. Boehm and Susan J. Terrio, 45–57. New York: New York University Press, 2019.

———. "U.S. Immigration Policy and Family Separation: The Consequences for Children's Well-being." *Social Science & Medicine* 132 (2015): 245–51.

Eagleton, Terry. *Sweet Violence: The Idea of the Tragic*. Malden, MA: Blackwell, 2003.

Emmanouilidou, Sophia. "Border-Crossings and the Subject in Abeyance in Irene Beltrán Hernández's *Across the Great River*." *Close Encounters of an Other Kind: New Perspectives on Race, Ethnicity, and American Studies*, edited by Roy Goldblatt et al., 159–79. Joensuu, Finland: University of Joensuu Press, 2005.

Ensor, Marisa O., and Elżbieta Goździak. *Children and Migration: At the Crossroads of Resiliency and Vulnerability*. New York: Palgrave Macmillan, 2010.

Eysturoy, Annie O. *Daughters of Self-Creation: The Contemporary Chicana Novel*. Albuquerque: University of New Mexico Press, 1996.

Foley, Elise. "Deportation Separated Thousands of U.S.-Born Children from Parents in 2013." *The Huffington Post*, June 26, 2014. Accessed July 28, 2014. www.huffingtonpost.com/2014/06/25/parents-deportation_n_5531552.html

Freed Wessler, Seth. "Nearly 205K Deportations of Parents of U.S. Citizens in Just Over Two Years." *Colorlines: News for Action*, December 17, 2012. Accessed July 28, 2014. colorlines.com/archives/2012/12/us_deports_more_than_200k_parents.html

Fukunaga, Cary, dir. *Sin Nombre*. Focus, 2009.

García, San Juanita. "Living a Deportation Threat: Anticipatory Stressors Confronted by Undocumented Mexican Immigrant Women." *Race and Social Problems* 10 (2018): 221–34.

García McCall, Guadalupe. *All the Stars Denied*. New York: Lee & Low, 2018.

——. *Shame the Stars*. New York: Tu Books, 2016.

Gibler, John. "Mexico's Ghost Towns: The Other Side of the Immigration Debate." *In These Times*, May 29, 2008. Accessed March 28, 2015. inthesetimes.com/article/3693/mexicos_ghost_towns

Glasgow, Godfrey F., and Janice Gouse-Sheese. "Themes of Rejection and Abandonment in Group Work with Caribbean Adolescents." *Social Work with Groups* 17, no. 4 (1995): 3–27.

Golash-Boza, Tanya Maria. *Due Process Denied: Detentions and Deportations in the United States*. New York: Routledge, 2012.

——, ed. *Forced Out and Fenced In: Immigration Tales from the Field*. New York: Oxford University Press, 2018.

González, Daniuska González. "*En el tiempo de las mariposas*, de Julia Álvarez: Escribiendo el espacio de lo femenino." *Filología y Lingüística* 27, no. 1 (2001): 99–112.

González, Gabriela. *Redeeming La Raza: Transborder Modernity, Race, Respectability, and Rights*. New York: Oxford University Press, 2018.

Goodman, Adam. "Mexican Migrants, Family Separation, and US Immigration Policy Since 1942." *Forced Out and Fenced In: Immigration Tales from the Field*, edited by Tanya Maria Golash-Boza, 43–50. New York: Oxford University Press, 2018.

Government Accountability Office. *Illegal Immigration: Southwest Border Strategy Results Inconclusive; More Evaluation Needed* (GAO-GGD 98-21), Prepared by Evi L. Rezmovic, et al., December 11, 1997. Accessed March 28,

2020. www.gao.gov/assets/230/224958.pdf

Gramlich, John, and Luis Noe-Bustamante. "What's Happening at the U.S.–Mexico Border in 5 Charts." Pew Research Center, November 1, 2019. Accessed March 21, 2020. https://www.pewresearch.org/fact-tank/2019/11/01/whats-happening-at-the-u-s-mexico-border-in-5-charts

Grande, Reyna. *Across a Hundred Mountains: A Novel.* New York: Washington Square Press, 2006.

———. *Dancing with Butterflies: A Novel.* New York: Washington Square Press, 2009.

Green, Melanie C. "Transportation into Narrative Worlds: The Role of Prior Knowledge and Perceived Realism." *Discourse Processes* 38 (2004): 247–66.

Green, Melanie C., et al. "Emotion and Transportation into Fact and Fiction." *Scientific Study of Literature* 2, no. 1 (2012): 37–59.

Guerrero, Diane, and Michelle Burford. *In the Country We Love: My Family Divided.* New York: St. Martin's Griffin, 2017.

Guerrero, Diane, and Erica Moroz. *My Family Divided: One Girl's Journey of Loss, Hope, and Home.* New York: Henry Holt, 2018.

Guidotti-Hernández, Nicole M. *Unspeakable Violence: Remapping U.S. and Mexican National Imaginaries.* Durham, NC: Duke University Press, 2011.

Gzesh, Susan. "Central Americans and Asylum Policy in the Reagan Era." *Migration Policy Institute*, April 1, 2006. Accessed March 30, 2020. www.migrationpolicy.org/article/central-americans-and-asylum-policy-reagan-era

Hakemulder, Jemeljan. *The Moral Laboratory: Experiments Examining the Effects of Reading Literature on Social Perception and Moral Self-Concept.* Amsterdam: John Benjamins, 2000.

Haney López, Ian. *White by Law: The Legal Construction of Race.* New York: New York University Press, 2006.

Harlow, Barbara. *Resistance Literature*. New York: Methuen, 1987.

———. "Sites of Struggle: Immigration, Deportation, Prison, and Exile." *Criticism in the Borderlands: Studies in Chicano Literature, Culture, and Ideology,* edited by Héctor Calderón and José David Saldívar, 149–63. Durham, NC: Duke University Press, 1991.

Heidbrink, Lauren. "Criminal Alien or Humanitarian Refugee: The Social Agency of Migrant Youth." *Children's Legal Rights Journal* 33, no. 1 (2013): 133–90.

Herrera, Juan Felipe. *Super Cilantro Girl/La Súperniña del Cilantro*. San Francisco: Children's Book Press, 2003.

Hondagneu-Sotelo, Pierrette. *Gendered Transitions: Mexican Experiences of Immigration*. Berkeley: University of California Press, 1994.

Hondagneu-Sotelo, Pierrette, and Ernestine Avila. "'I'm Here, but I'm There': The Meanings of Latina Transnational Motherhood." *Women and Migration in the U.S.–Mexico Borderlands: A Reader,* edited by Denise A. Segura and Patricia Zavella, 388–412. Durham, NC: Duke University Press, 2007.

Huang, Keilin. "An Interview with Award-Winning YA Author Guadalupe García McCall." Lee & Low Books The Open Book Blog, November 15, 2018. Accessed January 9, 2020. https://blog.leeandlow.com/2018/11/15/an-interview-with-award-winning-ya-author-guadalupe-garcia-mccall

Huerta, Jorge, et al. "A Conversational Review of Josefina López's *Detained in the Desert*." *Gestos* 52 (2011): 173–79.

Iacoboni, Marco. *Mirroring People: The Science of Empathy and How We Connect with Others*. New York: Picador, 2009.

Ibarrola-Armendáriz, Aitor. "The Burden of the Old Country's History on the Psyche of Dominican-American Migrants:

Junot Díaz's *The Brief Wondrous Life of Oscar Wao*." In *Trauma in Contemporary Literature: Narrative and Representation*, edited by Marita Nadal and Mónica Calvo, 134–47. New York: Routledge, 2014.

Jacobs, Elizabeth. "Undocumented Acts: Migration, Community and Audience in Two Chicana Plays." *Comparative American Studies* 14, nos. 3–4 (2016): 277–88.

"Japanese-American Internment During World War II." *National Archives*, n.d. Accessed March 29, 2020. www.archives.gov/ education/lessons/japanese-relocation#documents

Jaramillo, Ann. *La Línea: A Novel*. New Milford, CT: Roaring Brook Press, 2006.

Johnson, Benjamin Heber. *Revolution in Texas: How a Forgotten Rebellion and Its Bloody Suppression Turned Mexicans into Americans*. New Haven, CT: Yale University Press, 2003.

Johnson, Dan R., et al. "Potentiating Empathic Growth: Generating Imagery while Reading Fiction Increases Empathy and Prosocial Behavior." *Psychology of Aesthetics, Creativity, and the Arts* 7, no. 3 (2013): 306–12.

Jordan, Miriam. "Family Separation May Have Hit Thousands More Migrant Children Than Reported." *New York Times*, January 17, 2019. Accessed February 15, 2019. www.nytimes. com/2019/01/17/us/family-separation-trump-administra- tion-migrants.html.

Kanstroom, Daniel. *Deportation Nation: Outsiders in American History*. Cambridge, MA: Harvard University Press, 2007.

Kanstroom, Daniel, and M. Brinton Lykes. "Introduction, Migration, Detention, and Deportation: Dilemmas and Response." *The New Deportations Delirium: Interdisciplinary Responses*, edited by Daniel Kanstroom and M. Brinton Lykes, 1–30. New York: New York University Press, 2015.

Keen, Suzanne. "Empathetic Hardy: Bounded, Ambassadorial,

and Broadcast Strategies of Narrative Empathy." *Poetics Today* 32 (2011a): 349–89.

———. *Empathy and the Novel*. New York: Oxford University Press, 2007.

———. "Empathy Studies." In *A Companion to Literary Theory*, edited by David S. Richter, 126–38. Hoboken, NJ: Wiley-Blackwell, 2018.

———. "Introduction: Narrative and the Emotions." *Poetics Today* 32 (2011b): 1–53.

———. "Life Writing and the Empathetic Circle." *Concentric: Literary and Cultural Studies* 42, no. 2 (2016): 9–26.

———. "Narrative Empathy." In *the living handbook of narratology*, edited by Peter Hühn et al. Hamburg University. January 22, 2013. Accessed September 20, 2019. www.lhn.uni-hamburg. de/printpdf/article/narrative-empathy

———. "Narrative Empathy: A Universal Response to Fiction?" University of Connecticut Literary Universals Project, October 7, 2017. Accessed September 20, 2019. literary-universals. uconn.edu/2017/10/07/narrative-empathy-a-universal-re-sponse-to-fiction

———. *Narrative Form*. Revised and Expanded Second Edition. New York: Palgrave Macmillan, 2015.

———. "Readers' Temperament and Fictional Character." *New Literary History* 42 (2011c): 295–314.

———. "Strategic Empathizing: Techniques of Bounded, Ambassadorial, and Broadcast Narrative Empathy." *Deutsche Vierteljahr Schrift für Literaturwissenschaft und Geistesgeschichte* 82, no. 3 (2008): 477–93.

———. "A Theory of Narrative Empathy." *Narrative* 14 (2006): 207–36.

Koopman, Emy. "Reading the Suffering of Others: The Ethical Possibilities of 'Empathic Unsettlement.'" *Journal of Literary*

Theory 4, no. 2 (2010): 235–52.

Koss, Melanie D. "Young Adult Novels with Multiple Narrative Perspectives: The Changing Nature of YA Literature." *ALAN Review* 36, no. 3 (2009): 73–80.

LaCapra, Dominick. *Writing History, Writing Trauma.* Baltimore: Johns Hopkins University Press, 2001.

Limón, Graciela. *In Search of Bernabé.* Houston: Arte Público, 1993.

———. *The River Flows North.* Houston: Arte Público, 2009.

Lomelí, Francisco A. "Contemporary Chicano Literature, 1959–1990: From Oblivion to Affirmation to the Forefront." *Handbook of Hispanic Cultures in the United States: Literature and Art,* edited by Francisco A. Lomelí et al., 86–108. Houston: Arte Público, 1993.

Lomelí, Francisco A., et al. "Trends and Themes in Chicana/o Writings in Postmodern Times." In *Chicano Renaissance: Contemporary Cultural Trends,* edited by David R. Maciel et al., 285–312. Tucson: University of Arizona Press, 2000.

López, Josefina. *Detained in the Desert and Other Plays.* Madison, WI: WPR, 2011.

———. "Detained in the Desert." Indiegogo. 2012. Accessed April 2, 2015. www.indiegogo.com/projects/detained-in-the-desert

———. "Josefina López's New Play: *Detained in the Desert.*" KPBS News. August 30, 2013. Accessed February 20, 2019. www.youtube.com/watch?v=sfPMb7nfHBA

Lorenzen, Matthew. "The Mixed Motives of Unaccompanied Child Migrants from Central America's Northern Triangle." *Journal on Migration and Human Security* 5, no. 4 (2017): 744–67.

Lytle Hernández, Kelly. *Migra!: A History of the U.S. Border Patrol.* Berkeley: University of California Press, 2010.

Maciel, David R., and María Herrera-Sobek, eds. *Culture Across*

Borders: Mexican Immigration & Popular Culture. Tucson: University of Arizona Press, 1998.

Maciel, David R., et al., eds. *Chicano Renaissance: Contemporary Cultural Trends.* Tucson: University of Arizona Press, 2000.

Mar, Raymond, et al. "Emotion and Narrative Fiction: Interactive Influences Before, During, and After Reading." *Cognition & Emotion* 25, no. 5 (2011): 818–33.

Marshall, Serena. "Obama Has Deported More People Than Any Other President." *ABC News*, August 29, 2016. Accessed March 30, 2020. abcnews.go.com/Politics/obamas-deportation-policy-numbers/story?id=41715661

Martin, Yolanda C. "Gendered Exclusion: Three Generations of Women Deported to the Dominican Republic." In *Forced Out and Fenced In: Immigration Tales from the Field*, edited by Tanya Maria Golash-Boza, 151–60. New York: Oxford University Press, 2018.

Martínez, Demetria. *Mother Tongue.* New York: Ballantine, 1994.

Martínez, Óscar. *The Beast: Riding the Rails and Dodging Narcos on the Migrant Trail.* New York: Verso, 2013.

Martínez, Rubén. *Crossing Over: A Mexican Family on the Migrant Trail.* New York: Metropolitan Books, 2001.

Massey, Douglas S., and Karen A. Pren. "Unintended Consequences of US Immigration Policy: Explaining the Post–1965 Surge from Latin America." *Population and Development Review* 38, no. 1 (2012): 1–29.

Massey, Douglas S., Jorge Durand, and Nolan J. Malone. *Beyond Smoke and Mirrors: Mexican Immigration in an Era of Economic Integration.* New York: Russell Sage Foundation, 2002.

McCracken, Ellen. *New Latina Narrative: The Feminine Space of Postmodern Ethnicity.* Tucson: University of Arizona Press, 1999.

Mendoza, Sylvia. "Detained in the Desert: Protesting the Unjust through the Power of a Pen." *The Hispanic Outlook in Higher Education*, March 14, 2014. Accessed February 20, 2019. www.sylvia-mendoza.com/pdf/Detained-in-the-Desert-March-10-2014.PDF

Menjívar, Cecilia. "'Liminal Legality': Salvadoran and Guatemalan Immigrants' Lives in the United States." *International Migration Review* 36, no. 2 (2002): 437–66.

Menjívar, Cecilia, and Leisy J. Abrego. "Legal Violence: Immigration Law and the Lives of Central American Immigrants." *American Journal of Sociology* 117, no. 5 (March 2012): 1380–421.

Miller, Nancy K., and Jason Tougaw. "Introduction: Extremities." *Extremities: Trauma, Testimony, and Community*, edited by Nancy K. Miller and Jason Tougaw, 1–21. Champaign: University of Illinois Press, 2002.

Molina, Natalia. *How Race Is Made in America: Immigration, Citizenship, and the Historical Power of Racial Scripts.* Berkeley: University of California Press, 2014.

Morán González, John, and Laura Lomas. "Introduction." In *The Cambridge History of Latina/o American Literature*, edited by Morán González and Lomas, 1–30. New York: Cambridge University Press, 2018.

Morrison, Toni. "Unspeakable Things Spoken: The Afro-American Presence in American Literature." *Michigan Quarterly Review* 28, no. 1 (1989): 1–34.

Muñoz, José Esteban. *Disidentifications: Queers of Color and the Performance of Politics.* Minneapolis: University of Minnesota Press, 1999.

Muñoz Martinez, Monica. *The Injustice Never Leaves You: Anti-Mexican Violence in Texas.* Cambridge, MA: Harvard University Press, 2018.

Muñoz Ryan, Pam. *Esperanza Rising.* New York: Scholastic, 2000.

Nance, Kimberly A. *Can Literature Promote Justice? Trauma Narrative and Social Action in Latin American* Testimonio. Nashville: Vanderbilt University Press, 2006.

———. "Reading Human Rights Literature in Undergraduate Literature Classes: Professorial Desire, Disciplinary Culture, and the Chances of Cultivating Compassion." *Journal of Human Rights* 9, no. 2 (2010): 161–74.

National Immigration Law Center. "SB 1070 Four Years Later: Lessons Learned." April 23, 2014. Accessed March 28, 2020. https://www.nilc.org/issues/immigration-enforcement/sb-1070-lessons-learned/

Nazario, Sonia. *Enrique's Journey: The Story of a Boy's Dangerous Odyssey to Reunite with His Mother.* New York: Random House, 2006.

———. *Enrique's Journey: The True Story of a Boy Determined to Reunite with His Mother.* (Adapted for young people.) New York: Delacorte, 2013.

Neil, Emily. "Writing the Story of Central American Migrants for Young Readers." [Q&A with Alexandra Diaz.] Al Día Literature, August 29, 2018. Accessed March 30, 2020. aldianews.com/articles/culture/literature/writing-story-central-american-migrants-young-readers/53725

Ngai, Mae M. *Impossible Subjects: Illegal Aliens and the Making of Modern America.* Princeton, NJ: Princeton University Press, 2014.

Nowrasteh, Alex. "Deportation Rates in Historical Perspective." CATO at Liberty, September 16, 2019. Accessed March 30, 2020. www.cato.org/blog/deportation-rates-historical-perspective

Oatley, Keith. "Emotions and the Story Worlds of Fiction." *Narrative Impact: Social and Cognitive Foundations,* edited by Melanie C. Green, et al., 39–69. Mahwah, NJ: Lawrence Erlbaum Associates, 2002.

Oliver-Rotger, Maria Antònia. "Ethnographies of Transnational Migration in Rubén Martínez's *Crossing Over*." *MELUS* 31, no. 2 (2006): 181–205.

Ong Hing, Bill. *Defining America through Immigration Policy*. Philadelphia: Temple University Press, 2004.

Palacio, Melinda. *Ocotillo Dreams*. Tempe, AZ: Bilingual Press, 2011.

Passel, Jeffrey S., and D'Vera Cohn. "Children of Unauthorized Immigrants Represent Rising Share of K-12 Students." Pew Research Center, November 17, 2016. Accessed March 28, 2020. www.pewresearch.org/fact-tank/2016/11/17/children-of-unauthorized-immigrants-represent-rising-share-of-k-12-students

——. "Mexicans Decline to Less Than Half the U.S. Unauthorized Immigrant Population for the First Time." Pew Research Center, June 12, 2019. Accessed March 21, 2020. https://www.pewresearch.org/fact-tank/2019/06/12/us-unauthorized-immigrant-population-2017

Passel, Jeffrey S., et al. "Number of U.S.-born Babies with Unauthorized Immigrant Parents Has Fallen Since 2007." Pew Hispanic Center, November 1, 2018. Accessed March 21, 2020. pewresearch-org-develop.go-vip.co/fact-tank/2018/11/01/the-number-of-u-s-born-babies-with-unauthorized-immigrant-parents-has-fallen-since-2007

Pérez, Amada Irma. *My Diary from Here to There/Mi diario de aquí hasta allá*. San Francisco: Children's Book Press, 2002.

Perez, Domino Renee. *There Was a Woman: La Llorona from Folklore to Popular Culture*. Austin: University of Texas Press, 2008.

Peterson Beadle, Amanda. "All the Action on Immigration

is (Still) in the States." American Immigration Council Immigration Impact, May 8, 2014. Accessed July 30, 2014. immigrationimpact.com/2014/05/08/all-the-action-on-immigration-is-still-in-the-states

Portillo Trambley, Estela. *Trini*. Tempe, AZ: Bilingual Review Press, 1986.

Preston, Julie. "Alabama: Tough Immigration Measure Becomes Law." *New York Times*, June 9, 2011. Accessed June 29, 2011. www.nytimes.com/2011/06/10/us/10brfsAlabama.html?_r=2&ref=illegalimmigrants

———. "Deportations from U.S. Hit a Record High." *New York Times*, October 6, 2010. Accessed July 20, 2014. www.nytimes.com/2010/10/07/us/07immig.html?_r=0

Quintero Weaver, Lila. "Book Review: *Pancho Rabbit and the Coyote: A Migrant's Tale* by Duncan Tonatiuh." Latinxs in Kid Lit, March 20, 2014. Accessed March 28, 2020. latinosinkidlit.com/2014/03/20/libros-latinos-pancho-rabbit-and-the-coyote-a-migrants-tale-2/

Radford, Jynnah. "Key Findings about U.S. Immigrants." Pew Research Center, June 17, 2019. Accessed March 21, 2020. pewresearch-org-develop.go-vip.co/fact-tank/2019/06/17/key-findings-about-u-s-immigrants

Rebolledo, Tey Diana. *The Chronicles of Panchita Villa and Other Guerrilleras: Essays on Chicana/Latina Literature and Criticism*. Austin: University of Texas Press, 2005.

———. *Women Singing in the Snow: A Cultural Analysis of Chicana Literature*. Tucson: University of Arizona Press, 1995.

Riggen, Patricia, dir. *La misma luna*. Weinstein Company, 2007.

Rocco, Raymond A. *Transforming Citizenship: Democracy, Membership, and Belonging in Latino Communities*. East Lansing: Michigan State University Press, 2014.

Rodríguez, Ana Patricia. "Refugees of the South: Central

Americans in the U.S. Latino Imaginary." *American Literature: A Journal of Literary History, Criticism, and Bibliography* 73, no. 2 (June 2001): 387–412.

Rodríguez, R. Joseph. "Guadalupe García McCall: 'Books as Small Offerings.'" *Teaching Culturally Sustaining and Inclusive Young Adult Literature: Critical Perspectives and Conversations*, 161–78. New York: Routledge, 2019a.

Rodríguez, R. Joseph. *Teaching Culturally Sustaining and Inclusive Young Adult Literature: Critical Perspectives and Conversations*. New York: Routledge, 2019b.

Rodriguez, Sanjuana C., and Eliza Gabrielle Braden. "Representation of Latinx Immigrants and Immigration in Children's Literature: A Critical Content Analysis." *Journal of Children's Literature* 44, no. 2 (2018): 46–61.

Rodríguez, Sonia Alejandra. "Conocimiento Narratives: Creative Acts and Healing in Latinx Children's and Young Adult Literature." *Children's Literature* 47 (2019): 9–29.

Root, Maria P. P. "Reconstructing the Impact of Trauma on Personality." In *Personality and Psychopathology: Feminist Reappraisals*, edited by Laura S. Brown and Mary Ballou, 229–65. New York: Guilford Press, 1992.

Rosas, Ana Elizabeth. *Abrazando el Espíritu: Bracero Families Confront the US-Mexico Border*. Oakland: University of California Press, 2014.

Roth, Michael S. *Memory, Trauma, and History: Essays on Living with the Past*. New York: Columbia University Press, 2012.

Rumbaut, Rubén G. "The Americas: Latin American and Caribbean Peoples in the United States." In *Perspectives on Las Américas: A Reader in Culture, History, and Representation*, edited by Matthew C. Guttmann et al., 90–113. Hoboken, NJ: Blackwell, 2003.

Sacchetti, Maria. "Still Separated: Nearly 500 Migrant

Children Taken from Their Parents Remain in U.S." *Washington Post*, August 31, 2018. Accessed February 15, 2019. www.washingtonpost.com/local/immigration/still-separated-nearly-500-separated-migrant-children-remain-in-us-custody/2018/08/30/6dbd8278-aa09-11e8-8a0c-70b618c98d3c_story.html

Saldívar-Hull, Sonia. *Feminism on the Border: Gender Politics and Literature.* Berkeley: University of California Press, 2000.

——. "Feminism on the Border: From Gender Politics to Geopolitics." *Criticism in the Borderlands: Studies in Chicano Literature, Culture, and Ideology,* edited by Héctor Calderón and José David Saldívar, 203–20. Durham, NC: Duke University Press, 1991.

Sampaio, Anna. *Terrorizing Latina/o Immigrants: Race, Gender, and Immigration Politics in the Age of Security.* Philadelphia: Temple University Press, 2015.

Secretaría de Gobernación Instituto Nacional de Migración. *Guía para los migrantes,* n.d. Accessed March 27, 2020. www.inm.gob.mx/static/grupos_beta/GUIA_MIGRANTES.pdf

——. *Políptico de riesgos,* n.d. Accessed March 27, 2020. www.inm.gob.mx/static/grupos_beta/POLIPTICO.pdf

Secretaría de Relaciones Exteriores. *Guía del migrante mexicano,* 2005. Accessed March 28, 2015. www.cfif.org/htdocs/legislative_issues/federal_issues/hot_issues_in_congress/immigration/mexican-booklet.pdf

Segura, Denise A., and Patricia Zavella, eds. *Women and Migration in the US-Mexico Borderlands: A Reader.* Durham, NC: Duke University Press, 2007.

Smelser, Neil J. "Psychological Trauma and Cultural Trauma." In *Cultural Trauma and Collective Identity,* edited by Jeffrey C. Alexander et al., 31–59. Berkeley: University of California Press, 2004.

Soboroff, Jacob, and Dennis Romero. "Finding All Migrant Children Separated from Their Families May Be Impossible, Feds Say." NBC News, February 2, 2019. Accessed February 15, 2019. www.nbcnews.com/news/us-news/finding-all-migrant-children-separated-their-families-may-be-impossible-n966266

Socolovsky, Maya. "Cultural (Il)literacy: Narratives of Epistolary Resistance and Transnational Citizenship in Julia Alvarez's *Return to Sender.*" *Children's Literature Association Quarterly* 40, no. 4 (2015): 386–404.

Sontag, Susan. *Regarding the Pain of Others.* New York: Picador, 2003.

Stumpf, Juliet. "The Crimmigration Crisis: Immigrants, Crime, and Sovereign Power." *American University Law Review* 56, no. 2 (2000): 367–419.

Suárez-Orozco, Carolina, et al. "Making Up for Lost Time: The Experience of Separation and Reunification among Immigrant Families." *Family Processes* 41, no. 4 (2002): 625–43.

Szeghi, Tereza M. "Literary Didacticism and Collective Human Rights in US Borderlands: Ana Castillo's *The Guardians* and Louise Erdrich's *The Round House.*" *Western American Literature* 52, no. 4 (2018): 403–33.

Taylor, Diana. "Trauma and Performance: Lessons from Latin America." *PMLA* 121, no. 5 (2006): 1674–77.

Thompson, Amy, et al. "Re-conceptualising Agency in Migrant Children from Central America and Mexico." *Journal of Ethnic and Migration Studies* 45, no. 2 (2019): 235–52.

Thompson, Ginger. "Crossing with Strangers: Children at the Border; Littlest Immigrants, Left in Hands of Smugglers." *New York Times*, November 3, 2003. Accessed April 29, 2009. query.nytimes.com/gst/fullpage.

html?res=9A03EEDA1130F930A35752C1A9659C8B6

Thronson, David B. "Unhappy Families: The Failings of Immigration Law for Families That Are Not All Alike." In *The New Deportations Delirium: Interdisciplinary Responses*, edited by Daniel Kanstroom and M. Brinton Lykes, 33–56. New York: New York University Press, 2015.

Tonatiuh, Duncan. *Dear Primo: A Letter to My Cousin*. New York: Abrams, 2010.

———. *Pancho Rabbit and the Coyote: A Migrant's Tale*. New York: Abrams, 2013.

———. *Undocumented: A Worker's Fight*. New York: Abrams, 2018.

Trump, Donald. "Presidential Campaign Announcement." YouTube, uploaded by C-SPAN, June 15, 2015. www.youtube.com/watch?v=apjNfkysjbM

Turner, Jennifer D. "Diverse Literature from Duncan Tonatiuh and Violet J. Harris." *Language Arts Invited Dialogue* 94, no. 2 (2016): 124–29.

United Nations High Commissioner for Refugees (UNHCR). "Children on the Run: Unaccompanied Children Leaving Central America and Mexico and the Need for International Protection." UNHCR The UN Refugee Agency USA, 2014. Accessed January 18, 2020. www.unhcr.org/56fc266f4.html

United Nations Office on Drugs and Crime (UNODC). "Global Study on Homicide: Homicide Data Set 2019." DATAUNODC, July 2019. Accessed March 31, 2020. dataunodc.un.org/GSH_app

Urrea, Luis Alberto. *The Devil's Highway: A True Story*. Boston: Little, Brown and Company, 2004.

US Border Patrol. "Border Patrol Strategic Plan 1994 and Beyond: National Strategy." *Homeland Security Digital Library*, July 1994. Accessed March 28, 2020. www.hsdl.org/?abstract&did=721845

U.S. Customs and Border Protection. "U.S. Border Patrol

Southwest Border Apprehensions by Sector Fiscal Year 2016." Accessed March 30, 2020. www.cbp.gov/newsroom/stats/southwest-border-unaccompanied-children/fy-2016

———. "U.S. Border Patrol Southwest Border Apprehensions by Sector Fiscal Year 2020." Accessed March 21, 2020. www.cbp.gov/newsroom/stats/sw-border-migration/usbp-sw-border-apprehensions

———. "U.S. Border Patrol Total Monthly UAC Apprehensions by Sector (FY 2010–FY 2019)." U.S. Customs and Border Protection Stats and Summaries, 2019. Accessed March 31, 2020. www.cbp.gov/newsroom/media-resources/stats

van der Molen, Maarten. "The Tequila Crisis in 1994." Rabobank RaboResearch, September 19, 2013. Accessed September 29, 2020. https://economics.rabobank.com/publications/2013/september/the-tequila-crisis-in-1994/

Viramontes, Helena María. "The Cariboo Café." *The Moths and Other Stories*, 65–79. Houston: Arte Público, 1985.

Wagner, Alex. "America's Forgotten History of Illegal Deportations." *The Atlantic*, March 6, 2017. Accessed March 29, 2020. www.theatlantic.com/politics/archive/2017/03/americas-brutal-forgotten-history-of-illegal-deportations/517971

Wilson, Christopher, and Pedro Valenzuela. "Mexico's Southern Border Strategy: *Programa Frontera Sur*." Wilson Center Mexico Institute, July 11, 2014. Accessed March 30, 2020. www.wilsoncenter.org/sites/default/files/media/documents/publication/Mexico_Southern_Border_Strategy.pdf

Zolberg, Aristide. *A Nation by Design: Immigration Policy in the Fashioning of America*. Cambridge, MA: Harvard University Press, 2008.

Index

321